ANNE TYLER

ANNE TYLER

Credit: Diana Walker

ANNE TYLER

A Bio-Bibliography

Robert W. Croft

Bio-Bibliographies in American Literature, Number 5

GREENWOOD PRESS
Westport, Connecticut • London

PS
3570
.Y5
Z634
1995

Library of Congress Cataloging-in-Publication Data

Croft, Robert William.
      Anne Tyler : a bio-bibliography / Robert W. Croft.
         p.   cm.—(Bio-bibliographies in American literature, ISSN
0742–695X ; no. 5)
      Includes bibliographical references and index.
      ISBN 0–313–28952–2
      1. Tyler, Anne—Bibliography. 2. Women and literature—United
States—Bibliography. I. Title. II. Series.
Z8895.5.C76   1995
[PS3570.Y45]
016.813′54—dc20   94–42115

British Library Cataloguing in Publication Data is available.

Library of Congress Catalog Card Number: 94–42115
ISBN: 0–313–28952–2
ISSN: 0742–695X

First published in 1995

Greenwood Press, 88 Post Road West, Westport, CT 06881
An imprint of Greenwood Publishing Group, Inc.

Printed in the United States of America

The paper used in this book complies with the
Permanent Paper Standard issued by the National
Information Standards Organization (Z39.48–1984).

10 9 8 7 6 5 4 3 2 1

3165 5838

To Melody, Christian, and Britanny--

My anchors in the storm.

Contents

Preface and Acknowledgements

In October 1989 as I was beginning my graduate study at the University of Georgia and already searching for a topic for my dissertation, I wrote Anne Tyler a letter inquiring about her literary influences. To my surprise and great delight, she responded with a short letter that cited Eudora Welty as her chief influence and directed me to read her autobiographical essay "Still Just Writing." From that point on, I was hooked on Anne Tyler. During the next five years I began to investigate the life and works of this fascinating contemporary author. The book which resulted is, I hope, a fairly accurate and honest portrayal of the life of a superb writer and an extraordinary human being.

This book is divided into two major sections, biography and bibliography. The biographical half contains four sections. The first, entitled "A Setting Apart," describes Tyler's childhood in a North Carolina commune, her high school years in Raleigh, her college days at Duke, and her earliest writing efforts. The second section, "The Only Way Out," explains how, through her marriage, motherhood, and early novels and short stories, she managed to break out of her isolation. "Rich with Possibilities," the third section, chronicles her life in Baltimore, her new career as a book reviewer, and the composition of her middle novels. The final section, "A Border Crossing," explores her rise to fame and the themes of her major novels.

The last half of the book consists of a bibliography of works by and about Anne Tyler. The first part of this section lists primary sources in the following order: Tyler's novels, short stories, nonfiction articles and essays, poetry, children's books, and book reviews, and, finally, a listing of manuscripts (published and unpublished) in the Anne Tyler Papers at Duke University. In the second half of this section are listed secondary sources, including annotated entries on books, articles and interviews, dissertations, and theses written about Tyler's life and work. In addition, this section catalogues bibliographical citations for selected book reviews of Tyler's twelve published novels.

Each work in the bibliography is designated by an alpha-numeric code, according to the following key:

Primary Sources

N	Tyler's novels
S	Tyler's short stories
NF	Nonfiction articles and essays by Tyler
P	Tyler's poetry
C	Children's books written by Tyler
R	Book reviews written by Tyler

Secondary Sources
B   Books on Tyler's life and work
A   Articles and interviews
D   Dissertations and theses
V   Reviews of Tyler's novels

Following the bibliography is an index of subjects, people, and places discussed in the text and in bibliographical entries. References to the text come first and are given in Arabic numerals. Page numbers preceded by an asterisk (*) refer to sections in the text devoted exclusively to that subject or work. Alpha-numeric citations in the index direct the reader to entries in the bibliography related to particular subjects. The code listed above is used to denote the location of these entries.

During the past five years, while working on this book, I have received invaluable help, encouragement, and advice from many people. I would like to express my sincerest, heartfelt thanks to each of them:

At the University of Georgia, Hugh Ruppersburg, Rosemary Franklin, Russ Greer, Rebecca Sexton, Dezö Benedek, William S. McFeely, the excellent staff of the Interlibrary Loan Office, and the library's superb research staff. At Gainesville College, Glenda McLeod and Deb Lilly.

In North Carolina, the fine staff of the Special Collections Library of Duke University, especially Dr. Linda McCurdy; Mr. Thomas F. Harkins, of the Duke University Archives; Ms. Ann Barnes, school librarian at Needham B. Broughton High School in Raleigh; Judi Gaitens; and the following, who have all kindly granted me permission to quote from their letters: Fred Chappell, Carl L. Anderson, David Salstrom, Bob Barrus, Peg Neal, and Harry Abrahamson; as well as Ernest Morgan, who has granted permission to quote from the history of Celo Community.

Special thanks to the amazingly generous fellow Tyler scholars with whom I have corresponded during my research: Alice Hall Petry, of the Rhode Island School of Design; Elizabeth Evans, formerly of Georgia Tech; C. Ralph Stephens, of Essex Community College, Baltimore; Clarinda Harriss Raymond, director of the New Poets Series, who granted permission to quote from her letter, as well as Joseph C. Voelker, Stella Nesanovich, Frank W. Shelton, Wendy Lamb, and Patricia Rowe Willrich, the latter two who graciously granted me permission to quote from their articles on Tyler.

In New York, thanks to Judith B. Jones, Anne Tyler's editor at Knopf, for helping put together a publishing history of Tyler's novels and for permission to quote from her letters; Kathy Zuckerman, Ms. Jones's able assistant; and Toinette Lippy, for information on the history of the paperback rights to Tyler's novels.

In Baltimore, Tim Warren, book editor for the *Baltimore Sun*, and Ms. Frances Proutt, executive secretary of the Homeland Association. Most particularly, thanks to Anne Tyler herself for her patience and willingness to answer my seemingly endless questions and for permission to quote from the Anne Tyler Papers as well as her letters to me so long as I agreed to "sprinkle them throughout [my] text, rather than reproducing them all in one block or in a Q[uestion] & A[nswer] format." I know it was hard for her sometimes, being the private person that she is, but she was almost always unfailingly diligent in responding to my queries and amazingly kind. More specifically, I would like to thank her, on behalf of myself and her many readers, for the pleasure her novels have given us over the past thirty years.

Finally, but most importantly, I would like to thank my family. Melody, Christian, and Britanny, thanks for your love and patience and constant faith and support. I love you.

Abbreviations

After initial full citations, Tyler's novels will be cited in the text, using the following abbreviations:

AT   *The Accidental Tourist*
BL   *Breathing Lessons*
CN   *Celestial Navigation*
CW   *The Clock Winder*
DHR   *Dinner at the Homesick Restaurant*
EP   *Earthly Possessions*
IMEC   *If Morning Ever Comes*
MP   *Morgan's Passing*
SM   *Saint Maybe*
SC   *Searching for Caleb*
SDL   *A Slipping-Down Life*
TCT   *The Tin Can Tree*

CRITICAL BIOGRAPHY

"A Setting Apart"

Anne Tyler's life began as a series of journeys. At first, such a beginning may seem paradoxical. After all, for over a quarter of a century, Tyler has been identified almost exclusively, both in her novels and in her personal life, with only one place--Baltimore. Yet, in order to reach that one place in her life and work, she has had to live and work in many others. Indeed, these early physical wanderings served to set her apart, allowing her to gain the psychological insight and emotional depth necessary to take later imaginative journeys in her writing.

THE MIDWEST

Tyler's parents, Lloyd Parry Tyler and Phyllis Mahon Tyler, are Quakers and social activists. They were both born in Minnesota, Lloyd in Minneapolis on August 3, 1915, and Phyllis in Nashwauk on June 22, 1917. They were married in the Minneapolis Friends Meeting on January 3, 1940. Anne, their first child, was born in Minneapolis a year and a half later, on October 25, 1941. Both Lloyd and Phyllis worked in professional capacities--he as a chemist for the state of Minnesota and she as a social worker for the Family Welfare Association of Minneapolis.

In the years just prior to World War II, the Tylers concerned themselves with social issues and joined several groups opposed to war, particularly the Twin Cities Pacifist Action Fellowship, which worked to educate the public about alternatives to war and to the draft, such as non-combatant service.[1] The couple's idealism led them to search for a better place to raise their growing family. A second child, Israel Lloyd (nicknamed Ty), was born fourteen months after Anne, followed in 1949 by another son, Seth. The place they sought would, they hoped, instill in their children a solid foundation of simple values and hard work, outside the mainstream of an American society they perceived as intrinsically materialistic.

Beginning in June 1942, the Tylers made the first of several moves in search of that place. Their first move took them to Coldbrook Farm in Phoenixville, Pennsylvania, but they remained there only two years, moving again in 1944 to a suburb of Chicago. During the next four years they relocated twice, first to Duluth, Minnesota, and then back to the Chicago area.[2] Finally in 1948, their search seemed over. While living in Minnesota, they had learned of a settlement in the mountains of North Carolina called Celo. With its natural beauty and isolation from urban influences, such a setting, they felt, would provide the best atmosphere in which to raise their children in accordance with their ideals, away from the corrosive influences of modern society.

CELO

In the summer of 1948, when Anne was six, the Tyler family moved to the Celo Community, near Burnsville, North Carolina. Lying close to the foot of Mount Mitchell, the highest point in the eastern United States, Celo is the oldest land trust community in the nation still operating today. From its beginning in 1937, the community has operated on a shared labor basis, while striving to maintain the individual autonomy of each family. The Tylers' motives for moving to Celo closely parallel the founders' reasons for establishing the community. According to "Notes on the Beginnings of Celo Community," an unpublished manuscript recording the early history of the settlement, members of the community were to

> extricate themselves from the intricate economic relationships in which the current economy was involved . . . . to find whether they might, by simple living and hard work, maintain a considerable degree of freedom from the pressures and compulsions of the going economic regime, with the aim of using that freedom to try to orient themselves to the economic world in ways that would be in harmony with what they considered to be fundamental ethical considerations.[3]

Such an emphasis on individualism, hard work, and simplicity drew Lloyd and Phyllis Tyler to Celo. Once there, they tried to pass this idealistic philosophy on to their children.

Another motivation for moving to Celo was Lloyd's involvement in Celo Laboratories, a research firm dedicated to developing natural vitamins and drugs, in particular a drug to combat the RH factor, a blood antigen which causes serious complications in some pregnant women.[4] In Chicago, Lloyd had worked for the Chemical Products Division of National Cooperatives, Inc.; as a result, he brought a great deal of valuable experience and expertise to the new company. Lloyd's partner in the venture, Harry Abrahamson, recalls that development of the RH Hapten ultimately proved successful, although production halted when more cost-effective drugs were developed elsewhere.[5]

At Celo, the Tylers lived in their own home and, using organic farming techniques, tended a small garden that provided a good portion of their food. In addition, they raised some livestock. Bob Barrus, a co-resident at Celo during part of the Tylers' stay there, recalls that the one time he and his wife ate dinner with the Tylers they had roast beef, a special treat. During the course of the meal, Anne spoke up and asked, "Is this Nancy?" (Nancy was the family cow, at the time residing in the family's deep freezer.) Barrus remembers his amazement that Anne, despite her youth, seemed to have a clear insight into the complex interrelationships of farm life.[6]

Educating their precocious children provided a challenge to the Tylers. Because of Celo's remoteness and the inferiority of the local schools, Phyllis and Lloyd chose to teach Anne and Ty at home, using the Calvert School Correspondence Program, a home school program developed in Baltimore. This Baltimore connection was one of the first of a series of coincidences seemingly pointing to Anne's future literary home base. Home schooling, however, had its limitations. In particular, the children missed interaction with other children, so eventually the Tylers allowed Anne and Ty to attend the small local public school at Harvard. Unfortunately, Ty had a poor teacher, so the Tylers had to resume teaching him at home. Anne, on the other hand, apparently flourished at the small school. According to a local story, whenever the school's principal would need to leave for an hour or so to look after his cows, he would put Anne in charge, paying her a nickel for her services.[7]

Other families in the community contributed to the children's education as well. Children in the settlement received lessons in art, carpentry, and cooking. One longtime Celo resident, Dave Salstrom, remembers Anne and Ty visiting his private art class as a "guest" after school hours.[8] This class could have encouraged Tyler's developing interest in art.

Tyler's early artistic interest contributed to the development of her burgeoning literary imagination. By age seven she was writing stories in notebooks with the inscription "Written and Illustrated by Anne Tyler."[9] Furthermore, art seems to have stimulated her imagination, for she remembers "in the daytime . . . draw[ing] people on my blackboard and imagin[ing] what their lives were like and what unified them," thus forming her habit of "beginning to wonder what it would be like to be other people."[10] The visual process of drawing seems to have acted as a springboard for verbal expressions of her imagination. Even as an adult writer she often doodles while thinking of what to write, as one can see in the margins of some of her manuscripts. She sometimes draws sketches of her characters when she encounters trouble because "it helps me understand them."[11]

Appropriately for a future novelist, some of Tyler's earliest childhood memories also involve language. As a young girl, she would lie in bed, making up stories to entertain herself when she could not sleep. In a 1983 interview, Tyler remembered that most of these early stories concerned "lucky, lucky girls who got to go west in covered wagons."[12] An early bedtime provided Anne with opportunities to use her imagination in the creation of these stories. Later, as an adult who still suffers from insomnia, she recalled the experience in detail: "I pulled my knees up under the blanket and pretended I was a doctor and patients were coming to me with broken legs and arms and they had to tell me how they'd gotten them."[13] In her review of a children's book years later, Tyler proved that she had not forgotten this imaginative aspect of childhood by recommending the book to people of "any age . . . if they can remember how it once felt to dream a doll alive."[14] It was not long before Tyler took the next step from imagining stories to actually writing them down. She remembers starting that process "as soon as I knew how to put words on paper."[15]

Phyllis Tyler actively encouraged her children's imaginations, reading to them often, sometimes at night outside under the stars. Tyler has never forgotten the impact of her mother's reading aloud to her. In particular, one book, *The Little House* by Virginia Lee Burton, impressed Anne's young mind because "it has everything that matters: insidious change, the passage of time, giving in to change, struggling against change . . . ."[16] In 1986 Tyler published an essay in the *New York Times Book Review* entitled "Why I Still Treasure 'The Little House.'" Here she explains her early fascination with this book and its continued influence on her as she has reread it over the years, first for herself, then later for her children, and finally as she rereads it even now. From the book she claims she gained the "dawning knowledge that all moments are joined, each moment linked inexorably to the one that follows."[17] The book's effect on her as a young child is clear, for Tyler recalls "the feeling of elderly sorrow" that she felt and how listening to the book gave her

> a sudden spell of . . . wisdom . . . . It seemed I'd been presented with a snapshot that showed me how the world worked, how the years flowed by and people altered and nothing could ever stay the same. Then the snapshot was taken away. Everything there is to know about time was revealed in that snapshot, and I can almost name it, I very nearly have it in my grasp . . . but then it's gone again, and all that's left is a ragged green book with the binding fallen apart.[18]

Tyler's continuing interest in the effect of time and her use of objects to portray the passage of time perhaps stem from the early lessons taught her by this children's book.

The most important effect of living in an isolated community such as Celo, however, was the development of her sense of being an outsider. Although she flatly discounts any notion that her unconventional upbringing was odd, Tyler conceded, in a 1982 interview, that living in Celo did affect her: "There was nothing very unusual about my family life, but I did spend much of my older childhood and adolescence as a semi-outsider--a Northerner, commune-reared, looking wistfully at the large Southern families around me."[19] This developing sense of being an outsider helped sharpen her observational skills. Even more importantly, Tyler credits her experiences at Celo with developing in her the requisite sense of objective distance needed for effective writing. In her most revealing autobiographical essay, "Still Just Writing," published in 1980, Tyler recalled that someone had once told her that in order to become a writer a person must have had rheumatic fever as a child. Tyler noted, however, that "any kind of setting-apart situation" could create the sensibility needed to become a writer. For her, the feeling of being set apart came when she left Celo and attempted to find her place in the "outside world."[20]

Not surprisingly, then, Tyler set two of her earliest published short stories in isolated Quaker communities like Celo. Her first published short story, "Laura," in Duke University's literary magazine, the *Archive*, is set in just such a nonspecific place called "the Community." The interdependence of the members of this community is evident, as the eleven-year-old narrator recounts the community's reaction to the death of one of its members, an older woman named Laura, whose conservative religious views set her apart from the rest of the community. In her immaturity, the story's young narrator unexpectedly laughs when she hears of Laura's death. Not until later does she realize that her inappropriate behavior occurs because she has no other way of expressing her feelings of loss. In the case of this close-knit community, the interconnectedness of the people's lives makes the loss of even such a marginal member of the community significant. Despite their age and inexperience, the community's youngest members also feel that loss.

In a later story, appropriately titled "Outside," published in the *Southern Review* in 1971, the protagonist, young eighteen-year-old Jason McKenna, leaves a similar community (this time it has a name--Parsley Valley, North Carolina). In "Outside" Jason leaves the valley to work as a tutor for the son of a wealthy and dysfunctional New England family. In Pulmet, New Hampshire, Jason reacts with surprise when the townspeople mistake him for "a mountain boy." Back home in North Carolina, he had been the outsider, and real mountain boys had thrown rocks at him and his friends when they left the insular community to go into town to school. Here Jason's feelings of being an outsider seem to reflect Tyler's own memories of Celo.

Interestingly, the parents' reasons for moving to Parsley Valley parallel Lloyd and Phyllis Tyler's own motivations for moving to Celo. Jason's mother explains that she and her husband relocated their family to this secluded area to give their children "a better world"[21] and warns Jason that he does not know what the world is like outside. Jason, however, must find out for himself. At the end of the story, having been away, he is returning home by bus. Like many of Tyler's later characters, he returns home after a brief period of escape. These escape-and-return paradigms are repeated in various forms in such later novels as *The Tin Can Tree*, *The Clock Winder*, *Earthly Possessions*, and *The Accidental Tourist*. Whether or not Jason's return is a failure because he has not managed to break away from his family or a success because he has realized the value of his family remains uncertain. As he rides the bus home, however, one thing is certain. Jason's encounter with the outside world has drastically and irrevocably changed him. He now understands that the world outside his insular community is more complex than he had imagined and that he needs his family more than he thought he did.

Tyler was affected just as deeply by her Celo experience. The legacy of Celo was a sense of distance that years later, in "Still Just Writing," she admitted having given up hope of ever losing. In fact, she wrote that she had begun to value highly the privacy brought about by this characteristic of her personality.

CHILDHOOD

At Celo the growing Tyler family soon expanded into an extended family. Both Lloyd's and Phyllis's parents moved to the community, creating a close three-generational family unit that provided Anne and her brothers with an abundance of love and attention. In such an environment, Anne flourished, developing into a "loving and loveable, calm, thoughtful and 'private' child."[22] Tyler's love for her grandparents is apparent in her treatment of elderly characters in her work, particularly Daniel Peck in *Searching for Caleb*, who was modeled after her grandfather Tyler.

Despite Celo's nurturing environment and the closeness of her family life, this "private" child found childhood hard. Books provided both an escape from her private self and an entrance into another private world--the imaginary world of literature. In "Still Just Writing," Tyler explains that she herself disliked childhood and that even as a young child she felt that the action in books was "much more reasonable, and interesting, and *real*," than life itself; thus she spent most of her childhood with her head in a book waiting for the arrival of adulthood.[23] Later she admitted that "for some reason the thought of going back to childhood--even long enough to think of brief information about it--depresses me."[24] The reason for her fear of returning to that world, however, is not based on any bad memories of her own nearly idyllic childhood. Rather it seems to convey her sense of what she calls in *Saint Maybe* the "powerlessness" and "outsiderness"[25] inherent in childhood itself.

In many of her short stories, Tyler exhibits a keen understanding of children's feelings. Often she focuses on the child's perspective in her stories, sometimes choosing a child to narrate the story. Such is the case not only in "Laura," but also in Tyler's second published story (also printed in the *Archive*), "The Lights on the River." This story again recounts a child's reaction to death, but this time the death of people much closer to her--a father and brother. Characteristically, Tyler does not concentrate on the violence of these deaths; instead she explores their effects on the living. In "The Lights on the River," a young girl and her mother must listen all night to the sound of machines dragging the river for her brother's body (the father's having been found earlier). This narrative structure allows Tyler to portray the inner feelings of the child as she remembers her brother and contemplates death for the first time, even imagining herself in her brother's place at the bottom of the muddy river. From this perspective, it is the sound of the motors stopping, rather than her mother's gentle words later, that confirms the news of her brother's death. Tyler invests the child with intelligence and insight. The end result is that the reader perceives the child's loss more deeply because Tyler presents it from within the child's consciousness.

Tyler's own extraordinary insight was apparently obvious to many of those around her when she wrote these early stories. An opening biographical remark in the *Archive* placed as a headnote to "The Lights on the River" reads: "Anne Tyler sits quietly but attractively in most of her courses, saying little to demonstrate her intellectual and emotional depth. She is the kind of person who would be lost to all but her closest friends if it were not for her writing."[26] This brief description is interesting for two reasons. It reinforces the general perception of her insight and intelligence even at the age of eighteen, and it also supports Tyler's own view of herself as an outsider. The shell of privacy that she had drawn about herself, her sense of distance, was already intact.

Five years later, Tyler remembered her own reaction to childhood when she looked back in "Youth Talks about Youth," a personal reminiscence published in *Vogue*. Here she conveys her feelings through the use of an object: her family's old Model A Ford with a leaky radiator. The family used to drive this old car through the mountains, stopping at roadside waterfalls to refill the radiator. As they drove, Anne would listen to the swishing sound made by newer, fancier cars as they passed, wishing for the day when her family would buy a new car. When that day came, she remembers her disappointment that the new car did not make the swishing sound when she rode inside it. Only when listening from the outside could one hear it. Likewise, only when observing from an objective distance could she gain her artistic perspective.

Continuing in a reflective mood, Tyler expresses a similar disappointment in her new status as an adult, which, so far, had not met her expectations any better than the new car had. Having anticipated being "old and certain of things" by age twenty,[27] Tyler wonders whether the changes she is continually undergoing will ever make it possible for her to understand life completely. If she could have her way, she would prefer being "young and *sure* of things," but, with her more objective (and slightly older) perspective, she realizes that in a few years she will view her youth as "a perfect, separate island in time" and forget that "youth is no distinct time at all."[28] Tyler's childhood had been much like that island: safe and idyllic, yet isolated. From her childhood she gained a sense of independence and self-confidence, but she also acquired a sense of distance that she has had to struggle to break through for most of her life.

RALEIGH

Tyler was not quite seven when her family moved with such high hopes to Celo. By the time she turned twelve, however, the Celo experience had begun to sour for her parents. They found themselves increasingly dissatisfied by the authoritarian behavior of one of the community's members and withdrew first from the land association and eventually from the Quaker meeting. This was not the first time that such power struggles had led to problems at Celo. In the ten years prior to the Tylers' coming to Celo, there had been disputes concerning the allocation of resources, timber depletion, lack of agricultural prosperity, and pacifism during the war, all of which had resulted in other residents leaving the settlement.[29] The community's stated goal was to foster the development of "some elements of common philosophy and policy" through its "belief that life is too complex and too large to fit into any formal ideology; that if sincere, normal people will work together in reasonableness they will make day by day and year by year decisions which will tend to emerge into something like a desirable pattern."[30] But such a goal apparently could not be realized in a community composed of such highly individualistic and idealistic people.

Additionally, Tyler's parents decided that they needed to move to a larger city with more economic opportunities. Celo Laboratories had not been as profitable as Lloyd had hoped, and he found it increasingly difficult to provide for a growing family.[31] By the time the family moved to Raleigh at Christmas in 1953, all their resources had been exhausted by the years at Celo. Yet the couple's decision was not an easy one. It was further complicated by the sadness Lloyd and Phyllis felt in having to leave their parents behind.

But the move did not take the Tylers too far away. Lloyd secured employment with the State Water Resources Commission in Raleigh just over two hundred miles to the east. There Phyllis also began working as a social worker with the Juvenile Court Division. The Tyler family, which was finally complete with the birth of a third son, Jonathan, in 1954, began making the transition to city life, first renting houses and then buying a small home at 2512 Kenmore Drive when Anne was in eighth grade.

During the next thirty-five years, while Anne grew up and then moved away, Lloyd and Phyllis lived in Raleigh and established themselves as leaders in the Quaker community. They became active in pacifist causes, for many years holding a weekly noon-hour vigil on the steps of the State Capitol in opposition to the production of the B-1 bomber. Phyllis worked very hard in lobbying against the death penalty in general, and in particular became deeply involved in the case of a woman on death row.[32] Mrs. Tyler's efforts in conjunction with the American Civil Liberties Union to save the woman, Velma Barfield, however, ultimately proved unsuccessful. Yet Phyllis Tyler did succeed in a more personal campaign. Her actions taught her own children a deep sense of the value and uniqueness of every individual. Consequently, this sincere respect for the humanity of all people is evident in both Anne's life and in her fiction.

Both Lloyd and Phyllis also worked to promote the agenda of the American Friends Service Committee, and, after their retirement, travelled to the Gaza Strip to work with Palestinian refugees. In view of her parents' social activism, Tyler's seeming lack of any overt political or social agenda in her novels may seem odd. Still, while Tyler's social activism may not be as obvious as that of her peripatetic parents, her fiction does contain evidence of the lessons taught by her parents: a deep concern with ethical matters and a commitment to social justice.

Though much larger than Celo, Raleigh was not yet a large city. In the 1950s, it still retained much of the small-town feel of an earlier era, as well as a rural atmosphere. Even so, the move to Raleigh proved a challenge to Anne, who at the time had never used a telephone but could strike a match with her toe.[33] During the summer of her twelfth year, she worked on a tobacco farm outside Raleigh as a hander and recalls being jealous of the stringers, all of whom were grown women.[34] Tyler later used her firsthand knowledge of tobacco work in *The Tin Can Tree*, especially in creating the character Missouri. The move from the mountains of western North Carolina to the piedmont region at the center of the state also brought her into close contact with several new dialects, notably the black dialect. The ever observant Anne listened carefully to the voices around her and remembered their sounds when she wrote her North Carolina books. This aural connection remains an important aspect of her writing. Years later she confessed that she probably could not set another novel in North Carolina unless she could return there for an extended visit to listen to the way people were talking.[35]

In the larger setting of Raleigh, Anne began to develop further her interests in art and literature. She took art lessons and harbored dreams of becoming a painter.[36] More significantly, in high school she came under the influence of a nurturing teacher who challenged her to read widely and to develop her writing abilities.

From 1955 to 1958, Tyler attended Needham B. Broughton Senior High School in Raleigh, where she was active in many extracurricular activities including dramatic and literary groups. She participated in "The Golden Masquers," Broughton's dramatic society, serving as treasurer her senior year. That year the group helped produce the play *My Three Angels* and presented a shorter one-act play, *Two Crooks and a Lady*, at the Carolina Dramatics District Festival. In her sophomore year Tyler worked on a production that might have had a more significant impact on her, Thornton Wilder's *Our Town*. The poignancy and, more importantly, the relentless sense of the passage of time in that play must have reinforced ideas about time and change that *The Little House* and her own experience had already planted in her.

Even more than her participation in The Golden Masquers, Tyler's connection with Broughton's literary magazine, *Winged Words*, encouraged her development as a young writer. The magazine had been founded in 1950 by Phyllis Peacock, the English teacher who was to become so influential to Tyler. Mrs. Peacock, whom the 1958 school annual *Latipac* describes as "lead[ing] the line" of the hardest teachers at the school,[37] set high standards for her pupils. She had encouraged an earlier pupil, Reynolds Price, to pursue a career as a writer.

In an excerpt from his reminiscence, *Clear Pictures*, printed in the Raleigh *News and Observer*, Price remembered Mrs. Peacock as "not only a formidable guardian at the gates of good old censorious, rule-ridden, clear English" but also as "the rarest of unicorns--a magical teacher, the kind who works an inexplicable and unrepeatable voodoo . . . from a combination of effortless command of the subject, the discipline of a field marshal, the theatrical skills of classroom mastery and, most crucial, a fervent belief in the life-or-death importance of her subject."[38] From Peacock, Price learned several lessons that this master teacher must have also taught Tyler: clarity of style and respect for one's audience. Price wrote that Mrs. Peacock showed him how "no narrative can hope to succeed unless it takes invisible pains to make its story as visible to the audience as a good *clear* movie."[39] In the area of style, Peacock insisted upon "straightforward American English, stripped of shorthand, jargon and code and as lucid and entertaining as the complexity of the subject allowed."[40] Last, Peacock convinced Price that "enduring literature was made by individual men and women much like us."[41] Tyler's emphasis on the ordinary in her later writing is proof that she has never forgotten Mrs. Peacock's lesson either.

Tyler herself remembers Mrs. Peacock's dramatic teaching techniques, including "acting out Shakespeare . . . lying down on the floor and whispering as she died" or rewarding extra effort or creativity with the phrase "Orchids to you" in red ink on a student's paper, or "Onions to you" for inferior work. Tyler always sensed that Mrs. Peacock loved teaching and literature: "I never felt she was an ordinary woman who just needed to make money."[42] Most importantly, Tyler remembers Mrs. Peacock's enthusiastic encouragement. Although her parents, especially her mother, were supportive of her writing, Tyler recalls, "Mrs. Peacock got really excited and that made a huge difference."[43]

For her part, Mrs. Peacock, when interviewed after the publication of Tyler's first novel, remembered her former student as "always very sensitive--not only to people around her, but also to other writers--particularly to great writers. She seemed to have an understanding of their purpose." Discounting her own influence, Mrs. Peacock modestly attributed Tyler's creativity to her family life: "I think that the freedom of her home life has made her feel free to write. Hers is a thinking family. They are interested in ideas, people and great causes." Tyler did not forget Mrs. Peacock either. From Montreal she sent her a copy of *If Morning Ever Comes* inscribed "To Mrs. Peacock, for all that you've done. Anne."[44]

Another major influence on Tyler, even during her teenage years, was Eudora Welty, whose short stories Anne discovered in the school library. Tyler devoured Welty's short story collection *The Wide Net and Other Stories*, as well as her other works, and soon "knew her by heart."[45] From Welty's stories and novels Anne discovered the possibilities of writing about such ordinary people as Edna Earle Ponder, who could sit for hours and contemplate the mystery of how the letters of a Coca Cola sign intertwined. Anne remembers thinking that she knew people like Edna Earle and realizing that such people provided appropriate subjects for writers. She credits Welty with teaching her this lesson on the value of the ordinary: "A major influence, not just on my style but on the fact that I write at all, was Eudora Welty. Her short stories gave me my first inkling that it was possible to make literature out of the everyday people all around me."[46] From Welty, Tyler also learned the importance of carefully chosen details. In particular she admired "the way [Welty] can take the . . . smallest details to make the story come alive" and "convinced me that I should put them in my own stories."[47] These insights from Welty's writing into the usefulness of the ordinary and the importance of detail have never left Tyler.

Reading Eudora Welty's stories about the South also strengthened Tyler's connection to the region and helped her transcend her position as an outsider. Years later, in a review of *The Collected Stories of Eudora Welty*, Tyler recalled the experience of reading them for the first time: "For me as a girl--a Northerner growing up in the South, longingly gazing over the fence at the rich, tangled lives of the Southern neighbors--Eudora Welty was a window upon the world. If I wondered what went on in the country churches and 'Colored Only' cafes, her writing showed me, as clearly as if I'd been invited inside."[48]

DUKE

Perhaps because Durham was so close to home, Duke was not Tyler's first choice of colleges--Swarthmore was. Since she had won an Angier B. Duke Scholarship that paid full tuition and because her parents, with three younger children--all sons--coming along behind her (all of whom did go to Swarthmore), felt that it was more important for boys to get a good education, Tyler wound up at Duke. Although she noted a hint of bias in her parents' decision, characteristically, she made the best of the situation, finally conceding that everything worked out for the best: "That was the first and last time that my being female was ever a serious issue. I still don't think it was just, but I can't say it ruined my life."[49]

At Duke, Anne immediately benefitted from contact with her freshman English professor, Reynolds Price, whom Tyler describes as "the only person I ever knew who could actually teach writing."[50] Tyler was a member of the first class Price taught at Duke. Years later she wrote a reminiscence of her teacher for *Vanity Fair*. At the time Price had recently returned to teaching after undergoing radiation therapy for spinal cancer. Tyler remembered her favorite professor as a dashing figure. She always pictured him in her memory walking across campus in a black cape with a scarlet lining, although, actually, he simply wore a navy blue coat thrown around his shoulders. From her perspective as a student, his appearance was dramatic, as was his effect on the way she felt about writing. A master teacher, Price considers teaching his "serious hobby" and offers to his writing students what he must have offered Tyler then--"*strategy* . . . practical, concrete advice for getting on with the job of writing."[51]

In 1986, nearly three decades after being a student in his first class, Tyler attempted to analyze exactly what made Price such a successful teacher and writer. She concluded that he

> has had the great good fortune to know his place, geographically speaking. More than any other writer I'm acquainted with, except perhaps for Eudora Welty, he has a feeling for the exact spot on earth that will properly contain him, and he has never let himself be lured away from it any longer than necessary.[52]

From his perspective as a teacher, Price described Tyler as "frighteningly mature at 16," who "of all the young writers I have known . . . was the most prematurely skilled."[53] Eudora Welty, who had become friends with Price after meeting him on a visit to Duke during Price's undergraduate years there, remembers with amusement Price's bragging that first year that "teaching is going to be great" if all his students were to be as good as Anne.[54] Years later, in a 1983 interview, Price, older and wiser with more students to compare her to, declared Tyler "almost as good a writer at age sixteen as she is now; and she's now one of the best novelists alive in the world."[55] Price further characterizes Tyler as "the nearest thing we have to an urban Southern novelist."[56]

One assignment Price gave to the students in his first class was to write about their earliest memory. Predictably, the observant Anne's memory stretched back farther than any of the other students could remember--to before the age of one. She recalled her feelings about a jacket she disliked because it did not allow enough arm movement, as well as her frustration in trying to convey her feelings to her mother. Only later did she realize that she had been too young to convey her feelings in words and that she had only "thought [she] could talk."[57]

In her sophomore year at Duke, Tyler took a second course with Reynolds Price, an advanced course in short story writing. Recognizing her talent, Price soon began to give Tyler individualized assignments that allowed her to follow her own instincts. Instead of writing the critical papers Price assigned to the rest of his class, Tyler was allowed to write whatever she wanted. At first she wrote prose sketches about growing up in Celo that, according to Price, usually involved

> this wide-eyed extremely watchful girl child, who was not so much watching the community itself as watching the mountain people who lived around the community, with whom they would go mountain climbing, or flower picking. My memory is of this outsider child, this very watchful child recording, recording, recording the world.[58]

Price's comment reveals his understanding of Tyler's developing sense of distance, as well as her use of imagination in her composition method. And, of course, he also noticed her keen observation skills.

In addition to her classes with Price, Tyler took courses in advanced fiction writing with William Blackburn and C. R. Sanders. By the time she arrived at Duke in the late 1950s, Blackburn had already become a nearly legendary figure, having come to the university just two years after its founding in the mid 1920s. It was he who, at the request of a group of students, inaugurated the school's first course in composition in 1932. Disliking the term "creative writing," Blackburn stressed reading, believing that all writers stand in a long, noble literary tradition, in which his students might one day take part. Like Mrs. Peacock, he also emphasized mastery of the craft of writing, although not any particular style, allowing for diversity and individuality. The college catalogue entry for his advanced writing class "stated bluntly that only those students able to write 'with facility and correctness are expected to enroll.'"[59] Besides Tyler, Blackburn's students included such writers as William Styron, Reynolds Price, Fred Chappell, James Applewhite, and Josephine Humphreys. One particularly innovative technique of Dr. Blackburn's was to send out "one-year follow up" reminders with which he checked on the progress of his former students and encouraged them to keep writing. Tyler remembers receiving such notices following her graduation.[60]

Ironically, however, Tyler's major at Duke was not English. Instead she chose Russian because she wanted to "embark on something new and different and slightly startling"[61] and "because I thought the best literature--Dostoevsky, Chekhov--was in Russian."[62] From her Russian studies Tyler learned "a lot of the really obvious techniques and craftsmanship in [Russian novels] that were brought to our attention when we were studying them" and admits that those techniques "[come] up in my own stuff sometime."[63]

Although Tyler now laments that she has lost most of her knowledge of the Russian language, her love of Russian literature remains with her. Each summer she rereads *Anna Karenina*.[64] Of this classic novel she writes,

> It's one of those exactly perfect things to read in the summer, maybe because you can slow down for a novel like that. It doesn't have something happening on every page and maybe in the winter when I'm rushing I wouldn't appreciate it as much. I also happen to think it's about the best book ever written.[65]

Tyler's interest in Russian literature spilled over into other literary venues. While she was still in college, she began to write fiction in earnest. Twice she won the university's prestigious Anne Flexner Creative Writing Award. Carl L. Anderson, Tyler's freshman advisor and a member of the 1960 Flexner Award committee, recalls that she won "hands down."[66] The award had been established in 1947 by the family of a 1945 Duke graduate, Anne Flexner, who had died, tragically, two years later from injuries sustained in a fall from a horse. She too had been a student of Dr. Blackburn's and had aspired to be an "authoress."[67] The Flexner Award was first offered in 1948, and, at the time Tyler won, entries were limited to 5000 words for a short story, 100 words for a poem, and 3000 words for an essay.

In 1960 Tyler submitted to the competition the first two chapters of a novel. The chapters reveal her early skill with characterization and dialogue, as well as her use of memory as a narrative tool. The first chapter describes the relationship between a mother and her grown daughter. The mother, a divorcee who works as a music teacher, is somewhat irresponsible, whereas the daughter is the epitome of efficiency and assurance. As the mother awaits the arrival of her daughter, who has rearranged the kitchen for greater efficiency (reminiscent of Rose Leary's orderliness in *The Accidental Tourist*), she ponders the changes that time has brought about in her life.

Typically for a Tyler character, the mother, who even dislikes locking her doors at night, exhibits a desire to escape from her restrictive environment. Her feelings here anticipate later Tyler characters who yearn for escape (most notably Charlotte Emory in *Earthly Possessions*). Her relationship with her daughter also anticipates in some ways the role reversals one finds in *Saint Maybe* as Ian Bedloe gradually replaces his parents, or in *Dinner at the Homesick Restaurant* as Ezra Tull takes on the role of parent to his mother, Pearl. Of course, the chapters also anticipate later Tylerian themes such as isolation and miscommunication, as well as her fascination with the tension between order and chaos, stasis and change.

The novel's second chapter introduces Tyler's reflexive technique of moving into the past through memory. As the mother sits on the porch, she recalls the night her own mother died three days after giving birth, attended only by an old, drunken country doctor. Her father, who seems like Lloyd Tyler because he "had wanted to go far away in the mountains and live like Mr. Henry David Thoreau, who had gone off by himself a long time ago and didn't believe in cities,"[68] blames the doctor for his wife's death, but the daughter, sent away on an errand at the crucial moment, blames herself for failing to return in time to save her mother.

The second chapter ends with a typical Tylerian epiphany, a mutual moment of grace between two human beings. After the doctor reassures the girl that the mother's death was his fault, not hers, the girl extends her sympathy to him: "We were so unhappy . . . . And we didn't realize that even if we had succeeded in there we still would have failed in the end."[69] Here a young Tyler reveals her capacity for understanding the complex emotions of despair, regret, loss, and grief. Neither the doctor nor the girl can change the fact of the mother's death, so their only options lie in tempering the loss with a humane response. Each extends to the other what comfort and understanding that he or she can, given the limitations of all human beings to ever completely understand someone else. Such a response is by nature tenuous and frail, but it nevertheless produces the conditions necessary for endurance.

The next year Tyler again won the Flexner Award, this time for her short story "The Saints in Caesar's Household," which was later printed in the *Archive* and of which Reynolds Price has said, "It was the most finished, most accomplished short story I've ever received from an undergraduate in all my thirty years of teaching."[70] The story's title, though it has nothing to do with the time or setting of the story itself, suggests that Tyler's Quaker background had provided her with a fair knowledge of the Bible. The story's title alludes to Paul's request for prayer for the saints in Caesar's household who were suffering persecution because of their new Christian faith. The story's characters, however, suffer not because of their faith but because of a lack of it, and because of their resulting feelings of alienation and isolation.

In Tyler's story the saints of the title symbolize mankind in general, all of whom suffer from isolation from each other and from themselves. After a long absence from home, Mary Robinson, a young woman who works in a publishing firm in New York, returns to her small hometown in the South for a vacation. Through a series of increasingly revelatory letters, Mary's mother has attempted without success to inform Mary that an old friend of hers, Laura Gates, has suffered a nervous breakdown. Consequently, Mary does not hear the news until she runs into another old friend during the busride home. Once home, Mary, filled with conflicting emotions, avoids going to see Laura for several days. When Mary does finally visit her friend, Laura reacts defensively. Laura starts talking about the lack of connections between people and then confronts Mary: "Who did *you* ever reach out for as they went by?"[71] Shaken by her encounter, Mary leaves Laura sitting in the rain. Laura's newfound vision of the isolation of man severely disturbs her. She is unable to make the effort to reach out to her friend and, consequently, suffers from the same feeling of loneliness.

Although she spent much of her time writing, Tyler also participated in many other less solitary activities during her years at Duke. She worked on the *Archive*, the student literary magazine. Writer Fred Chappell, then the editor of the *Archive*, remembers how Tyler contributed to the magazine by offering her opinions about which pieces should be published. Most of all, he recalls admiring "her ease of expression and ability to articulate thoughts and feelings for characters not particularly articulate themselves."[72]

In addition to her work on the *Archive*, Tyler pursued her interest in drama by participating in the Wesley Players, a campus theatrical group that staged original productions. During her three years at Duke, Tyler played several major roles in Wesley productions. She played Laura in Tennessee Williams's *The Glass Menagerie*, Mrs. Gibson in Thornton Wilder's *Our Town*, and the female lead in an original student production.[73]

The burgeoning civil rights movement did not pass unnoticed by Tyler either. She was one of the first Duke students to join the black student protests. Anne's interest in civil rights had been fostered by her parents, who had encouraged their children to become involved in both the pacifist movement and the struggle for integration. But such involvement did not come without sacrifice and danger. The Tyler family endured threats and even violence during these years for standing up for their convictions.

Despite the turmoil around her, Tyler plugged away at her studies. By attending summer school both years, she was able to graduate early at the age of nineteen. Along the way, in addition to courses in Russian and English, she also took courses in Italian and comparative literature, continuing to pursue her interest in languages. But the speed with which she worked her way through her courses did not harm the quality of her work. In 1961, having made mostly A's, she graduated Phi Beta Kappa, twenty-sixth in a class of 271.

"I KNOW YOU, RIDER"

While working towards her degree, Tyler continued to write. In 1961 she completed her first novel, "I Know You, Rider." Its somewhat derivative imitation of the Southern literature of the day might explain why, despite several attempts, Tyler could not secure a publisher. The manuscript remains unpublished and is held in the Anne Tyler Papers at Duke University's Special Collections Library. The novel is important because of what it reveals about Tyler's early literary tastes and for its introduction of recurrent themes and character types used more extensively in her later works.

"I Know You, Rider" presents the exploits of several misfits in a small North Carolina city similar to Raleigh. Typed on the back of scrap paper from her father's workplace, the North Carolina Sewage and Industrial Waste Association, the story reads like Carson McCullers, complete with a version of the Sad Cafe called Darleen's Grill. The novel also contains many examples of the grotesque, in a style reminiscent of another Southern writer, Flannery O'Connor. Tyler, however, disclaims any influence from either of these writers. Though she does admit to having read both authors by the time she wrote "Rider," she expresses a firm distaste for O'Connor's "willful cruelty to her characters, despite her brilliance as a stylist." More important as an influence, she avers, was "the music I was listening to at that time."[74] The book's music is a mixture of folk songs and blues guitar. Its gritty tone reinforces the theme of missed connections and miscommunication. One song in particular provides the novel with its title. It is a song about a "rider," a man who lives off a woman.

In the story, Danny Ponder, a restless free spirit searching for a "listener's job,"[75] looks at an old print of settlers going west in covered wagons and contemplates how to spend the money he has won in a card game. He could get his guitar out of hock or buy his girlfriend Maggie a red dress. The larger issue of what Danny should do with his life is further complicated by his friend Todd Landis, who attempts to get Danny to accept a responsible job and settle down. This conflict between the responsible, well-meaning Todd and the free-spirited Danny introduces Tyler's concern with the tension between stability and freedom.

While Danny is trying to decide what to do, he roams the town and meets Spirit Farraday, a character who seems straight out of Flannery O'Connor. Spirit is a former circuit preacher who has given up preaching because of a "spiritual headache" (50) and now works as a shirt salesman. His religious past, however, is still very much with him. He tells Danny: "God is my business. And a real down-to-*earth* business, too, where you got to figure out for yourself what Christ would say to Khrushchev if they were to meet on the sidewalk someday" (53). Spirit is the forerunner to the more sedate preachers who populate Tyler's later fiction. Unorthodox and backslidden though he is, Spirit nevertheless retains some of the dogmatism Tyler condemns in those other ministers: "I sell God, I don't sell him cheap, and I don't sell him easy" (53).

Tyler also uses an approach to narrative structure in "I Know You, Rider" that anticipates her later works. She divides the novel into three parts with each section shifting the narrative focus to another character. In later novels such as *Celestial Navigation*, *Breathing Lessons*, and *Saint Maybe* she uses this shifting point of view more effectively and skillfully. Even at this early stage in her career, she understood that, in order to convey life's complexity, she would have to present it from a variety of perspectives in her writing. Whereas Part I concentrates on Danny, in Part II the focus shifts to Maggie, who wonders if Danny is just a "rider," using her for his own purposes. Maggie's sense of responsibility contrasts with Danny's free spirit. Maggie complains, "I'm the sensible half of the world and he's the pretty half and all I do is wish for things but I'm too sensible" (90). This conflict between the two lovers illustrates the essential difference between these two characters. One craves stability and the other desires freedom.

Predictably, when Danny appears under her window that night, Maggie ignores him. Instead, she telephones to invite her family for a visit. Her family arrives the next day, the first of Tyler's big, boisterous, and slightly embarrassing families. This one is definitely Southern in speech and actions, complete with a Great Aunt Mayola, who insists on calling Maggie by her full name--Maggie Joan--in the Southern tradition of two-part names. At this stage of her career, Tyler, deny it if she will later, is clearly a Southern writer. Her characters wander past "Negro women rocking . . . on their porches and old brown men talking tobacco work and knifings on the curb" (11), and they speak in a heavy dialect filled with "what-all" (52), "glory be" (123), and a host of other Southern expressions. Tyler's heavyhanded use of such regionalisms borders on stereotype.

While Maggie lacks the nerve to break away from her responsibilities, she does venture to get Danny's guitar out of the pawn shop. Spirit then convinces her that Danny needs her, explaining that the world is divided into thirds, with Spirit and her "the treasuring third" (139), whose job it is to comfort and believe in people like Danny. With a new understanding of Danny, Maggie leaves the guitar for him and goes home to wait for his next visit.

In Part III, the focus shifts to Spirit, who is in trouble with his landlady for not paying his rent. Spirit searches for Danny, who has been walking through the streets playing the same four notes over and over on a whistle. Danny's musical talent anticipates later artist characters such as Jeremy Pauling and Macon Leary, who need artistic outlets for their creative spirits. In addition, Danny is a Thoreauvian figure, marching, literally, to his own tune. His friend Todd, however, stuck in the temporal world, intervenes. He is angry with Danny for failing to show up for a job interview.

Finally, Danny acquiesces to the demands of his friend and of the mercenary world, but, ironically, he dies in a spectacular wreck on his way to the interview. His scooter hits a post and he is launched high into the air, indicative of his transcendence of the material world. Spirit, deeply moved by Danny's death, attempts to discuss his feelings with several people, but language fails him. With no words to express himself, Spirit's one recourse is to take up Danny's whistle and march through the streets of the city, announcing the coming of spring. Tyler's use of music here, and throughout the novel, reveals her belief in the limitations of language to express feelings adequately.

NEW YORK

In 1961 Tyler won a Woodrow Wilson Fellowship in Slavic Studies at Columbia University, and she moved to New York. There she continued her Russian studies, completing all the required coursework for a master's degree. She never completed her thesis, however, and, a year later, she left New York without a degree.

Yet her year in New York was not without its rewards. In the city, Tyler continued to develop her "life apart" in the anonymity of the city's crowds. She developed the habit--in her words, the "addiction"--of riding the city's trains and subways. As she rode she felt that she was "nothing but an enormous eye, taking things in, and turning them over and sorting them out."[76]

Tyler's observant eye later helped her to compose several short stories related directly or indirectly to characters she observed on her train rides in New York. In fact, her first story to be published in a national periodical includes such an experience. "The Baltimore Birth Certificate" was published by the *Critic*, a Catholic review, in February 1963. The story, set in New York (the title is simply another coincidental allusion to Tyler's future home), chronicles the attempts of an old woman, Miss Maiselle Penney, to obtain a copy of her birth certificate from Baltimore. After writing to the Baltimore records office with no success, Miss Penney enlists the aid of her niece, who suggests that they go to the Legal Aid office in New York for further help. To get there, they take the subway, and as they ride along, Miss Penney recalls other train journeys from her past. By using the journey motif, Tyler is able to follow Miss Penney's memory as it travels through time. This trope is reinforced when, as the train stops, Miss Penney's niece "[holds] the whole train back, just by stopping those doors from shutting."[77] Just as her niece is holding back the train, Miss Penney's memories are holding back time. Tyler's use of memory as a narrative tool for controlling time in this story anticipates later applications of the technique in novels such as *Breathing Lessons* and *Dinner at the Homesick Restaurant*, in which large blocks of time are narrated through memory.

Tyler's next published story, "I Play Kings," printed in *Seventeen* in 1963, though not set in New York, nevertheless utilizes a New York memory as well. The setting is Raleigh, but the most important section of the story recounts the narrator's memory of a trip she and her brother took to New York. Their ostensible purpose for going there was to buy her brother a cello. But they also visit Francie Shuford, the daughter of their neighbor in Raleigh, who had moved to New York a year earlier to pursue an acting career. They find Francie, now pregnant, singing in a nightclub. The song she sings is reminiscent of the folk songs that so interested Tyler in "I Know You, Rider." In particular, Francie sings "500 Miles," which begins with the line "If you miss the train I'm on." The words of the song seem like a message to the narrator, telling her that Francie has no plans to return to Raleigh, possibly because of her condition and possibly because she is happy and fulfilled in New York.

MAINE

Having left Columbia, Tyler was not anxious to return to North Carolina. Instead, in the summer of 1962, she moved to the coastal town of Camden, Maine, where she worked scrubbing the decks of a fishing boat and proofreading for the local newspaper. Her interest in boats is evident in several later short stories such as "The Bride in the Boatyard" and "A Street of Bugles," but particularly in the ending of *Celestial Navigation* when Mary Tell lives in Brian's boathouse on the edge of a river. In fact, Tyler has subsequently daydreamed about living such an existence beside the water: "I often wonder what it would be like to live all alone in a shack by the sea and work 23 hours a day."[78]

The first product of Tyler's Maine sojourn, however, was her short story, "A Street of Bugles." The opening headnote from the story, published in the *Saturday Evening Post* in 1963, reads:

> "A Street of Bugles" grew out of a summer I spent in a small coastal town in Maine. One of the many ways in which the town seemed unusual was that no one, not even the young people, appeared to want to leave it. Most of them seemed bound to that one place forever . . . . It was about this situation that I wanted to write as soon as I left the town.[79]

Tyler must have indeed been fascinated by a situation in which there was seemingly no desire for change--a perfectly static existence.

"A Street of Bugles" tells the story of Sammy, a young ship's engine mechanic who yearns to escape the restrictiveness of Balton, Maine. While helping to launch a new yacht, Sammy suddenly decides to head the boat out into the open sea, another example of Tyler's use of the escape motif. Sammy, like so many later Tyler heroes, feels the restrictiveness of his situation. Like Ian Bedloe in *Saint Maybe* and Ira Moran in *Breathing Lessons*, Sammy has had to give up the dream of going to college in order to support his family. In Sammy's case, family means just him and his mother, who is one of the first Tyler women to have been abandoned by her husband. Sammy also feels a pride in workmanship exhibited by other Tyler heroes. As the boat is launched, he feels "like some god, standing where no one else could stand, above all the ordinariness of iron and boat grease."[80] But that very ordinariness and the human connections that it involves eventually call Sammy back. When he hears the bugles blowing to commemorate the boat's launching, he turns it around and returns to his ordinary life. Despite Balton's restrictiveness, Sammy realizes that it is "such a *damned* loving town."[81] So he returns, like Charlotte Emory in *Earthly Possessions*, to the familiar and to the love that, although imperfect, is nevertheless somehow necessary to him.

Such contradictory feelings about home may have motivated Tyler to return to North Carolina after the end of that summer. There she found a use for her Russian training in her work as the Russian bibliographer in the Perkins Library at Duke University. She found the work to her liking. For the most part, it entailed ordering books from the Soviet Union. Best of all, it required only menial labor that did not drain her mentally and emotionally. Thus she could devote the greater part of her energies to writing.

Although, as one might expect, Tyler's earliest efforts at writing lack the maturity in style and content of her later fiction, her first short stories and novels do exhibit some of the themes and narrative techniques of her later work. Like her later novels, these works begin to explore the Tylerian themes of isolation, miscommunication, and endurance. They present their protagonists as individuals essentially alone in the world, yet continually striving to overcome that isolation. Although their attempts at communication prove insufficient, these characters usually still attempt to make connections with other human beings. It is this willingness to try, despite the inevitability of failure, that Tyler admires most and that gives her characters hope for endurance.

In these early works Tyler also experiments with narrative techniques found in her later novels. From the first, Tyler's emphasis has been on character, not plot. In these early stories she creates vivid, extremely individualized characters but often fails to show anything important happening to them. There is a sense of stasis in the plot. Perhaps this emphasis on *who* rather than *what* stems from the essentially Southern quality of her early fiction. Southern literature does tend to rely more heavily on characterization than on plot. Interestingly, Tyler's overdependence on character continued as long as she set her novels in the South, especially North Carolina. By the time she began to set her novels in Baltimore, her plots had become more intricate and interesting. Yet, even in the later work, she still maintains her emphasis on character.

Additionally, Tyler's early work introduces her technique of using memory to connect the past with the present. She seems to agree with Faulkner that the past is not dead. Every moment is linked to the moments before and after it in a long, unbroken line. Memory is the method Tyler uses to move back and forth along that line in her fiction. But her view of time also includes the possibility, though not the probability, of change. Thus she senses the need to explore life from more than one perspective, whether that vantage point be a point in time or the viewpoint of different characters. Consequently, in these early works she began to experiment with multiple perspectives and time-frames.

Endnotes

1. Letter from Peg Neal to the author, 17 Oct. 1993.

2. Elizabeth Evans, *Anne Tyler* (New York: Twayne, 1993): xiii.

3. Arthur E. Morgan and Griscom Morgan, "Notes on the Beginnings of Celo Community," unpublished manuscript: 1.

4. Letter from Dave Salstrom to the author, 25 June 1993.

5. Letter from Harry Abrahamson to the author, 2 Aug. 1993.

6. Letter from Bob Barrus to the author, 27 July 1993.

7. Letter from Bob Barrus to the author, 27 July 1993.

8. Letter from Dave Salstrom to the author, 30 June 1993.

9. Patricia Rowe Willrich, "Watching through Windows: A Perspective on Anne Tyler," *Virginia Quarterly Review* 68 (Summer 1992): 499.

10. Betty Hodges, "Interview with Anne Tyler," *Durham Morning Herald* (12 Dec. 1982): D3.

11. Kendall Guthrie, untitled article, Duke University *Chronicle* (6 Dec. 1982): 6.

12. Laurie L. Brown, "Interviews with Seven Contemporary Writers," *Southern Quarterly* 21 (Summer 1983): 11.

13. Hodges D3.

14. Anne Tyler, review of *The Indian in the Cupboard* by Lynne Reid Banks, *New York Times Book Review* (11 Oct. 1981): 38.

15. Brown 4.

16. Brown 11.

17. Anne Tyler, "Why I Still Treasure *The Little House*," *New York Times Book Review* (9 Nov. 1986): 56.

18. Tyler 56.

19. Sarah English, "An Interview with Anne Tyler," in *The Dictionary of Literary Biography Yearbook: 1982* (Detroit: Gale Research, 1983): 193-94.

20. Anne Tyler, "Still Just Writing," in Janet Sternburg, ed. *The Writer on Her Work* (New York: Norton, 1980): 13.

21. Anne Tyler, "Outside," *Southern Review* NS 7 (Autumn 1971): 1131.

22. Letter from Harry Abrahamson to the author, 2 Aug. 1993.

23. Tyler, "Still Just Writing" 13.

24. Willrich 498.

25. Anne Tyler, *Saint Maybe* (New York: Knopf, 1991): 115. Subsequent references will be cited in the text.

26. Anne Tyler, "The Lights on the River," *Archive* (Oct. 1959): 5.

27. Anne Tyler, "Youth Talks about Youth: 'Will This Seem Ridiculous?'" *Vogue* (1 Feb. 1965): 85.

28. Tyler 206.

29. E.R. Ohle, "The History of Celo Community," unpublished manuscript: 45-75.

30. Morgan and Morgan 10.

31. Letter from Harry Abrahamson to the author, 2 Aug. 1993.

32. Letter from Peg Neal to the author, 28 July 1993.

33. Anne Tyler, "Still Just Writing" 13.

34. Letter from Anne Tyler to the author, 19 Mar. 1993.

35. Bruce Cook, "New Faces in Faulkner Country, *Saturday Review* (4 Sept. 1976): 41.

36. Letter from Anne Tyler to the author, 19 Oct. 1989.

37. *Latipac*, 1958 Yearbook of Needham B. Broughton Senior High School, Raleigh, NC: 149.

38. Reynolds Price, "Permanent Lessons: A Writer Remembers Two of His Teachers," Raleigh *News and Observer* (29 Jan. 1989): D8.

39. Price D8.

40. Price D8.

41. Price D8.

42. "Peacock: 'Orchids to You,'" Raleigh *Times* (17 May 1985): B2.

43. Hodges D3.

44. Roy Martin, "Her Student Had That Special Touch," Raleigh *Times* (31 Oct. 1964): Features 1.

45. Anne Tyler, "Olives Out of a Bottle," *Archive* 87 (Spring 1975): 78.

46. Letter from Anne Tyler to the author, 19 Oct. 1989.

47. Michael Ballantyne, "Novel No. 1 Published, No. 2 Typed, No. 3 Is Jelling," *Montreal Star* (21 Nov. 1964): Entertainments 4.

48. Anne Tyler, "The Fine, Full World of Welty," *Washington Star* (26 Oct. 1980): D7.

49. Tyler, "Still Just Writing" 14.

50. Tyler 14.

51. Anne Tyler, "Reynolds Price: Duke of Writers," *Vanity Fair* (July 1986): 85.

52. Tyler 82-83.

53. Guthrie 6.

54. Barbara Lazear Ascher, "A Visit with Eudora Welty," *Yale Review* 74 (Autumn 1984): 149.

55. Willrich 501.

56. Cook 40.

57. Willrich 502.

58. Willrich 502.

59. "Duke: To Cross a Threshold, The Capital Campaign for the Arts and Sciences," The William M. Blackburn Endowment for Imaginative Writing, Duke University, 1984: 4.

60. Tyler, "Olives" 74.

61. Willrich 501.

62. Joan Forsey, "An Author at 22," Montreal *Gazette* (2 Oct. 1964): 18.

63. Tyler, "Olives" 78.

64. Anne Tyler, "The Private Life of Count Tolstoy," *Washington Post Book World* (19 Jan. 1986): 2.

65. Alice Steinbach, "The Books of Summer: Who Reads What When Days Are Hot," *Baltimore Sun* (13 July 1982): C1.

66. Letter from Carl L. Anderson to Robert Byrd, 23 Mar. 1985, in the Anne Tyler Papers, Special Collections Library, Duke University.

67. Victor Strandberg, "Anne Flexner: More Than Just a Name," Duke University *Chronicle* (3 May 1971): 5.

68. Tyler, chapter two of her 1960 entry to the Flexner Award competition: 18.

69. Tyler 22.

70. Willrich 502.

71. Anne Tyler, "The Saints in Caesar's Household," *Archive* (Apr. 1961): 10.

72. Letter from Fred Chappell to the author, 19 Dec. 1992.

73. Willrich 503.

74. Letter from Anne Tyler to the author, 7 Apr. 1993.

75. Anne Tyler, "I Know You, Rider," unpublished manuscript, the Anne Tyler Papers, Special Collections Library, Duke University: 45. Subsequent references will be cited in the text.

76. Tyler, "Still Just Writing" 14.

77. Anne Tyler, "The Baltimore Birth Certificate," *Critic* (Feb. 1963): 43-44.

78. Anne Tyler, "Because I Want More than One Life," *Washington Post* (15 Aug. 1976): G7.

79. Anne Tyler, "A Street of Bugles," *Saturday Evening Post* (30 Nov. 1963): 64.

80. Tyler 66.

81. Tyler 66.

"The Only Way Out"

The reasons why a person becomes a writer can never be fully understood, for the forces of environment, influence, heredity, and creativity all combine to shape the conditions that form a writer's perception. In Anne Tyler, nature--a talent inborn--and nurture--of her innate abilities along the way--both must have been at work. More particularly, environment and family seem to have influenced and encouraged Tyler's objective perception. At first this objectivity created in Tyler a sense of distance, a setting apart, which she continues to struggle to overcome even today. Very early, however, she discovered a way out of her isolation. First imagining and then writing about the ordinary life around her provided an escape for her. Thus, as she once revealed in an interview, "For me, writing was the only way out."[1]

Yet, during the years immediately following her graduation from college, Tyler discovered other means of overcoming her isolation. Her life soon changed dramatically in two very significant ways. These changes, marriage and motherhood, ultimately helped her to achieve and then maintain a balance between her artistic detachment and her need for connections to the real world.

MARRIAGE

The year 1963 proved a watershed in Tyler's life. While she was working as the Russian bibliographer in the Duke library, she met Taghi Modarressi, an Iranian medical student ten years her senior and a resident in child psychiatry at the Duke School of Medicine.

Five years earlier, at the age of 25, Taghi had fled his native country after being interrogated by the Shah's secret police and detained briefly as a suspected political agitator. At the time of the incident, he was working in a remote village studying the children of a primitive tribe. Even then he was already an accomplished young man, having finished his preliminary medical studies and published his first novel. Badly shaken by his experience with the police, Taghi left his country and his family, which he later described as "religious but not obsessive,"[2] to come live in America with a brother, also a doctor, in Wichita, Kansas. After a year and a half, he obtained a residency in child psychiatry at Duke University in Durham, North Carolina.

There he met a quiet, dark-haired young woman with gray-blue eyes who shared his interest in literature. A relationship began to develop between the young writer and the intriguing foreigner. Tyler seems to have been surprised when the relationship grew serious. Her first thought when Taghi asked her to marry him was not an unqualified, unhesitant "Yes!" but rather "Oh, well, why not?"[3] Later, reminiscing about her seemingly cavalier response to such a momentous question, Tyler wryly commented, "Fortunately, of course, it worked out."[4] At this stage in her life, she seems to have viewed marriage as a mystery, an inevitable event but a relationship about which she lacked the insight she would display twenty-five years later in her best novel about married life, *Breathing Lessons*.

In her 1978 short story "Linguistics," Tyler explores a marriage similar to her own. An American college student, Claire, meets a foreign graduate student at a party and becomes involved with him. She is especially intrigued by the foreignness of his language. They marry despite the worries of Claire's family that they have no "shared history."[5] Years pass; they have twins, whom they plan to raise bilingually but who wind up speaking only English (like Tyler's daughters). Eventually the husband becomes more Americanized, so that on a visit to his own country he discovers that he "doesn't speak the language anymore."[6] In their marriage, however, he and Claire have developed their own shorthand vocabulary, as well as a "shared history." Such human connections, Tyler was to discover in her own marriage, overcome both linguistic and cultural barriers.

Following their wedding in May 1963, Anne accompanied Taghi on a visit to Iran to meet his family. On the plane she surprised her new husband by speaking Persian, which she had been studying secretly to surprise him and to impress his family. Years later she recalled her study methods and her apprehensive feelings about this trip: "I taught myself Persian from a book before going to Iran to meet my husband's 300 relatives, shortly after we were married; sheer panic made the book method uncharacteristically effective."[7] Apparently, the month-long visit went well, for Tyler described it favorably a year later:

> I had 350 in-laws to meet. It was quite an experience, but I love the country. It's not that there are that many more people in the family, but they keep in touch. For example, you may not know who your second cousin married, or who your second cousin is, but they do.[8]

In later stories and novels, Tyler has used language barriers to illustrate the limitations of communication. Although the events in her 1976 short story "Your Place Is Empty" are fictional, Tyler's own Iranian mother-in-law provided the "seed" of the story about the visit of an Iranian mother to her son in America after a twelve-year separation.[9] This story is particularly interesting because it presents the problem of language barriers from the foreigner's viewpoint. Additionally, the story illustrates Tyler's attempt to view the world from a variety of perspectives.

In the story, the mother-in-law, Mrs. Ardavi, attempts to learn some English during her seven-month-long visit, but she grows impatient: "What she wanted was the language to display her personality, her famous courtesy and her magical intuition about the inside lives of other people,"[10] but, of course, with her limited command of English, words fail to meet her high expectations. Mere words cannot convey anyone's true self. In Mrs. Ardavi's case, she cannot convey the essence of her personality to her son in her own native tongue, much less explain it in a strange language to her foreign daughter-in-law. Thus, at the end of her visit as she boards the plane to return home to Iran, she remains "undeniably a foreigner"[11] both to the unfamiliar country and to her family. The story illustrates Tyler's view of the essential isolation inherent in the human condition. Ironically, words, which attempt to record that condition, cannot adequately express life's complexity or overcome its isolation.

By contrast, in "Linguistics," although Tyler again examines the limitations of language, she concentrates on the underlying human connections and emotions that make possible partial communication. At the end of this story, the American woman, Claire, who has been married to a foreigner for many years, receives a phone call from her husband's aunt, who speaks little English. Without her nephew to act as interpreter, the woman, like Mrs. Ardavi, cannot convey her message to her foreign relative, but that does not completely block communication. Instead she says the only thing she knows how to say in English: "Kellaire . . . I love you very much," to which Claire responds (later not remembering in which language): "I love you too."[12] The story's ending suggests the possibility that, despite the inherent limitations of language, human emotions and connections might prove adequate compensation for the inadequacy of words.

When Taghi's visa to the United States expired in 1963, he and Anne faced a decision. Not having completed his residency, he was not ready to return to Iran, even though, eventually, he planned to open a psychiatric clinic there. His other option was to find a residency in another country. The closest country was Canada, so he applied to and was accepted by the Allan Memorial Institute in Montreal. Once again, Tyler was off on another journey.

IF MORNING EVER COMES

Tyler had already begun writing a new novel (*If Morning Ever Comes*) before her move to Montreal. Her initial interest in the book was slight. In fact, she seems to have cared so little for it that on the plane to Montreal she actually misplaced the first part of the manuscript and didn't even bother going back to the airport to look for it. Fortunately, however, the airline recovered it; a month later, while at the airport on another errand, Taghi retrieved the lost manuscript.[13] During the next few months, while Tyler searched unsuccessfully for a job in Montreal, she also worked to finish the novel. She finally completed it in October 1963, after just six months of writing.

If Morning Ever Comes, like "I Know You, Rider," is set principally in North Carolina. Yet it opens in New York, where Ben Joe Hawkes, the novel's protagonist, is attending law school at Columbia, after having worked several years to support his family following his father's death. The extended Hawkes family, which consists of a mother, grandmother, and six sisters, is another one of Tyler's large families, although this one, interestingly, is headed by strong female characters.

At the beginning of the novel, Ben Joe, mistakenly thinking that this family of lone females needs his help with a crisis, returns home to Sandhill, North Carolina. The crisis is the return of Ben Joe's oldest sister, Joanne, who has left her husband after seven years of marriage and one child. Upon his arrival, however, Ben Joe quickly learns that his family is faring just fine without him. He is further surprised to discover that he is the one who needs the sense of security and identity that his family represents.

If Morning Ever Comes reveals Tyler's feelings about place. Like Ben Joe, she had been away from home long enough to miss it when she wrote the novel. An interview from this period includes her enthusiastic comment about anticipating her family's Thanksgiving visit to Montreal, their first to the city.[14] The novel also reveals her continued affinity for North Carolina settings. Like Tyler, Ben Joe has to settle for spending his undergraduate years at a North Carolina school, although (again like Tyler) he eventually winds up at Columbia.

The novel also introduces familiar Tyler themes of missed connections and the isolation of individuals, even within large families. Ben Joe is not "sure" about his role in his family; indeed, he feels uncertain about his position in life. He laments, "A hundred years ago, maybe, you could look at a Carolina white man and know what he would have for supper that night, in what kind of house and with what sort of family sitting around him. But not anymore--not in his case, at least."[15] Ben Joe's approach to overcoming that isolation is to stop changing. At the end of the novel, he enacts a reversal of Tyler's escape/return paradigm, leaving home rather than returning to it. In another sense, though, he is returning home because he takes "his own little piece of Sandhill transplanted" (*IMEC* 265) back to New York with him in the form of his old girl friend, Shelley Domer. This action represents his attempt to recreate a part of his unchanged past in the new home he plans to make with Shelley. Even the train conductor reinforces this idea when he takes their tickets and says, "Won't have to change" (*IMEC* 266). Ben Joe's lack of change reinforces Tyler's own belief that "each person has a fairly immutable self, issued before birth, and heavily influenced by various earnest decisions made during early childhood. Not that change beyond that isn't possible--and very interesting to a novelist--but I tend to be skeptical about wholesale transformation of the self much beyond childhood."[16]

Tyler also attributes this unwillingness to change to Ben Joe's Southern character. In an interview following the novel's publication she commented, "The most Southern thing about Ben Joe is his inability to realize that time is changing. This is a very typical Southern fault. People were trying to live on the surface as a family--the way it's supposed to be."[17] In the interview Tyler also expressed for the first time her preference for character over plot. Such an emphasis reinforces her kinship with other Southern novelists, who in her words, "concentrate on these little threads of connections between people."[18] And her own affinity with the South is clear, for even though at this time she intended to move to Iran with Taghi after he completed his medical training, she still planned to write about the South: "It seems silly to live in Iran and write about a place you came from 40 years ago, and yet I can't picture writing about a Persian market place."[19]

Three years earlier Tyler had written a short story that anticipated *If Morning Ever Comes*, "I Never Saw Morning," which had been published in the April 1961 *Archive*. The story is set during the years before Ben Joe (here called Hayes, not Hawkes) went off to Columbia, when he was first dating Shelley Domer. The story also examines the changes that time is bringing about in its characters. The two young people return from a date one night to find an old friend of Shelley's mother at the house. During the visit the friend belittles her husband in front of everyone, and Shelley, flush with the thoughts of her idealized love for Ben Joe, suddenly runs upstairs. Her rudeness, however, does not scandalize the visitors; instead they begin to reminisce about the early days of their marriage. Time seems to collapse upon itself, revealing that these contrasting relationships have more in common than Shelley might think. Generational cycles keep repeating themselves. At the end of the story Shelley's younger sister wonders why Shelley and Ben Joe walk up the porch steps so slowly when they come home after a date: "Does it just come to you *naturally*, to climb that slowly?"[20] Tyler seems to think, and reinforces her point through the perspective of three different generations in the story, that time works cyclically and that one's perspective on love changes with the passage of time.

Another story, "Nobody Answers the Door," published in the *Antioch Review* in 1964, also anticipates *If Morning Ever Comes*. It centers around the reaction of Ben Joe (now with the last name of Hawkes) to the news of his sister Joanne's marriage. By this time Ben Joe is working in the local bank to support his mother and sisters. When Joanne calls with the news, Mrs. Hawkes is initially angry and hangs up. Later, though, she tries to call Joanne back. But Joanne, whose feelings have been hurt, refuses to answer her phone. For his part, Ben Joe does not even want to talk to his sister. Words cannot express his own feelings of loss, so he leaves the house before anyone can come get him to talk to Joanne.

Both of these stories involve reactions to changes wrought by time--people moving away from home, children growing up, relationships developing and changing, old familiar situations evolving into new, often uncertain or even frightening ones. During the 1960s, as Tyler struggled with her own emotions about leaving home for good and establishing a new family of her own, she poured these emotions into her writing.

If Morning Ever Comes was published by Knopf on October 19, 1964. It sold well for a first novel (13,000 copies), and Bantam bought the paperback rights in December 1965. Most reviewers praised the book as a fine first novel, especially one by a writer of only twenty-two. Reviewer after reviewer mentioned Tyler's youth as an excuse for any faults in the book; many simply marveled that a person so young could produce such a book, despite its uneven quality. Orville Prescott, whose review in the *New York Times* Tyler's editor Judith Jones credits with giving the book its "send-off," described the young author as one of those seemingly "born knowing how . . . to write good fiction."[21] In Tyler, Jones believes, Prescott recognized "a genuine new voice."[22] Katherine Gauss Jackson, writing in *Harper's*, echoed the amazement of a male friend: "'It scares me. How can a twenty-two-year-old girl know so much about how a man feels?'"[23] Finally, Walter Sullivan, reviewing the book for the *Sewanee Review*, declared it "more than a respectable beginning for an author . . . just barely old enough to vote."[24]

Most reviewers of *If Morning Ever Comes* also noted Tyler's strong characterizations. Clifford A. Ridley observed that "Tyler tells us a lot about people. Her eye for the minutiae of human behavior and for the complex human relationships in a large family is right on focus; her ear for the attitudes and patois of the South is just as keen."[25] But while they praised Tyler's characters, many reviewers considered the book's plot rather slight. Rollene Saal summed it up succinctly: "Nothing momentous happens,"[26] while the *Virginia Quarterly Review* dismissed the book as "little more than a series of character sketches."[27] Years later, in a 1979 interview, Tyler explained her emphasis on character: "[A]s far as I'm concerned, character is everything. I never did see why I have to throw in plot too."[28]

At this point in her career, Tyler's attempt to treat both sexes equally in her writing is already apparent, although still not yet fully developed. In the *Saturday Review*, Julian Gloag suggested that Ben Joe's mind "is only vestigially masculine."[29] Tyler, however, certainly did not feel that her gender limited her to writing only from the viewpoint of a woman. In an interview soon after the publication of *If Morning Ever Comes*, she recalled how "galling" to her the notion of one of her college professors was that a woman "should never try to write from a man's point of view, because a woman doesn't know how a man thinks."[30] As if to prove her teacher wrong, Tyler wrote the novel from the viewpoint of a man. Since then she has written convincingly from the viewpoint of both genders in her novels.

The day after receiving the news that *If Morning Ever Comes* had been accepted for publication, Tyler finally found a job in Montreal. No one had needed a Russian bibliographer, but the McGill University Law Library had an opening for someone with library experience, and Tyler began to work full-time there. The work was just the kind of job she had been looking for, not too physically or emotionally draining. It left her plenty of energy to begin working at night and on weekends on her next novel, *The Tin Can Tree*. And the job proved fruitful in another way. Almost ten years later Tyler remembered one of her coworkers at the library, a man who was painfully shy around women, when she created the character of Jeremy Pauling in *Celestial Navigation*.[31]

THE TIN CAN TREE

In her second novel, *The Tin Can Tree*, Tyler expanded her range in both tone and content. Though the setting is still North Carolina and the subject another family crisis, even at the time of its publication Tyler considered *The Tin Can Tree* "more serious" because in *If Morning Ever Comes* she had been "afraid to be too serious."[32] In the novel, which recounts the repercussions of the death of six-year-old Janie Rose Pike, three families live in an unusual triplex house. The first family consists of Mr. and Mrs. Pike, their son Simon, and the Pikes' grown niece, Joan. The second family is the Greens, James, a photographer, and his dependent brother Ansel. The final family consists of Misses Lucy and Faye Potter, two elderly spinster sisters.

Following their daughter's death in a tractor accident, Mr. and Mrs. Pike attempt to deal with their grief and resume their normal lives. Mrs. Pike, however, cannot overcome her grief and retreats within herself psychologically and into her bedroom physically. Her retreat indicates weakness, because it suggests lifelessness. Such an existence is unacceptable to Tyler. While her characters may live individual lives, they cannot exist without connections to others.

In the novel's subplot, Tyler also explores the issue of connectedness. Joan, who loves James but cannot convince him to leave his hypochondriacal brother, decides that she will leave. But when Simon, who has also been feeling the isolation and neglect of his mother's withdrawal, runs away, Joan abandons her own plans in order to help find the boy. This crisis precipitates both Joan's return and Mrs. Pike's emergence from her bedroom. By the end of the novel, they finally understand that life is for the living and that they must maintain the ties that bind them even in the face of death. Missouri, the old black woman who works in tobacco with Joan, conveys this truth to her early in the novel: "Bravest thing about people . . . is how they go on loving mortal beings after finding out there's such a thing as dying."[33]

Each of the characters in *The Tin Can Tree* also realizes his or her own essential isolation. At the end of the novel, though Joan is taking a photograph of the whole family, she is herself both physically and emotionally separate from the group. And even the people posing in the photograph seem isolated to Joan, "each clutching separately his glass of wine" (*TCT* 273). Thus, Joan reaches the conclusion that "whole years could pass, they could be born and die, they could leave and return, they could marry or live out their separate lives alone and nothing . . . would change. They were going to stay this way" (*TCT* 273).

To Knopf's disappointment, *The Tin Can Tree* did not fare as well as *If Morning Ever Comes*, selling just 8500 hardback copies, although Bantam again picked up the paperback rights in November 1966. Reviews of *The Tin Can Tree* continued to focus on Tyler's Southern qualities and her youth. Katherine Gauss Jackson noticed occasional "echoes of Carson McCullers or Harper Lee or Truman Capote,"[34] while Millicent Bell was reminded of Carson McCullers, who "also wrote of human disconnection and the need for love in a stagnant community."[35] To Mary Stack McNiff, Tyler's Southernness rested in her creation of "a strong sense of place."[36] Years later in a review of T. R. Pearson's *Off for the Sweet Hereafter*, Tyler herself summed up the Southern qualities of that book in a similar fashion: "this story could have been told in just this way only by a Southerner. Certainly the constant straying from 'What Happened' to 'Who, Exactly, It Happened To' (and 'Who His Grandfather Was,' besides) seems distinctly if not uniquely Southern, as does the ambling, wry tone."[37] To the extent that Tyler concentrates on character almost exclusively in her first two novels, by her own definition, she was definitely still a Southern writer at this stage of her career.

As in *If Morning Ever Comes*, however, *The Tin Can Tree* really revolves around characters in a family--in this case an extended family symbolized by the unusual three-family house they inhabit. Reviewers generally liked Tyler's characters. One found them "as real as the neighbors next door."[38] Others thought that Joan is "the eternal 'guest' of the household";[39] that Simon, who is "part stubbornness, part lack of comprehension, part clear observation uncluttered by sentiment,"[40] provides "the fulcrum of the story";[41] and that Janie Rose, though dead, "haunts the book, even though she is portrayed realistically."[42]

Tyler's style also continued to impress reviewers. Clifford Ridley loved her "muted and suggestive . . . directness and economy of style," "uncanny" command of dialogue, and "truly remarkable" ear.[43] *Booklist*, similarly, felt that the book "quietly discloses through authentically caught conversation and highly individual characters the poetry and humor of life."[44] To Katherine Gauss Jackson, the book's resolution had "the intricacy and delicacy of satisfying music."[45]

John Conley was intrigued by the choices made by several characters--Joan's decision to stay with James, James's to look after Ansel, and Mrs. Pike's to resume care of her son. Conley observed that *The Tin Can Tree* "enforces the traditional insight that man lives meaningfully and truly becomes himself . . . only if he lives by principle as specified in acts of choice."[46]

Finally, D.E. Richardson emphasized the endurance of each of the families who "must learn to live with each other, and [who] succeed, although at the cost of personal sacrifice and a measure of personal defeat."[47] This emphasis on endurance, especially within families, interests Tyler tremendously. As she admitted fifteen years after the publication of her first two novels, the family, in particular, portrays "how people manage to endure together--how they grate against each other, adjust, intrude and protect themselves from intrusions, give up and start all over again in the morning."[48]

Tyler's own subsequent appraisal of her first two published novels has been harsh: "*The Tin Can Tree* and *If Morning Ever Comes* should be burned."[49] As for her motivations for writing them, she once explained, "I wrote them because I wanted to write books. There's no flame in them. They're of little value. There's no real trip, no investment in them. I'd like to be rich and eccentric enough to buy all the copies."[50] Luckily, though, the books survive. Although in comparison to Tyler's later novels they now seem slight and underdeveloped, they nevertheless provide insight into Tyler's early themes and illustrate the direction in which her writing style would progress.

Tyler's thoughts on the writing process at this formative stage in her career reveal both a writer struggling to express herself as well as a writer who already exhibits a great deal of self-discipline. In a 1965 interview, she described the process of writing as "agonizing." Even more difficult for her was seeing her work in print: "You think you have an idea but when you sit down to write you discover it's not as developed as you think it is. But the harder part is to read it in print--that's usually about a year later. By that time you hate it because it's too long ago, and you're too embarrassed about the whole thing. I think that's much harder than writing."[51]

Tyler's dedication to writing is also apparent in other early interviews. In fact she admitted feeling "almost guilty if I don't do some writing every day. I think you have an obligation to do more than just look at life." After her first two novels, she planned to move on to other subjects and to "get away from the South. I don't want it to turn into a crutch. One thing I don't want to do is forget how to write short stories. I found that after I finished *If Morning Ever Comes* the first few stories I wrote were much too long. But I've got a one-track mind and I can't do both kinds at the same time."[52]

Living in Canada caused Tyler to feel even further apart from the outside world than her early experience at Celo had. Living in another country created even more distance from which she could observe the world. The culture of Canada itself she later described as "half foreign, half familiar."[53] She disliked Montreal's cold winter weather, and she must have found the city's French language a further barrier, at least at first, although with her aptitude for languages she eventually managed quite well.

The only story Tyler ever set in Canada is "A Flaw in the Crust of the Earth," a short story published in 1967. The story depicts the isolation of a young college dropout named Peter, who lives in Montreal and works in the copying room at the library. He likes the job for the same reason that Tyler liked her job at the McGill Law Library: he can leave at the end of the day and not have to think about work anymore. Then one day his apartment is burglarized. The robbery symbolically marks the start of the breakdown of his isolation. Most interestingly, the thief inexplicably steals a photograph of Peter. That night, unable to sleep, he watches a woman in the next apartment building and imagines erecting a bridge with an ironing board over to her apartment. In his isolation he yearns for connections.

The next day Peter decides to leave Montreal, not planning to go anywhere in particular but just to escape. Whether he is escaping from his isolation or fleeing for fear of losing that isolation is unclear. At the train station, however, he meets a woman who is also leaving the city because she believes Montreal is built on an enormous flaw in the crust of the earth and expects a cataclysmic earthquake at any moment. The woman's foolishness makes Peter realize that his impulse to flee is equally foolish. Wherever he might go he would still find the universal human condition of isolation and fear. Rather than depressing him further, this knowledge makes him feel better, so he gets up and returns home. In Tyler's view of the universe, the flaws and cracks in life are no reason for not living life as best as one can. To her, the act of endurance itself is a virtue.

Despite the Montreal setting, the story's location is really nonspecific. The particular city of Montreal does not come to life because Tyler mentions no specific landmarks and makes no attempt to reproduce the speech patterns or customs of the city in her characters. The story could have taken place in any large city. Tyler could never write about the real Montreal because she did not live there long enough to understand its people in the way she had understood North Carolina, or in the way she would one day feel about Baltimore.

MOTHERHOOD

Any isolation that Tyler might have felt in Montreal was irrevocably broken with the birth of her first daughter, Tezh, in 1965. Tezh proved to be an insomniac like her mother, so her arrival dramatically changed Tyler's world. Staying up all night to walk the baby left Anne without the energy or time to write on a schedule. Instead her schedule was dictated by feeding and nap times. As Tyler quickly discovered, motherhood was a fulltime job and an exhausting one. The birth of a second daughter, Mitra, two years later further limited Tyler's creative time.

Tyler must have remembered the enormous amounts of time and energy required of new mothers when years later in *Saint Maybe* she wrote a scene in which Rita, who has never had a child, tries to convince Ian, who has spent most of his adult life raising his brother's three children, that babies are not too much trouble, especially if she and Ian have a girl rather than a boy. Ian replies, "Neither is easy" (*SM* 311), and then evaluates his parenting experience:

A lot of it was just plain boring. Just providing a warm body, just *being* there; anyone could have done it. And then other parts were terrifying. Kids get into so much! They start to matter so much. Some days I felt like a fireman or a lifeguard or something--all that tedium, broken up by little spurts of high drama. (*SM* 312)

But like Ian, Tyler usually found the experience of parenthood rewarding. She refused to relinquish her children's care to anyone else. Although some housekeepers do a fine job raising children, she wrote in "Still Just Writing," every child she has seen brought up like that seems "dulled and doesn't use words well."[54] She determined that such would not be the fate of her children. These maternal concerns and her deep love for her daughters made her set aside her own work temporarily.

Tyler's self-imposed, partial sabbatical from writing lasted from 1965 to 1970 (the years from the birth of her first daughter until her second daughter began nursery school). The greatest portion of her time was fully occupied in caring for her daughters. She sometimes wondered whether this period of her life was ever going to end and whether her writing skills would decline. In retrospect, however, she realized that the time passed rather quickly. A few years later when her daughters were past infancy, she was able to put the seemingly overwhelming responsibilities of raising children into clearer perspective. She encouraged an Iranian cousin who had just had a baby by telling her that this stage would not last more than three years and that having a child made all the sacrifices worthwhile.[55]

Somehow, despite the limitations on her time and the drain on her energy, Tyler did continue to write a little. With the many demands and interruptions of motherhood, however, she concentrated primarily on the less time-consuming task of writing short stories. Stories published during this period include "As the Earth Gets Old," "Two People and a Clock on the Wall," "The Genuine Fur Eyelashes," "The Tea-Machine," "The Feather Behind the Rock," "A Flaw in the Crust of the Earth," "Who Would Want a Little Boy?," and "The Common Courtesies," a story, interestingly enough, about a mother's less-than-enthusiastic acceptance of her daughter's pregnancy and motherhood. Many other unpublished stories in the Anne Tyler Papers attest to her efforts to keep writing during this period.

Motherhood, however, was not without certain benefits. Even as it drained her emotionally and physically, it also had a maturing effect. She explained the paradox years later when her children were teenagers: "Since I've had children, I've grown richer and deeper. They may have slowed my writing for a while, but when I did write, I had more of a self to speak from."[56] In subsequent novels, her portrayals of mothers have grown deeper and richer. She has moved from stereotype to fully-realized characterizations of the mothers in her novels. In contrast to the one-dimensional Ellen Hawkes of *If Morning Ever Comes* and the juvenile immaturity of Evie Decker in *A Slipping-Down Life*, Tyler's mothers have become increasingly multilayered and complex. Her understanding of the demands of motherhood and her sensitivity for the feelings of mothers improve steadily from her portrayal of the caretaker Elizabeth Abbott in *The Clock Winder*, to Mary Tell in *Celestial Navigation*, whose "natural state" is pregnancy,[57] to Muriel Pritchett and Sarah Leary, whose conflicting feelings about motherhood Tyler explores in *The Accidental Tourist*.

In her new role as mother, Tyler began to relish the role of caretaker. Although motherhood sometimes proved exhausting, she discovered an inner need to nurture others. In a 1972 interview she admitted this interest in nurturing, yet also expressed a seemingly contradictory belief in not interfering in other people's lives: "I must find the idea of taking care of others very attractive; there must be a place in life for people who do that. If I have to take a moral stand, though, I feel terribly strongly that nobody should do anything, that you should leave your hands out of other people's business."[58] Perhaps, in some way, Tyler's writing allows her to exercise both contradictory needs. It provides her the opportunity to take absolute care and control of the lives of her characters, but, since her characters are not actual people, she does not feel that she has intruded upon another person's privacy.

Tyler soon learned that she had to separate her writing life from her real life. Her futile attempts to combine motherhood and writing produced several confusing situations. In "Still Just Writing," Tyler recalls one particularly amusing scene. Having discovered that she often thought of some of her best ideas while she was doing housework, she started carrying around a tape recorder to record ideas as she was vacuuming. But she found that such a mixing of her two lives never quite worked, so she returned the tape recorder to the store. Instead, she found it more productive to keep her two lives (writer and housewife) separate, like two different pieces of string that she picks up at different times.[59]

Such a partitioning of her life helped Tyler maintain her sense of objectivity and distance. Later she even wondered whether, having "spent so long erecting partitions around the part of me that writes--learning how to close the door on it when ordinary life intervenes" she "could fit the two parts of myself back together now."[60] Such a partitioning of her life provided her the necessary time and place for her writing. Conversely, maintaining the other half of the partition, her family life, allowed her to meet the responsibilities of motherhood and marriage. These ties to her family Tyler has called her "anchors to reality."[61] Thus, with herself firmly anchored in the real world of her family, she felt free to journey, imaginatively, into the lives of the families she was creating in her fiction.

"WINTER BIRDS, WINTER APPLES"

Tyler's one attempt at writing anything longer than a short story between the births of her daughters, consequently, proved disappointing. After Tezh's birth, Tyler began writing "Winter Birds, Winter Apples" (1966). The novel's plot involves another family of women, this one living alone on the North Carolina seacoast. As in *If Morning Ever Comes*, the women are strong, independent characters. They have been forced to become strong by a history of desertions by male family members. One of the women, a young pregnant woman named Bridgett, thus becomes concerned when her husband Daniel fails to return on time from a trip. Thinking that he too has deserted her, Bridgett takes the initiative and moves out without leaving a note.

When Daniel returns late from his trip due to an accident, he must search for Bridgett, who has moved to her aunt's house. The miscommunication between the sensitive, pregnant wife and the well-meaning husband is somewhat reminiscent of Eudora Welty's story "The Wide Net." In that story a pregnant wife gets mad and hides from her husband. He comes home and mistakenly thinks she might have drowned, so he drags the river to look for her body. In Tyler's story, the misunderstanding is resolved when Daniel finally finds Bridgett and explains the purpose of his trip: to fetch a cradle as a surprise for Bridgett. Even with the misunderstanding cleared up, however, Bridgett initially refuses to take Daniel back. Finally, though, she gives in. In the end, miscommunication does not prove more powerful than human connections and mutual understanding.

"Winter Birds" anticipates the escape-and-return paradigm in *Searching for Caleb* and *Earthly Possessions*. It also continues the theme of the limitations of language and communication between people. On this issue Bridgett's expressions of independence when Daniel returns are particularly interesting. She tells her husband bluntly, "I won't be kept in a box for you,"[62] mirroring perhaps Tyler's own feelings of being restricted by the enormous responsibilities of her new role as mother and her feelings about this self-imposed hiatus from her writing. Tyler felt that her stories were bottled up within her and feared that they might be lost. With the exception of a few short stories, she published nothing. The manuscript for "Winter Birds" remains in the Anne Tyler Papers and will probably never be published.

Still, Tyler always managed to maintain an objective perspective. Though Taghi's work as a doctor took him away from the family often, leaving Anne as the primary caretaker, she realized that he made great sacrifices too. In "Still Just Writing" she describes the mutually dependent and beneficial relationship that developed between them: Taghi became the family's "liaison with the outside world, bringing in money"; Anne served as the "caretaker," who read bedtime stories to the children and kept the house in repair.[63]

BALTIMORE

In 1967, Taghi completed his residency at the Allan Institute. He received a job offer from the University of Maryland School of Medicine in Baltimore. So the Modarressi family packed up and moved to Baltimore, the setting of so many of Tyler's novels. At the time they did not consider the move permanent. Taghi still planned to return to Iran, but political conditions there were beginning to deteriorate.

The luck, or providence, of Taghi's Baltimore job offer was to prove monumental to Tyler's work, but not immediately. The city itself is so intrinsically associated with Tyler's work now that one can scarcely imagine what might have happened if Taghi's employment had taken the family anywhere else. Baltimore, with its many neighborhoods, its sense of history, and its diversity seems the perfect place for Tyler. At first, as with Montreal, Tyler needed time to get to know the city before she began to write about it.

A SLIPPING-DOWN LIFE

Despite having lived in Baltimore for over two years, when Tyler began to write her next book in 1969 she still chose a North Carolina setting. A newspaper story she had read years earlier provided the inspiration for the novel. The article recounted the story of a girl in Texas who slashed Elvis Presley's name on her forehead in an attempt to get his attention. From that germ of an idea grew A Slipping-Down Life (1970).

A Slipping-Down Life is Tyler's shortest novel, perhaps because she wrote it when she was "tied down by two infants, trying to work in snatched moments at night."[64] The novel tells the story of a young girl, Evie Decker, who carves the last name of a local rock singer, Drumstrings Casey, into her forehead to gain his attention. Drum first thinks of Evie's action as grotesque, but then later he decides that she is good publicity and eventually asks her to marry him. Evie responds to Drum's marriage proposal with the same words Anne used with Taghi, "Oh, well. Why not?"[65]

After her marriage to Drum, Evie begins to mature rapidly, especially after she becomes pregnant. Drum, on the other hand, fails to mature at all. Faced with the prospect of receiving no support from her husband, Evie Decker realizes that it is up to her to look after both herself and her baby. She is the first of Tyler's mothers to exhibit a strong sense of responsibility for a child, even if it means abandoning the father. By the end of the book, Evie has found a job (like Tyler in a library) and moved into the house she inherits from her father and out of her relationship with the unreliable (and unfaithful) Drum.

Despite the novel's short length and slight scope, Tyler's feelings about *A Slipping-Down Life* reveal its importance in the development of her writing. Though realizing that the book is "flawed," she nonetheless thinks of it as "a certain brave stepping forth."[66] In particular, she loves the characters. Drum is a special favorite. She loves him, "his family, everything about him. He's the direct inheritance of all the days on the tobacco farm."[67] Tyler was also pleased by another aspect of the book: "It's the one book of mine in which the characters do change."[68] Possibilities for change or the failure of characters to change continued to fascinate her.

Unfortunately, sales of *A Slipping-Down Life* were disappointing. It fared worse than even *The Tin Can Tree*, with only 7800 hardcover sales. Still Bantam bought the paperback rights in March 1971. Perhaps part of the reason for the book's dismal sales is that critics mistakenly labeled it as a book for teenagers. *Booklist* named the book one of its "Best Books for Young Adults, 1970." Consequently, fewer reviews appeared, and those reviews merely summarized the book's plot briefly without much analysis. Even so, the quality of Tyler's writing did not go unrecognized.

Although most critics found Evie and Drum somewhat depressing characters, Tyler's skill in characterization continued to draw the attention of reviewers. Carol Eckberg Wadsworth's review for *Library Journal* is typical: "the story does not seem very important; yet it is engrossing and shows insight into the psychology of some rather depressing lives."[69] Likewise, Martin Levin, in a brief review for the *New York Times Book Review*, dismissed the book as an "unassuming folk tale of two teenage losers" that nonetheless "takes the measure of their social climate."[70] Finally, Pauline J. Earl alluded to what was to become a trademark of Tyler's--eccentric characters--in describing the novel as "an offbeat, but rather human story."[71]

The first few years of living in Baltimore were busy, tiring, challenging times of transition for Tyler, years in which she had to take on new roles and adjust to her life in another place. But, while these changes may have seemed like an interruption in her writing career, they were actually quite beneficial. Once she developed roots in Baltimore, this place would provide her imagination with fertile ground so that she could launch out on greater journeys in the books that were to come.

Endnotes

1. J. D. Reed, "Postfeminism: Playing for Keeps," *Time* (10 Jan. 1983): 61.

2. Nora Frenkiel, "Writing to Find 'Absent People' and Himself," *Baltimore Sun* (25 Feb. 1986): B1.

3. Clifford Ridley, "Anne Tyler: A Sense of Reticence Balanced by 'Oh, Well, Why Not?'" *National Observer* (22 July 1972): 23.

4. Ridley 23.

5. Anne Tyler, "Linguistics," *Washington Post Magazine* (12 Nov. 1978): 39.

6. Tyler 46.

7. Letter from Anne Tyler to the author, 19 Mar. 1993.

8. Joan Forsey, "An Author at 22," Montreal *Gazette* (2 Oct. 1964): 18.

9. Letter from Anne Tyler to the author, 19 Mar. 1993.

10. Anne Tyler, "Your Place Is Empty," *New Yorker* (22 Nov. 1976): 49.

11. Tyler 54.

12. Tyler, "Linguistics" 46.

13. Laurie L. Brown, "Interviews with Seven Contemporary Writers," *Southern Quarterly* 21 (Summer 1983): 4.

14. Michael Ballantyne, "Novel No. 1 Published, No. 2 Typed, No. 3 Is Jelling," *Montreal Star* (21 Nov. 1964): Entertainments 4.

15. Anne Tyler, *If Morning Ever Comes* (New York: Knopf, 1964): 26. Subsequent references will be cited in the text.

16. Letter from Anne Tyler to the author, 29 Aug. 1992.

17. Jorie Lueloff, "Authoress Explains Why Women Dominate in South," Baton Rouge *Morning Advocate* (8 Feb. 1965): A11.

18. Lueloff A11.

19. Lueloff A11.

20. Anne Tyler, "I Never Saw Morning," *Archive* (Apr. 1961): 14.

21. Orville Prescott, "Return to the Hawkes Family," *New York Times* (11 Nov. 1964): 41.

22. Letter from Judith Jones to the author, 28 July 1993.

23. Katherine Gauss Jackson, "Mad First Novel, but Without Madness," *Harper's* (Nov. 1964): 152.

24. Walter Sullivan, "Worlds Past and Future: A Christian and Several from the South," *Sewanee Review* 73 (Autumn 1965): 719.

25. Clifford A. Ridley, "From First Novels to the Loves of William Shakespeare," *National Observer* (16 Nov. 1964): 21.

26. Rollene W. Saal, "Loveless Household," *New York Times Book Review* (22 Nov. 1964): 52.

27. *Virginia Quarterly Review* 41 (Winter 1965): viii.

28. George Dorner, "Anne Tyler: A Brief Interview with a Brilliant Author from Baltimore," *The Rambler* 2 (1979): 22.

29. Julian Gloag, "Home Was a House Full of Women," *Saturday Review* (26 Dec. 1964): 38.

30. Lueloff A11.

31. Helene Woizesko and Michael Scott Cain, "Anne Tyler," *Northeast Rising Sun* 1 (June-July 1976): 29.

32. Forsey 18.

33. Anne Tyler, *The Tin Can Tree* (New York: Knopf, 1965): 106. Subsequent references will be cited in the text.

34. Katherine Gauss Jackson, *Harper's* (Dec. 1965): 133.

35. Millicent Bell, "Tobacco Road Updated," *New York Times Book Review* (21 Nov. 1965): 77.

36. Mary Stack McNiff, *America* (30 Oct. 1965): 508.

37. Anne Tyler, "He Did It All for Jane Elizabeth Firesheets," *New York Times Book Review* (15 June 1986): 9.

38. Jackson 133.

39. Ian Flavin, *Books and Bookmen* (Feb. 1967): 30.

40. McNiff 507.

41. J. M. Stedmond, "Fiction," *University of Toronto Quarterly* 36 (July 1967): 384.

42. McNiff 508.

43. Clifford A. Ridley, "Spark and Tyler Are Proof Anew of Knopf Knowledge of Top Fiction," *National Observer* (29 Nov. 1965): 25.

44. *Booklist* (15 Oct. 1965): 196.

45. Jackson 133.

46. John Conley, "A Clutch of Fifteen," *Southern Review* NS 3 (July 1967): 782.

47. D.E. Richardson, "Grits and Mobility: Three Southern Novels," *Shenandoah* 17 (Winter 1966): 105.

48. Mary Ellen Brooks, "Anne Tyler," in James E. Kibler, ed. *The Dictionary of Literary Biography*: American Novelists Since World War II, vol. 6 (Detroit: Gale Research, 1980): 337.

49. Wendy Lamb, "An Interview with Anne Tyler," *Iowa Journal of Literary Studies* 3 (1981): 64.

50. Woizesko and Cain 28.

51. Forsey 18.

52. Ballantyne Entertainments 4.

53. Anne Tyler, review of *Crossing the Border, Fifteen Tales* by Joyce Carol Oates, *New York Times Book Review* (18 July 1976): 8.

54. Anne Tyler, "Still Just Writing," in Janet Sternburg, ed. *The Writer on Her Work* (New York: Norton, 1980): 7.

55. Tyler 9.

56. Tyler 9.

57. Anne Tyler, *Celestial Navigation* (New York: Knopf, 1974): 69. Subsequent references will be cited in the text.

58. Clifford Ridley, "Anne Tyler: A Sense of Reticence Balanced by 'Oh, Well, Why Not?'" *National Observer* (22 July 1972): 23.

59. Tyler, "Still Just Writing" 9.

60. Tyler 7.

61. Marguerite Michaels, "Anne Tyler, Writer 8:05 to 3:30," *New York Times Book Review* (8 May 1977): 43.

62. Anne Tyler, "Winter Birds, Winter Apples," unpublished manuscript, The Anne Tyler Papers, Special Collections Library, Duke University: 161.

63. Tyler, "Still Just Writing" 8.

64. Brooks 337.

65. Anne Tyler, *A Slipping-Down Life* (New York: Knopf, 1970): 131. Subsequent references will be cited in the text.

66. Brooks 340.

67. Ridley, "Anne Tyler" 23.

68. Ridley 23.

69. Carol Eckberg Wadsworth, *Library Journal* (15 Mar. 1970): 1050.

70. Martin Levin, "Reader's Report," *New York Times Book Review* (15 Mar. 1970): 44.

71. Pauline J. Earl, *Best Sellers* (1 May 1970): 58.

"Rich with Possibilities"

At the end of *Morgan's Passing*, Morgan Gower walks down the street holding a stack of letters given to him by a woman who mistakes him for a postman. The mistake pleases him because it reinforces his habit of stepping into different roles and allows him to learn the secrets contained in the letters before he mails them. The novel ends with Morgan's ebullient reverie: "Everything he looked at seemed luminous and beautiful, and rich with possibilities."[1]

Like Morgan's life, the next decade of Anne Tyler's life seemed rich with possibilities. Although she had stopped moving around and taken firm root in Baltimore, her new home provided more opportunities for exploring the tension between her seemingly contradictory desires to live other lives and to maintain a stable family life. Through her writing, although Tyler could not, like Morgan, step literally into other people's shoes, she did manage to live other lives imaginatively through her characters.

The title of Tyler's 1976 article for the *Washington Post*, "Because I Want More Than One Life," hints at her not-so-subtle desire to reach beyond the limitations of her life as wife and mother. Although happy in both of these roles, she apparently needed to live the richer, fuller life of the artist as well to make her life complete. In the article she explains, "Mostly it's lies, writing novels,"[2] lies which she invents and, strangest of all to her, sometimes gets paid for writing down. She says that she writes because she enjoys the escape of living "more than one life" and "insist[s] on a wider selection."[3]

In "Because I Want More Than One Life" and a 1977 interview with Marguerite Michaels, aptly titled "Anne Tyler, Writer 8:05 to 3:30," Tyler describes both her method of composition and the challenges she faced as a young mother and wife during this period of her career. She would rise at 6 or 6:30 to make her daughters' breakfasts and get them ready for school. Then she would cook the family's supper for the night so that the rest of her day she could devote to her writing. By 8:00 she would be up in her study, a starkly furnished white-walled room furnished with a daybed and a few bookcases that contain almanacs dating back to 1948 and a set of Time-Life history books covering each decade back to 1870. Tyler uses these books as reference sources to insure both the historical accuracy and immediacy of her work. In addition, the room's shelves contain several photography books for her to "just to sink into" and "fill up on when [she] feel[s] empty."[4] The presence of these books attests to her continuing interest in art.

The study's walls are covered with framed pictures of everything from family photographs to newspaper clippings. Most of the pictures, Tyler admits, "have to do with isolation: uninhabited houses, deserted courtrooms, stark old men staring into space."[5]   Two significant items among the framed objects are the photograph of her great-grandfather playing a cello in the hayloft of a barn, the source for the cover of *Searching for Caleb*, and a handwritten copy of Richard Wilbur's poem "Walking to Sleep,"[6] which admonishes its reader to "Step off assuredly into the blank of your mind," waiting confidently for the results.[7]

Tyler's method of composition follows the poem's admonition closely. Sitting cross-legged on her daybed, she sits and stares at the wall for the first thirty minutes or so, clicking her pen (always a fine-tipped black Parker ball-point) until her thoughts "snag on something--some passer-by . . . from years ago, or some intricate family situation."[8] Not since she was a teenager, Tyler claims, has she used "an actual living person" as the model for one of her characters. As she thinks about a character, she begins to imagine what it would be like to be that other person and soon her thoughts grow into fully realized characters. As a book or short story develops, she feels these characters becoming increasingly independent of her, until at times they refuse even to obey her and seem to take on separate lives of their own. Tyler alludes to this strange power of her characters when she describes her futile attempts to write scenes or situations that do not fit the characters. In the end, she always discovers that she must give in to the characters' demands. Once she finally lets "the plot go their way," then "everything falls into place."[9]

In order to hear her characters' distinctive voices, Tyler insists on writing in longhand. According to her, the "sound of the typewriter would stop my ears from working."[10] Two of her greatest fears are blindness (because she would not be able to see how the words look on the page) and arthritis (because she would not be able to hold a pen for long stretches of time). In recent years, however, she has made concessions to technology. She eventually acquired a word processor to type final drafts and book reviews. In the early stages of composing her fiction, however, she still writes out every word laboriously in longhand.

BOOK REVIEWS

In an almost prescient observation, the main character of Tyler's 1960 Flexner Award-winning entry ponders the shelves full of books in her house: "the books themselves were fine and solid, with good bindings and carefully kept pages. Row on row they marched, all around three walls and then another row in the hall. Who would ever have guessed she could have had time to read all those books in just one lifetime?"[11] Tyler might have been looking into her own future, for twelve years later she began another career--as book reviewer. In November 1972, her first review appeared in the *National Observer*, followed by two more in 1974; then in February 1975 she became a regular reviewer for the *National Observer*, writing an average of one review a month until the periodical ceased publication in July 1977. Her reasons for undertaking this new career seem as ambivalent as her response to Taghi's marriage proposal: "I started reviewing just because the various publications asked me to."[12] She does, however, admit to a secondary motivation. The money from reviewing helped "pay my children's school fees."[13] Tezh and Mitra attended a private Quaker school in Baltimore.

Apparently, when Tyler began reviewing for the *National Observer*, its editors considered her primarily a short story writer; in fact, her first five reviews for the *Observer* were of short story collections. As her reputation as a novelist and book reviewer grew, however, that perception changed. Her *Observer* reviewing expanded to include novels, and other publications also began to ask her to review as well. In 1976, she began reviewing for the *New York Times Book Review* and, two years later, the *New Republic*. Soon she was writing for a number of periodicals, including the

Saturday Review, *Vogue*, and the *Atlantic*, in addition to newspapers all over the country such as the *Washington Post*, *Chicago Tribune*, *Boston Globe*, *Baltimore Sun*, *Chicago Sun-Times*, *San Francisco Chronicle*, *Detroit News*, *Raleigh News and Observer*, and *USA Today*.

From 1972 to 1991, Tyler produced more than two hundred and fifty book reviews in which she reveals herself to be both a keen, if somewhat benign, critic and a seemingly omnivorous reader. Whenever she reviews a book, she appears to know not only the book she is presently reviewing, but the author's entire oeurve as well. As for the impact of review writing on her fiction, Tyler claims that it improved her analytical abilities: "I do believe reviewing has sharpened my thought processes. I used to read books like eating chocolates--I like it, I don't like it, toss it aside and reach for the next-- but reviewing has forced me to stop and analyze what makes a book work or not work."[14] Certainly the higher quality of Tyler's novels since she became a book reviewer suggests that this deeper analytical perception benefitted her own writing.

One of the most important aesthetic credos revealed in Tyler's book reviews is her belief in a pact between author and reader. In one of her earliest reviews she castigates a book's author who, in her opinion, has not lived up to this tacit agreement: "If a contract exists between writer and reader that the writer will do his best to draw the reader in and the reader will do his best to follow, [this author] has reneged on his part of the deal."[15] She particularly dislikes self-reflexive works that make no attempt to reach out to the reader because, as she describes a Susan Sontag book, "they turn too far inward, making no effort in the direction of the reader."[16] In Tyler's view, the author should make every effort to reach his or her audience so that "readers [do not] have to work so hard to find [a book's treasure]."[17]

Such a reader-centered philosophy of writing, however, does not preclude experimentation. Tyler often praises authors for their creativity, simply demanding sufficient craftsmanship to make such experimentation succeed. To meet her standards, a writer's experiments must never fail to draw the reader into the writer's world.

And for Tyler, what draws a reader into that fictional world is detail. Again and again in book reviews spanning the two decades of her reviewing career, Tyler praises authors who have mastered the skillful use of detail to create "a wonderful particularity."[18] Of Nadine Gordimer's mastery of this technique Tyler writes, "She has a special reverence for the particular, for that one small, glittering facet that will cast light on the whole."[19] In a later review, she finds that Gordimer's "active details, humming with motion" are "so concrete that you're tempted to slap at the mosquitoes."[20] Tyler also notices Penelope Mortimer's "gift for presenting the single, precise detail that implies a whole stream of other details flowing underground."[21] In still another review she lauds "the deliberate click of the exactly right, cooly appropriate detail upon the page," which creates "a treasure chest of pure moments."[22]

Details such as these bring the fictional world alive and make characters seem like real people rather than fictional stereotypes. Tyler notes that good details create "a sense of particularity--a granting of a full measure of individualism to the most incidental character, place or fact"[23] and seem "so thoughtfully selected, so exactly right, that they strike the reader as inevitable."[24] If the details are particular enough, then readers feel as if "they've gained a toehold on another world."[25]

Even so, Tyler disapproves of merely amassing details. Although she first praises one author's "talent for piling up observations, coloring in each leaf and blade of grass till you have no choice but to visualize the scene laid before you," she then notes the writer's need for "the gift of selection."[26] Tyler's favorite word to describe the effect of good details is "layers." Properly selected, the right kind of details creates "more layers" to the story,[27] "complicated underlayers,"[28] "a feeling of depth, of multiple layers,"[29] and "the effect . . . of layers--of the levels of knowledge through which we proceed in getting to know any living person."[30] Such narrative layers recreate "the complexity that we stub our toes on every day in real life"[31] and produce literature that "totally submerges us . . . . so deeply into another world that we almost fear we won't be able to climb out again."[32]

SOCIAL ISSUES

Tyler's failure to concern herself in her fiction with current social issues has caused some critics to dismiss her writing as limited, shallow, and shortsighted. For instance, her novels set in the 1960s and early 1970s mention the Vietnam War only in passing. Ian Bedloe's convenient heart murmur keeps him out of the conflict in *Saint Maybe*, and Peter Emerson returns home from the war with little comment in *The Clock Winder*. Other novels such as *Celestial Navigation* and *A Slipping-Down Life* do not mention the war at all. Because of Tyler's neglect of such important social issues, Susan Gilbert has gone so far as to claim that "Tyler's characters persist in ignorance of or indifference to social debates around them."[33]

The social topic seemingly most overlooked by Tyler, however, is the women's movement. This movement came to the forefront of the American scene at precisely the period when most of Tyler's novels are set, the 1960s through 1980s. Yet, according to her detractors, her female characters fail to move beyond traditional roles. Worse perhaps, these critics point out, when Tyler's women do encounter chances for escape, they often fail to seize them. After a brief sojourn, they usually return unscathed and unchanged by the experience back to the same often restrictive homes. Thus, in *A Slipping-Down Life* Evie Decker winds up in her father's home; Elizabeth Abbott becomes caregiver to the entire Emerson clan in *The Clock Winder*; Charlotte Emory, the character whose escape in *Earthly Possessions* seems, ostensibly, the most successful, returns to her conservative preacher husband Saul and even refuses his suggestion that they take a trip; Mary Tell simply moves from one man to another in *Celestial Navigation*; and Emily Meredith in *Morgan's Passing* switches partners but not her role within that relationship. Later novels, it seems, portray women as more content in their maternal and wifely roles. Jenny Tull, in *Dinner at the Homesick Restaurant*, becomes mother to a whole brood of children (in her pediatric practice and in her third marriage). Maggie Moran, never giving up on changing those she loves, sleeps peacefully beside her complacent husband at the end of *Breathing Lessons*. Bee Bedloe labors tirelessly to create holiday dinners of hors d'oeuvres in *Saint Maybe*.

In Tyler's vision, men and women are human beings first, males or females second. In her life and in her writing she emphasizes the humanity of people and de-emphasizes gender differences. In a book review of stories by women she explained:

> It's my personal feeling that only a portion of my life--and almost none
> of my writing life--is much affected by what sex I happen to be. And I
> can't imagine that even that portion would be affected in the same way for
> everyone.[34]

To Tyler, individuality and a healthy respect for each person's uniqueness (whether male or female) are of paramount concern.

Perhaps, Tyler, who grew up in a houseful of men (three brothers and a father) with only her mother as a fellow female role model, was rarely made conscious of the differences between the sexes, or of the societally imposed restrictions upon them. As a result, she seems to have developed a non-gender-specific view of life. Therefore, from the very beginning, in her novels she felt free to speak, convincingly, in the voice of both male and female narrators. *If Morning Ever Comes* presents the perspective of Ben Joe Hawkes, while *The Accidental Tourist* concentrates on the viewpoint of Macon Leary. Other novels treat life from the perspective of a female narrator. In *A Slipping-Down Life*, Evie Decker provides the focus, and in *Earthly Possessions*, Charlotte Emory takes center stage. More often, however, Tyler's novels utilize multiple perspectives, viewing life from the vantage points of both sexes. As early as 1961 in "I Know You, Rider," Tyler experimented with such an approach, continuing to develop it in *The Tin Can Tree* and *Celestial Navigation*. Finally, in her later novels she has seemingly become incapable of restricting herself to one perspective. Thus, in *Breathing Lessons* she penetrates the minds of both Maggie and Ira Moran, and in *Saint Maybe* she portrays the viewpoints of a variety of people, not only of both sexes but also of different ages.

Oddly enough, however, despite Tyler's belief that the possibilities for male and female characters are not determined by their sex, she often does portray women in her novels as intelligent but uneducated. From Evie Decker to Justine Peck to Maggie Moran, woman after woman has little or no college education, odd perhaps for a writer whose education includes study at two of the country's most distinguished universities-- Duke and Columbia. Later characters, however, break this trend, although uneducated female characters always remain. For example, in *The Accidental Tourist*, Sarah Leary is an English teacher, but Muriel Pritchett has barely finished high school. In *Saint Maybe*, Agatha finishes medical school (as has Jenny Tull in *Dinner at the Homesick Restaurant*), but Daphne floats from one deadend job to the next with just a high school degree.

In all fairness, few of Tyler's characters of either sex are overeducated. Tyler's men often lack formal higher education. Certainly Jake Simms, Caleb Peck, and Drum Casey never darken a college classroom door. Other men dream of continuing their studies, but circumstances prevent them. Ira Moran and Ian Bedloe abandon college plans to care for their families. Like their less ambitious counterparts, they have to settle for jobs that, like most people's, do not require a college education. Tyler's fascination with common jobs like these stems from her continuing interest in the ordinary. Such jobs place her characters squarely in the mainstream of ordinary life where they can encounter situations and people from ordinary life. Thus, her characters work shelving books at the local library (Evie Decker in *A Slipping-Down Life*), telling fortunes (Justine Peck in *Searching for Caleb*), framing needlepoint (Ira Moran in *Breathing Lessons*), or building furniture (Ian Bedloe in *Saint Maybe*).

For all her even-handedness, though, Tyler is not oblivious to the obstacles in the paths of women, nor does she readily forgive obvious sexism. She mocks one author's sexist description of a woman with "legs beginning at the hips" with the quip, "It's not clear where else they would begin."[35] In a review of a nineteenth century cookbook, she admires the recipes but notes the drudgery and toil that preparing them required: "none of this came easy. We are talking of the days when women (for it was never men, heaven knows) ground their own spices and roasted their own coffee beans, . . . beheaded their own pigs, and concocted their own food colorings."[36] Particularly in reviews of children's books, perhaps because children are not so set in their attitudes and still capable of change, she takes special care to note positive treatments of female characters. In a review of one children's book, she points out that the town doctor just happens to be a woman[37] and applauds another book's presentation of its "female characters in productive, unstereotyped roles."[38]

THE CLOCK WINDER

Tyler's fourth published novel, *The Clock Winder*, marks another "brave stepping forth." In it she examines the interaction of a caretaker, Elizabeth Abbott, who paradoxically does not "like people you can have so much effect on,"[39] with the "event-prone" (*CW* 172) Emerson family she eventually assumes responsibility for. The novel is the first example of Tyler's willingness to tackle larger time periods in her writing. She extends her scope to cover the entire decade of 1960-1970, although she denotes the passage of time rather arbitrarily by simply noting the year at the beginning of certain chapters.

Throughout the novel Elizabeth struggles with the dilemma of whether to involve herself in the lives of the ironically unself-reliant Emersons, pieces of whose lives and problems become "lodged within Elizabeth like shrapnel" (*CW* 150). Initially arriving simply to work as a handyman for Mrs. Pamela Emerson, the recently widowed matriarch of the clan, Elizabeth is soon drawn into the lives of the seven adult Emerson children. In fact, she eventually affects them so much that one, Timothy, commits suicide because of her; another, Andrew, shoots her in the arm; and still another, Matthew, marries her. As a result, her identity becomes inextricably joined to theirs.

Near the end of the novel, Elizabeth even loses the distinguishing label of her name. The doctor who treats her for a gunshot wound identifies her as a member of the accident-prone family: "You Emersons could support me single-handed" (*CW* 281). Following a stroke that causes a slurring of her speech, Mrs. Emerson begins calling Elizabeth "Gillespie," a name that sticks even after Mrs. Emerson's recovery. After her marriage to Matthew, Elizabeth's last name officially becomes Emerson. By the end of the novel, Elizabeth's original names are completely lost, and the transformation of her identity is complete.

Tyler herself must have identified with Elizabeth's situation, for she considered the novel self-revelatory. In an interview shortly after the novel's publication she stated, "I'm getting a little more and more willing to expose more of myself with each book. There's more of *me* in *The Clock Winder*--not autobiography, but more that I feel."[40] A few years later, in a panel discussion at Duke, however, she confessed that "a lot of the vagueness" she saw in her early novels such as *The Clock Winder* "was just wrapping cotton wadding so that no one could see me in the book in any way."[41] Yet such "cotton wadding" could not hide her feelings completely.

In the overall context of Tyler's canon, *The Clock Winder* is perhaps most significant for its setting. It marks the first time that Tyler chose Baltimore as the setting for a novel. The specific locale is Roland Park, an upscale neighborhood similar to her own Homeland. After five years in Baltimore, Tyler had assimilated enough of the city's atmosphere and people to feel comfortable setting a novel there. Despite beginning in Baltimore, however, Tyler could not at this point set the entire book there. Thus, in the middle of the novel, Elizabeth runs away to her home in Ellington, North Carolina, acting out yet another of Tyler's escape-and-return paradigms. Like Thomas Wolfe before her, what Elizabeth finds in North Carolina is that she can't go home again. Once there, her father, a repressive Baptist minister, attempts to force her to fit a preconceived mold and tries to marry her off to her old boyfriend Dommie (whose name sounds like "Dummy"). Elizabeth, however, rebels against such repression and leaves Dommie at the altar. After a brief sojourn teaching crafts in a reform school, she chooses to return to Baltimore and the Emersons.

Oddly enough, returning necessitates reassuming the caretaker role from which she had originally fled. Nevertheless, within a few years she is running the Emerson household with a seeming effortlessness and efficiency, managing to cook supper, rid the house of cicadas, and nurse a child all at once "like a broad golden madonna" (*CW* 309). Such a happy ending may indicate Elizabeth's acceptance of and contentment in her role. Tyler, however, viewed the ending with skepticism: "I think Elizabeth does herself irreparable damage in not going farther than she does, but on the other hand what she does is the best and happiest thing for her. I think of it as a sad ending, and I've been surprised that not everyone does."[42] Tyler's statement reveals two important aspects of her literary philosophy: 1) her characters are independent and 2) she accepts their right to live their own lives.

The Clock Winder's sales held steady with her previous novels, selling just 10,600. Once again Bantam bought the paperback rights in July 1973. Tyler's continuing emphasis on character at the expense of plot is reflected in the unenthusiastic reviews of *The Clock Winder*. Although, as Martin Levin observed, the "richly idiosyncratic characters . . . amble about in Chekhovian fashion" with a "gentle charm," nevertheless "one wishes their story had more substance."[43] The *Virginia Quarterly Review* echoed these sentiments, noting Tyler's creation of "a novel of vast interest entirely with character."[44]

In particular, reviewers criticized the structure and resolution of the novel. Elizabeth Easton, writing for the *Saturday Review*, commented: "The novel wanders aimlessly along much as its heroine did. The author doesn't seem to know quite what to do with her characters, any more than Elizabeth knew what she wanted to do with her life."[45] Similarly, Catharine Mack Smith, in her *New Statesman* review, found "the change in [Elizabeth's] attitude . . . psychologically credible, but even so the all-round redemption is a little too neat, particularly in the case of Andrew, whose mental derangement is implausibly transformed into happy domesticated sanity."[46] The novel's "too neat" resolution also troubled George Hill, who, writing for the London *Times*, nevertheless conceded that despite "the family redemption [being] remarkably comprehensive . . . the book holds up well till then."[47]

CELESTIAL NAVIGATION

When asked which book marks Tyler's first great novel, Judith Jones, her editor of thirty years, replied unhesitatingly, "*Celestial Navigation*."[48] What could make someone who has known Tyler for so long choose this book rather than one of her later, more mature works? Perhaps the answer lies in the main subject of this novel--the creation of art. After all, *Celestial Navigation* explores the contradictory impulses of the artistic sensibility (whether the artistic medium be paint, music, words--as in Tyler's case--or pieces of red fabric stolen from a child's pajamas--as in Jeremy Pauling's). Furthermore, Tyler explores this issue with a forthrightness and openness that is at times almost painful.

Tyler's admission that her previous work had contained some "cotton wadding" reveals her desire to protect her privacy. Yet, with *Celestial Navigation*, she stripped away most of this self-imposed cover and revealed in Jeremy Pauling a personality very similar to her own. In writing about Jeremy, Tyler was actually examining the paradox inherent in her life or any artist's or writer's life. Several years later, in a review of Annie Dillard's *The Writing Life*, Tyler defined the writer's dilemma: "in order to describe the world the writer must withdraw from it."[49]

Writing *Celestial Navigation* was in some ways both Tyler's means of proving this paradox as well as escaping it. As she was starting the novel, she was "fighting the urge to remain in retreat" despite having more time to write once her youngest daughter began school. To her, creating Jeremy was a way of investigating her own "tendency to turn more and more inward."[50] Just as Jeremy's sculptures become larger and more multidimensional as he withdraws deeper into his imagination, so too does Tyler feel that her imagination is "freest when [she is] most confined" and that "having to stay put, having to deal with the discouragements and rewards of family life without any means of escape, has somehow made [her] inner world richer and deeper."[51]

Jeremy Pauling, therefore, holds a special place in Tyler's cast of characters, for she considers him, of all her creations, the character most like herself: "Jeremy's life is more of mine. He's isolated, I'm isolated, but he's more so."[52] Tyler even developed psychosomatic illnesses like Jeremy's while she was writing the novel,[53] although she claims she "didn't know the condition 'agoraphobia' existed" at the time.[54] As someone who values her privacy and feels close to her characters, Tyler understandably developed a fierce protectiveness of Jeremy. So as not to "intrude, [or] violate his privacy," she found herself cutting one sentence for every two she wrote.[55] Tyler's reluctance to reveal too much about Jeremy's private life is one possible explanation for the novel's major flaw: the lack of information about Jeremy's sexual relationship with Mary, a union that produces five children.

Tyler's way of writing *Celestial Navigation* illustrates her method of composition. She keeps an index card file of ideas that she has jotted down as she encounters interesting people who provide her with ideas for characters or fictional situations. First she flips through the file and takes out cards which she thinks she might use. Usually she winds up with about ten or so. Then for the first month of work on the novel she thinks about these characters in those situations and begins to outline the plot.[56] What results, as the plan for *Celestial Navigation* illustrates, is not an intricate outline of every event in the book, but a brief sentence-length entry for each chapter. For instance, the entry for chapter nine reads "Jeremy, 3rd p. Life alone. Trip to boatyard."[57] Additionally, Tyler drew up an actual floorplan for Jeremy's boarding house, complete with a drawing of the front of the house, so that she could keep up with which boarders (and later children) occupied which bedrooms. She also made charts to record the children's ages in certain years.

The novel tells the story of sculptor Jeremy Pauling's failed attempt to escape from the island of isolation on which he is "marooned"[58] because of an overprotective mother and his fragmented artistic sensibility. As the novel opens, Jeremy's mother has just died, leaving him a boarding house filled with a collection of eccentric old people and a succession of medical students.

Into Jeremy's isolated life walks Mary Tell, a young mother with a child. Mary has run off to Baltimore with a married man, but her first husband will not give her a divorce. At first Mary's realness almost overwhelms Jeremy, but after her boyfriend returns to his wife, Jeremy gathers the courage to ask her to marry him. The location of this proposal is significant. In one of the few ventures outside his house, he follows Mary down the block to the grocery store and faints. When she reaches down to help him, he proposes. Of course, she cannot marry him because she is not yet divorced, but they agree to pretend to be married and proceed to have five children in the space of ten years.

Unfortunately, despite the encouraging signs of connection and identity that seem to be forming in Jeremy's life, the opposite actually occurs. Jeremy is "baffled" (*CN* 157) by the children. He sees them as "visitors from the outside world" (*CN* 158). Worse still, he views Mary as a "supplier, feeder, caretaker" (*CN* 160), a basically maternal role that Tyler must have felt she held in her own family. Jeremy and Mary therefore in some ways represent the two sides of Tyler's life as well--artist and homemaker.

The novel's crisis comes when, after ten years, Mary's husband finally divorces her. Yet, when she suggests that she and Jeremy can finally marry, he is not strong enough to abandon the status quo: his artistic isolation. He withdraws into his artistic shell mentally and into his studio physically and does not come out until the next day when hunger forces him to seek food. On the refrigerator door he finds a note from Mary explaining that she and the children have left.

Jeremy's response to this abandonment is significant. Rather than immediately going after his family, he retreats to his studio to continue working on his latest statue, "a man half running, glad to be gone" (*CN* 181). He fixes the statue's image "very firmly in his mind like some magnetic star that would guide him through this moment"-- his celestial navigation (*CN* 189). After working a while he stops, pleased that he now has the privacy he requires for his art; but then he wonders, "What is it I have been waiting to do?" (*CN* 189). Jeremy's situation here is the artist's dilemma. All artists need privacy to concentrate on their work. Yet they also need connections to the outside world. The degree to which any artist resolves these contradictory needs often determines his or her success as an artist and happiness as a human being.

Unfortunately, Jeremy cannot achieve a balance between the two contradictory needs. His one attempt to do so meets with abysmal failure. After six months, he finally gathers the courage to go after Mary, who has been living in a shack owned by Jeremy's art dealer, Brian O'Donnell. This "first and final act of heroism," Gail Godwin notes in her review of the novel, is "more valiant and terrifying to [Jeremy] than blasting off to Venus would be for an astronaut."[59] Unlike Jeremy, however, Mary and the children have adapted beautifully to their new situation. When Jeremy arrives, he attempts to prove his "efficiency and authority" (*CN* 268), first by winterizing the windows of the shack and then by airing out the sails on Brian's boat. But when he attempts to take the children out on the boat with him, Mary intervenes, fearing for their safety. Humiliated, Jeremy takes the boat out by himself but can succeed only in sailing the boat in a circle, a figure symbolic of his lifelong isolation. Like the circle, he remains forever enclosed, unable to break free.

Continuing her experimentation with narrative form and longer timeframes, Tyler covers slightly over a decade in *Celestial Navigation* (1960-71). She also relates the story in chapters alternating between Jeremy's perspective and those of other characters ranging from Jeremy's sister to Mary to various boarders. Yet while the chapters told from the perspective of the other characters utilize first-person narrators, Jeremy's chapters are narrated in third person. Such a narrative stance might at first, according to Alice Hall Petry, imply "some sort of psychic split," but actually, in Jeremy's case, it is perhaps "more accurate to say that Jeremy simply is acting on his artist's compulsion to stand apart, to study and evaluate people."[60]

Another affinity between Jeremy and Tyler involves their attitudes toward the production of their art. Neither feels that an artistic endeavor can be rushed or abandoned. Tyler's novels and Jeremy's sculptures are both like "olives out of a bottle"[61] (*CN* 228). Neither Tyler nor Jeremy can skip or choose not to complete a work, even an inferior one, such as Tyler's three unpublished manuscripts. Each work must be finished before the next, hopefully better, work can begin. Tyler feels compelled to complete each project before she can even begin to think about her next one. Both Jeremy and Tyler also experience the need for rest between creative periods. Jeremy needs "a regathering period, an idle space sometimes stretching into weeks" (*CN* 179). Likewise, Tyler "feel[s] used up and burnt out" after finishing a novel and in between projects "fill[s] in by having a lot of experiences."[62] For Tyler these experiences include gardening, cooking, being with her family, and generally re-establishing her ties with the world, which she has often neglected during the most intensive periods of writing a novel.

In the end, these reconnections ultimately make Tyler very different from Jeremy. Her artistic sensibility may mirror his, but her personal life is much better adjusted. She herself admits that she is "outwardly more balanced than Jeremy" and that she does "manage to cope and get things done."[63]   She achieves this equilibrium by exerting a great deal of control, organization, and discipline over both of her careers--writer and wife/mother.   While her children were small, she wrote according to a strict schedule, organizing her day so that she was free when they came home from school. With the demands of her writing, however, extra outside activities had to be put on hold. Although such an attitude may seem to make her "increasingly closed down, [and] self-protective," this system works for her, and as she so humorously puts it, "the PTA can get along without me."[64]

The end of *Celestial Navigation* was especially problematic for Tyler. First she and her editor disagreed about the need for the book's final chapter. Judith Jones wanted Tyler to cut the last chapter, which after all is very short and somewhat anticlimactic after the devastating finale of the previous chapter. Jones asserted that "everyone would understand what happened to Jeremy," but Tyler insisted that *she* "wouldn't understand" and that she also "wanted Jeremy to do his last, biggest sculpture."[65]   This exchange illustrates both Tyler's genuine love for her characters, as well as her determination not to end a novel until she knows what will happen to her characters in the future.

Unlike most of her other books, which offer at least the possibility of reconciliation or reaffirmation in relationships, *Celestial Navigation* ends in defeat. Tyler attempted to write a happy ending and, in fact, admits trying to write towards such an ending, but she found

> that writing felt wooden: my sentences were jerky when I looked back at them.
> In a way I felt I was trying to cover up a lie, and then I thought, I may as well
> tell the truth: the woman leaves the man. The problem in *Celestial Navigation*
> was that those characters were two absolutely separate people and they couldn't
> possibly have stayed together.[66]

Many readers were puzzled by the unhappy ending of the novel, but Tyler felt that no other ending would have been appropriate.

Sales for *Celestial Navigation* were especially disappointing.   Only 6300 hardcover copies were sold, and Bantam waited until July 1976 to pick up the paperback rights. *Celestial Navigation* also baffled most reviewers. Julian Barnes, writing for the *New Statesman*, noted that Tyler's "divid[ing] her narrative between six characters . . . causes (not surprisingly) a certain search for an author."[67]   The growing artistic depth of Jeremy Pauling also "strain[ed] plausibility" even more for Pearl K. Bell, who thought Tyler "overextend[ed] herself, asking us to believe that so maimed and helpless an individual could not only persuade an attractive . . . woman to marry him; but could also do what is necessary to sire five children in less than ten years."[68]

Tyler herself admitted that the sexual aspect of Jeremy's character needed further development: "As I look back upon that book I see that it must be hard for readers to credit Jeremy with any sexual capability, and that I really owed it to them to show how he managed it. But Jeremy is the character I've felt most protective of, and so I let the book down on that account."[69]

Despite this flaw, the book's main strength remains its characters. Gail Godwin, in the *New York Times Book Review*, found Mary Tell "an unlikely blend of Earth Mother and Maverick."[70]   Eileen Kennedy also praised Tyler's achievement in characterizing Jeremy, noting her accomplishment in "translat[ing] into words the mind that works with form, line, color" and her success in "penetrat[ing] the psyche of the artist who distances reality because that is the only way he can see reality."[71]

SEARCHING FOR CALEB

Despite her family obligations, Tyler continued to write with strict discipline, writing for seven hours a day four days a week. Within two years, she had produced her next novel, *Searching for Caleb*. It is an extension of Tyler's interest in time and the past, as well as another attempt to come to grips with the dichotomy of her own nature and her conflicting feelings about family.

The time frame of *Searching for Caleb* is the most ambitious of any Tyler novel, spanning almost a century, from 1880-1973 in the life of the Peck family, an upper class Baltimore family founded by the mysterious Justin Peck, who appeared out of nowhere after the Civil War to start an importing business and establish a dynasty. He married first one wife, who died bearing his first son, Daniel, and then promptly married another, who bore a second son, Caleb.

The two sons come to represent the two conflicting sides of the Peck family. Daniel, who complies with the conservative "Peckness" of the family, becomes a lawyer and eventually a judge. He dislikes "*difficult* names" and "foreignness"[72] and lives in the insulated Peck world symbolized by the massive, sturdy series of adjoining homes Justin built in Roland Park for his sons and their children. Caleb, however, represents a freer, less restrictive side of the family that surfaces in various characters from time to time. Caleb loves all kinds of music, but when he tells his father about his desire to pursue a musical career rather than taking over the family business, his father has a stroke. Caleb's mother blames him for "kill[ing] your half of your father" (*SC* 55).

Through the years these two sides of the Peck family character contend with each other. First, Daniel's wife, Margaret Rose, who has fulfilled her role as mother by producing six Peck children in quick succession, leaves Daniel. Daniel, too stubborn to go after her (like Jeremy at first in *Celestial Navigation*), remains immobilized and loses her when she runs away to a boarding house in Washington, D.C. There she eventually dies in a fire, but not before enjoying a brief life of freedom. In Washington, she works in a money laundering operation for the U.S. Department of the Treasury. Tyler got the idea for this quirky occupation from a newspaper clipping.[73] Perhaps spurred on by Margaret Rose's example, Caleb decides a few months later to follow his dream of a musical career. He leaves in 1912 without telling any family members of his plans. His whereabouts remain a mystery for the next sixty years.

When the novel opens in 1972, two descendants of the Peck family, Justine, daughter of the youngest daughter of Daniel and Margaret Rose, and Duncan, son of Justin Two, Daniel's oldest son, have seemingly broken out of the Peck mold. They have married each other in disobedience to the family's sense of propriety and are living an unsettled, nomadic life very different from what the Pecks expected. Duncan moves from job to job, ironically never staying with one longer than it takes to become successful. For her part, Justine likewise disappoints the family by taking up the disreputable profession of fortune telling. As a young woman, she had met a fortune teller, Madame Olita, who noticed her potential for clairvoyance. Madame Olita's profession appealed to Justine because the old woman assured her that she could change both the future and the past, "not what's happened . . . but what hold it has on you" (*SC* 129). Throughout the rest of the novel, all of the characters attempt to make changes in their lives in order to escape the bonds of the past.

This task is not an easy one, however, for each character retains characteristics of both sides of their Peck ancestry. Even as Duncan and Justine live their wandering life, their own marriage keeps them locked within the Peck family circle. The hold of heredity is reinforced by their daughter, Meg, whose obsessive desire for order and stability Justine sees as a reversion to "total Peckness" (*SC* 145). Meg eventually elopes with a milquetoast minister in a misguided attempt to find the order she missed growing up.

Even the older characters experience this duality. In his old age, Daniel finally allows the other side of his character to surface. He begins to search for his long-lost brother Caleb, symbolically the creative part of himself that he has repressed for sixty years. Daniel's search for his brother provides the title for the novel. Originally, Tyler considered several possible titles, including "Predictable Changes," "Careless Losses," "A Change of Fortune," "Sudden Departures," "Missing from the Family Album," and "Looking for Caleb."[74] She finally settled on "Hunting for Caleb," but her editor thought it would sound too much like James Dickey's *Deliverance*. Tyler later explained: "[My editor] took the word *hunting* literally. Where I was raised you could say, 'Go hunt your brother for supper.' It just meant you were going to find him."[75] Fortunately, her editor prevailed and the title was changed to *Searching for Caleb*.

To create the intriguing character of Justine Peck, Tyler did not go out and visit clairvoyants or palm readers, for she feared that such conduct would have "killed . . . off instantly" her imaginative response to the character. Rather she "bought a little dime-store Dell book--just to pick up the names of some of the card formations."[76] Thus, Justine is not based on any real person. Instead she is a creation of Tyler's artistic sensibility and a mirror of Tyler's feelings about time, the past, and the future.

Tyler did, however, base Daniel Peck on her own grandfather,[77] although she admitted to changing one aspect of his life. In a moment of grace, Tyler bestowed on Daniel a full set of perfect teeth as a gift to her own grandfather, who had lost most of his teeth and always complained about having to eat only applesauce.[78] Justine's feelings for both Daniel and Caleb Peck are a tribute to Tyler's love for her grandfathers.

Daniel Peck's vision of heaven also mirrors Tyler's own feelings for her characters. Daniel would prefer heaven to be a small town where he "would know everybody . . . and [no one] would ever die or move away or age or alter" (*SC* 190). Tyler, likewise, admits that one of her favorite fantasies is meeting all her old characters in heaven and catching up on what's been happening in their lives.[79]

At the end of the novel, the family hires a private detective, Eli Everjohn (who also turns up in *Saint Maybe*) to find Caleb. Eli quickly finds him in a rest home in Louisiana. Ironically, Daniel dies before he can see his brother. It is then left to Justine to make the journey to bring Caleb back to his family.

At this point the novel's focus shifts to Justine's search for wholeness. She realizes that through the years she has "mislaid . . . herself" (*SC* 258) and finally understands that her travels with her grandfather in search of Caleb have actually been her own journeys to come to grips with her own past and to reconcile the conflicting sides of her Peckness. Daniel had admitted in his letter to Caleb that his "ties to the present have weakened" (*SC* 247) and that the past still held him firmly in its grip. Caleb, on the other hand, had never dwelt on the past but "preferred the present" and was "happy where he was" (*SC* 268). Justine's task is to find a resolution between these two extremes.

In the end, Justine takes the advice she has been giving to her customers all these years: "Take the change. Always change" (*SC* 29). Therefore, she and Duncan accept jobs in a traveling carnival (he as fix-it man and she as fortune teller). This decision allows them to move forward with their lives rather than moving back into the insularity of the Peck world of Roland Park. Justine's choice, as Duncan puts it, is Tyler's favorite resolution, to "endure" and "adapt" (*SC* 229).

Searching for Caleb proved slightly more successful commercially than *Celestial Navigation*, although at this point in her career, sales for Tyler's novels seemed fated to hover around 10,000. *Caleb* held true to that pattern, selling just 9600 copies. One bright spot, however, was the purchase of the book's paperback rights in February 1977 by the Popular Library, which also picked up the renewals for Tyler's earlier novels and published them later that year. The one exception was *Celestial Navigation*, whose rights had been purchased by Bantam a year earlier. As a result, the Popular Library edition of *Celestial Navigation* did not appear until January 1980. The importance of these paperback editions during this period cannot be overestimated. At a time when her novels were going out of print in hardcover because of slow sales, the availability of paperback editions helped to maintain and build her popular audience, as well as her literary reputation. In fact, Judith Jones, her editor, credits these paperback editions with helping Tyler finally break through into higher hardcover sales: "Anne built up a devoted following through her paperback sales. Eventually her audience became so substantial that hardcover sales were affected--readers couldn't wait to get the next Anne Tyler so they bought her in hardcover."[80]

Reviews of *Searching for Caleb* suggest that it is perhaps Tyler's first really great novel, for in this book she seems finally to have brought together all the elements of fiction--character, plot, and theme--in a masterfully convincing way. So impressed was John Updike with Tyler's skill that he ended his review in the *New Yorker* with a statement of unqualified admiration: "This writer is not merely good, she is *wickedly* good."[81] Other reviews were equally enthusiastic. *Choice* called the book a "delightful, high-spirited novel . . . with a sure touch of realism."[82] Katha Pollitt heralded it in the *New York Times Book Review* as "Tyler's sunniest, most expansive book,"[83] and Walter Sullivan wrote, "Within the boundaries she has set for herself she is almost totally successful."[84]

More specifically, critics noted a growing depth of character and theme, as well as a less heavy-handed and obtrusive style. The Peck characters are left free to develop as they naturally would as individuals. There is no sense of authorial intrusion. Katha Pollitt sensed "at the center of Tyler's characters . . . a private, mysterious core which is left, wisely, inviolate."[85]

The character of Justine herself intrigued many reviewers. Walt Chura felt that she "grows from a perfect Peck young lady to Duncan's fortune-telling, Caleb-searching, mystery-loving soulmate."[86] Katha Pollitt described her quest as "a search for the self she has mislaid."[87] To Martha B. Tack, "hesitant Justine becomes a kaleidoscopic, perpetual motion machine."[88] Walter Sullivan went so far as to equate Justine's viewpoint with Tyler's: "Like Miss Tyler, Justine insists on nothing: believe, accept what you will; but the inscrutable depth of life is everywhere suggested."[89]

The responses of the novel's characters to their ancestry fascinated other critics. Philip Howard found Duncan "reckless, feckless, and Peckless . . . refus[ing] to be fenced in by regular work or the family's expectations of him."[90] On the other hand, proving that the tide of heredity runs strong, Justine and Duncan's daughter Meg "out-Pecks the Pecks" in her desire for order and in marrying, of all people, a fastidious preacher.[91] The role of heredity in shaping characters' lives also concerned Lynn Sharon Schwartz, who considered the Peck family "as a sealed unit, with an impervious grip on its members through the twin traps of heredity and environment" in which even Justine and Duncan, the family rebels, remain "dominated . . . by the tyranny of chromosomes."[92]

Most interesting, however, were reviewers' comments about Tyler as an author with a unique, individual vision that separated her from other, perhaps more "fashionable" contemporary writers. Ward Just wrote, "[Tyler] has quite a lot to say about alienation, but her characters are not alienated in the customary, fashionable ways."[93] Besides viewing alienation from a different perspective, Tyler, according to Katha Pollitt, also seemed to be stepping to a different drummer in relation to the prevailing feminist trend: "The current school of feminist-influenced novels seems to have passed [Tyler] by completely: her women are strong, stronger than the men in their lives, but solidly grounded in traditional roles."[94]

The critics thus found the novel to be a book about a highly individual family by a writer with a truly unique, individual perspective. Like their creator, the Pecks are "a family whose very conventionality borders on the eccentric."[95] Victor Howes, writing for the *Christian Science Monitor*, observed that "a little more of the fang and claw might put [Tyler] up there among the truly rare satirists," yet he also noted how Tyler contrasts "the goodness of dependable but dull vs. the spontaneous but irresponsible."[96] In the end, *Searching for Caleb* is, Philip Howard concluded, "a book about chasing rainbows, and finding happiness by enduring, adapting, accepting what comes along, and liking people."[97]

HOMELAND

When Tyler chose the upscale Baltimore neighborhood of Roland Park as the setting for the Pecks' solid houses in *Searching for Caleb*, she was right at home. Roland Park borders her own neighborhood of Homeland, which lies just across Charles Street from Roland Park. In fact, the same real estate company that had earlier developed Roland Park began to build houses on the old Perine Estate of "Homeland" in the mid-1920s. The Roland Park Company, however, encouraged more variety in its later development, moving away from the Victorian architecture of Roland Park towards more traditional architecture, especially "the style of the 18th century highlighting Georgian motifs . . . [but with] Norman, Tudor, French country and Early American [in combination] with Colonial."[98] These diverse styles utilized a variety of building materials. Some houses, such as Tyler's home on Tunbridge Road, are constructed of stone, but brick, frame, and stucco houses abound in other sections of the neighborhood.

Homeland's tree-shaded streets are named after English towns or Anglican saints. The subdivision lies between Charles Street and York Road, two main Baltimore thoroughfares often mentioned in Tyler's work. Yet Tyler never mentions Homeland, only Roland Park, in her work. It seems that Charles Street and York Road provide not only the boundaries for her fictional world, but the borders of her private life as well.

In her fiction Tyler incorporates the two separate worlds of Baltimore, upper-class Roland Park and lower-to-middle-class downtown. Yet the people who live in these vastly different settings are remarkably similar. In her article "The Two Worlds of Anne Tyler," Mary Anne Brush describes these two sections of Baltimore and notes that in both "worlds" Tyler's "characters are like the houses they live in, their lives shabby and cluttered and in constant need of repair. This is the human condition, according to Anne Tyler, and it is this vision that unites the two worlds of her fiction."[99]

EARTHLY POSSESSIONS

Tyler seems to have been ready to strike out into the world, literally, in her next novel, *Earthly Possessions*. To her, the book was "the work of somebody entering middle age, beginning to notice how the bags and baggage of the past are weighing her down, and how much she values them."[100] According to notations at the end of the manuscript, she began writing *Earthly Possessions* in the fall of 1975 and finished it on April 28, 1976. Less than a month later she had finished revising and typing it.[101]

Inspiration for characters once again came to Tyler from newspaper articles. Jake Simms's character was inspired by a *Baltimore Sun* piece entitled "Marylander Is Wonder Boy of the Demolition Derby."[102] An article about storefront ministers, "Some Storefront City Churches Grow Big; Few Seem Stereotype,"[103] provided the spark for Saul Emory. This article ends with a quotation from one of the ministers: "I knew nothing about organizing a church, but as I went step by step, God gave me the wisdom and made a way."[104] Saul's trusting philosophy in the novel closely mirrors the minister's.

Earthly Possessions continues Tyler's exploration of the contradictory effects of family on the individual. She illustrates this tension through the novel's narrative structure. Chapters set in the present, where Charlotte is seeking escape from her family, alternate with chapters about the past, where she struggles with the claustrophobic restrictiveness of that family. The irony of her situation is reinforced by the novel's opening. Charlotte, having taken the "Keep on Truckin'" badge she finds in a box of cereal literally as a sign to make her escape, goes to the bank to withdraw money so she can leave her "hellfire preacher"[105] husband Saul. Her decision to leave makes her feel "suddenly light-hearted, as if [she] were expecting something . . . . [or] were going on a *trip* (*EP* 7). At the bank, however, her plans change abruptly when Jake Simms kidnaps her during a botched bank robbery. Paradoxically, once she realizes that Jake is no physical threat to her, she is happy because he has facilitated her escape from her family.

Charlotte has experienced the same conflicting desires concerning family all her life, even before her marriage to Saul. As the child of a grotesquely obese woman and an ineffectual, passive father who ran a home photography studio, she grew up feeling insecure and ambivalent about her parents. She had two great fears: 1) finding out that she was not her parents' "true daughter" and being sent away, and 2) being their daughter and "never, ever manag[ing] to escape to the outside world" (*EP* 15). Her fears precisely coincide with Tyler's conflicting feelings about the effect of family on the individual.

The death of Charlotte's father during her first year of college prevents her from escaping from the restrictiveness of her family, despite her desire for normalcy. She comes home to look after her mother and to take over the photography business. Likewise, her next chance for escape is also foiled. She marries Saul, her next-door neighbor, expecting him to take her away, but instead he promptly announces that he plans to become a minister. To make matters even more claustrophobic for Charlotte, rather than establishing a new home for her, he moves into her house, bringing all his mother's furniture with him.

The furniture, every piece of which has "its shadow, a Siamese twin" (*EP* 100-01), thus becomes a metaphor for the familial responsibilities and restrictions that beset Charlotte over the next fifteen years. Her job as a photographer is her one respite from this restrictiveness because it allows her to escape, momentarily, into the lives of other people, who, paradoxically, come to her to be photographed in costumes that allow them the same type of escape. Charlotte does, however, make attempts, to rid herself of both the furniture and these burdens. As a result, her life becomes "a history of casting off encumbrances, paring down to the bare essentials, stripping for the journey" (*EP* 37). Ultimately, her most important possession becomes a good pair of walking shoes.

Charlotte finally succeeds in escaping from her family through the fumbling efforts of Jake Simms. But the kidnapping slowly develops into something else for both characters--a mutual journey of self-discovery. Jake, the "victim of impulse" (*EP* 43) and a sometime demolition derby driver, escapes from the county jail and robs a bank in order to get money to rescue his pregnant girlfriend, Mindy, from a home for unwed mothers in Georgia. Once he and Charlotte spring Mindy from the home, however, Jake becomes increasingly uncertain about taking on the responsibility of a wife and child.

It is left up to Charlotte to push Jake into accepting his new roles as husband and father. She accomplishes this feat by leaving him, even though he begs her to stay and help him establish his relationship with Mindy: "[I]t ain't so bad if you're with us. . . You act like you take it all in stride, like this is the way life really does tend to turn out" (*EP* 197). For her part, Charlotte returns home to Saul. She reassumes her role as caretaker of the family and her job as a photographer, recognizing that "all of us [live] in a sort of web, criss-crossed by strings of love and need and worry" (*EP* 182). With this knowledge she feels no need for escape and even rejects Saul's suggestion that they travel: "We have been travelling for years, travelled all our lives, we are travelling still. We couldn't stay in one place if we tried" (*EP* 200). Like Tyler's most mature characters, Charlotte gains a partial understanding of her place in a chaotic and everchanging world. Her response, like Justine's in *Searching for Caleb*, is to adapt and, most importantly, to endure.

Charlotte Emory's desire to shed her possessions and travel light mirrors a similar tendency in Tyler. Tyler admits to being a homebody who, paradoxically, is continuously preparing for travel. She always keeps her nightgown and travel-size toiletries packed.[106] Her desire to rid her life of all but the necessities is reflected in a 1978 piece she wrote, with some help from her daughter Mitra, for the *Homeland News*, published by the neighborhood homeowners' association. The article, "A Child's Tour of Homeland (or, The 120-Minute Mile)," explains how a "short" fifteen-minute walking tour of the neighborhood turns into an hour-and-forty-eight-minute marathon as her daughter stops to look at everything and finds interesting objects to bring home. These include discarded venetian blinds, gerbil cages, and, from a previous excursion, a set of eight wooden window shutters, at the time still cluttering up the back of Mitra's closet.

All this clutter must have seemed intrusive and diverting to such an organized person as Tyler. Yet these intrusions actually served to enrich her imaginative world. In fact, she admits that almost everything she knew about contemporary culture came to her through her daughters, who would drag the outside world into the house, not as they dragged shutters and gerbil cages, but through school and friends and children's general inquisitiveness about the world. Her children became her "ultra real ties to reality"[107] and her "anchors to reality."[108] When Tezh and Mitra came knocking at her study door, asking for bandaids, tetanus shots, and explanations about the facts of life,[109] Tyler's work would be interrupted. What the girls might not have known, though, is that they were also giving something to their mother in return, helping her to mature not only as a parent but also as a writer.

Sale figures for *Earthly Possessions* continued to categorize Tyler as a writer with a small audience. The book sold 10,900 hardcover copies and was quickly added to the Popular Library's paperback list in July 1978. Many reviewers of *Earthly Possessions* attempted to place it in the bored-housewife-escapes-prison-of-marriage genre. Most, however, usually wound up admitting that Tyler's seventh novel fails to conform to the restrictions of that format. Part of the problem lies in the characters themselves, whom most critics found less convincing than earlier Tyler characters. *Choice* commented, "A great deal of what is written here seems contrived, or invented, so characters never really take life."[110] Writing for the *New York Times Book Review*, Anatoyle Broyard labeled Charlotte "only a hope chest of negatives, a woman on the run from boredom toward an empty ambiguity."[111]

The relationship between Jake and Charlotte also rang hollow for many critics. John Leonard, in his *New York Times* review, voiced a complaint that has since been leveled repeatedly at Tyler--her lack of interest in her characters' sex lives: "As kidnappings go, this one is wholly without sexual tension."[112] To be fair, however, Tyler's choice to ignore the sexual tension inherent in the kidnapper/victim relationship may be due to the characters themselves; Jake, although he has gotten Mindy pregnant, is too young, inexperienced, and inept to interest a mature woman such as Charlotte. Tyler does deal more openly with the more mature sexual relationship between Charlotte and her husband. Every Sunday Charlotte wages a sexual battle against Saul's piousness. As she sits listening to him preach, she thinks up ways to seduce him: "There was something magical about that pew that sent all my thoughts swooning toward bed. Contrariness, I suppose. He was against making love on Sunday. I was in favor of it. Sometimes I won, sometimes he won. I wouldn't have missed Sundays for the world" (*EP* 110-11).

The ending of *Earthly Possessions*, which finds Charlotte back at home where she started, as well as its narrative structure, troubled other reviewers. *Choice* noted that "the ending reminds the reader of the end of the filmed *Wizard of Oz*: there's no place like home, though of course Tyler is drawing a kind of home of the spirit, in which there is constant spiritual voyaging."[113] The title of Nancy Gail Reed's review in the *Christian Science Monitor*, "Novel Follows Unpredictable Escape Routes," indicated the confusing nature of the book's resolution.[114] Gilberto Perez dismissed the book as "another exercise in confinement."[115] He felt that the use of two different narrative voices in the alternating chapters ("retrospective" first person and "eye-witness first person") fails because it confuses the reader. Most inexplicable, however, is how the narrator, who relates the story retrospectively, somehow still does not know the story's outcome.[116]

Still other reviewers found much to praise in *Earthly Possessions*, especially in its characterizations. The reviewer for *Progressive* felt that Charlotte's "final acceptance of her situation offers a truer portrayal of a woman's role than many of the more political feminist novels."[117] In her *Time* review, Angela Wigan praised Tyler's books for being "advocacies of affirmation" in which "profound gentleness and beauty can reside in the plainest people."[118] And Diane Johnson lauded Tyler's eye that reveals "the deep strangeness of people who would look ordinary if viewed in less detail by a more ordinary writer."[119]

IRANIAN ISSUES

In 1979, when Moslem extremists took over the American embassy in Teheran, the Modarressis were not surprised. For years Taghi had kept abreast through friends and relatives of the social and political upheavals in his native land. His mother's letters would arrive already opened. Such disturbing events and the growing political unrest had earlier convinced him to give up his plan to return to Iran to open a psychiatric clinic. For her part, Tyler was more concerned about the effect these events would have on her family.

And the American backlash against Iranians did affect her family, especially her daughters. In a 1980 interview, she described a name-calling incident at her daughters' school. Mitra came home crying because some classmates were whispering behind her back, saying that she was an Iranian. She confronted the children and told them that she was indeed an Iranian. Then once she arrived home, she was confused and told her parents: "'Yes, I am Iranian--but no, I'm not. I'm American.'"[120] Tyler had to comfort her daughter and try to help her through this identity crisis.

As for her own reaction to the Iranian revolution, Tyler felt "angry about the hostage business."[121] Two reviews written that year reveal her thoughts about conditions in Iran. In "Please Don't Call It Persia," a review essay in the *New York Times Book Review*, she characterized the problems in Iran as a "struggle to speak and be heard."[122]

Her sympathies were clearly with the anti-Shah forces. Even so, she deplored the increasing violence she saw on television and mourned the loss of the old Iran she had visited sixteen years before. Similarly, in a review of Caroline Richards's book on political repression in Chile, she seemed to be alluding to conditions in Iran when she wrote:

> For several days after finishing [the book], I traveled in a kind of swamp of despair; and I don't think I will ever again hear mention of Chile (let alone the CIA) without becoming faintly ill. But that was the whole purpose--all the more valuable when you think of other situations, in *other places* [italics mine], where similar events are occurring today.[123]

Taghi's response to the situation was much more stoic than Anne's. Having seen and heard of so many of his friends being "tortured and killed by the Shah's people," he did not "feel *that* angry"[124] about the hostage crisis. His seeming callousness shocked Anne and made her realize for the first time that they were "not from the same country."[125]

"PANTALEO"

The pending Iranian crisis and the increasing demands of raising older children made the next few years after writing *Earthly Possessions* a particularly difficult period during which Tyler found little time, and less focus, to write. She felt somewhat overwhelmed, describing herself in her revealing 1980 essay, "Still Just Writing," as a "woman/wife/mother" and "caretaker"[126] whose jobs included reading bedtime stories, preparing meals, plastering the dining room ceiling, painting the downstairs hall, taking pets and children for shots, fixing electrical switches, and, in her spare time, writing novels. Perhaps as a result of these many diversions, Tyler's next novel, "Pantaleo," proved unpublishable. Although she submitted it to her agent, he was unenthusiastic, so Tyler shelved it. As with "Winter Birds, Winter Apples," she did not press for publication of a novel that did not meet her high standards.

"Pantaleo," however, is an interesting departure for Tyler. It marks her attempt to master the genre of the mystery novel. The novel recounts the story of Sam Pantaleo, a young man who takes on the responsibility of raising Parker, his girl friend's three-year-old son, after she is killed in a car accident. At first Sam attempts unsuccessfully to find Parker's father (just as the Bedloes attempt to find Agatha and Thomas's relatives in *Saint Maybe*). Eventually, however, Sam grows to love Parker with "a permanent, gutting, racking anguish that made mere love seem as pallid as ghosts."[127]

Soon Sam begins to notice a strange man watching Parker. Afraid of losing the boy, Sam initiates a series of moves (similar to Duncan and Justine's in *Searching for Caleb*). With each move he takes on a new identity (like Morgan in *Morgan's Passing*, with whom Sam's character, especially at the beginning of the novel, has many affinities). Over the next sixteen years, Sam moves to a new town every time he notices the strange man. Finally, he learns that the man is a detective hired by Parker's real father, a married man who had been having an affair with the boy's mother. The novel's resolution comes too quickly, however. Tyler loses the suspense she had built up, by offering the innocuous explanation of the private detective and the revelation of the identity of Parker's real father. These seem anticlimactic after the rather complicated, circuitous, and overly long plot. The ending, therefore, seems forced.

THE MIDPOINT

During the mid-to-late 1970s, Tyler continued to write steadily, producing more novels, short stories, and reviews than at any other time in her career. She accomplished this feat through sheer determination and concentration. She dedicated Mondays through Thursdays to writing, leaving Fridays for "groceries and snow tires."[128] Yet commercial success continued to elude her. In fact, after *Celestial Navigation*, she still owed money to her publisher. As late as 1976, her best year to date, she made just $35,000 a year from her writing.[129] But she did not let her limited success upset her. Asked in a 1979 interview if she felt that her lack of popularity had anything to do with her failure to write about "fashionable" topics, Tyler responded, "No, I suspect it's more an issue of whether they like my work or didn't like my work, rather than anything to do with fashions."[130] Her response to the question prompted the same interviewer to ask whether she considered herself more a "writers' writer" who was not interested in commercial success. Tyler replied, "I figure I'm probably just read by people who like to get inside other people's lives" and suggested the term "eavesdropper's writer" to describe her appeal.[131]

In some ways Tyler relished her relative anonymity, especially insofar as it allowed her to maintain her privacy at home in Baltimore. Many of her neighbors did not even know she was a writer. As late as 1979, Tyler still stated, "Most people think I'm a housewife." This perception suited her because she did not "want an audience too close."[132] Her growing critical approval, however, compensated for her lack of commercial success. On May 18, 1977, the American Academy and Institute of Arts and Letters honored her with a citation "for literary excellence and promise of important work to come."

Summers continued to be fallow times for Tyler the writer and busy times for Tyler the mother. In a 1978 article for the *New York Times Book Review*, she listed three goals for her summer. Although prosaic, they reveal the focal points of her interests: she wanted 1) to "finally grow one perfect pot of basil, without whiteflies" (reinforcing her interest in gardening and its restorative effect on her), 2) to "take a brush to the dog and see if I can find out what her true shape is" (revealing her concern for the ordinary tasks of housekeeping and her love of pets), and 3) to finish reading *Lord of the Rings* to her youngest daughter (illustrating her commitment to her children).[133] In the midst of these mundane concerns, Tyler still subconsciously nurtured the characters in her work in progress [*Morgan's Passing*], "hop[ing] and trust[ing] that the characters [would] keep themselves going without me" and that they would not "have crumbled away to nothing as I always fear they will"[134] when she returned to her work after the summer break.

Tyler's fears were somewhat justified, however, by the events of that summer. She describes the summer in "Still Just Writing," her longest and most revealing personal essay. While working on *Morgan's Passing* in the spring, she suffered interruption after interruption (from car troubles to veterinary visits). When Tezh and Mitra got out of school for summer vacation, there was no time to write. Finally, she managed to get the girls off to camp, only to be called in the middle of the night when her older child became sick with what the doctors thought was typhoid fever. After she and Taghi drove all night to bring Tezh home from camp, she miraculously recovered in three days from what was apparently just a virus and was sent by train back to camp. By this time, however, Tyler was worn out, unable to concentrate. All the while Morgan was wandering in and out of her mind.

MORGAN'S PASSING

Tyler's trouble in writing *Morgan's Passing*, however, did not make the novel any less important to her. If anything, her worries increased her concern, for Morgan became "very real" to her. She came up with the ideas for the characters in *Morgan's Passing* from several newspaper clippings. She had always had a "great interest in imposters."[135] When she read an article in the *Baltimore Sun* ("Phony Doctor Practicing Medicine in Mexico") about a local con artist who had pretended to be a clergyman and then a doctor, she was intrigued enough to clip the article and save it for future reference. Likewise, she found inspiration from another article entitled "Puppeteer Couple Has Entertained 4 Generations Here." This article provided the inspiration for the characters of Emily and Leon Meredith. Finally, Tyler's love of catalogues also proved fruitful. In one she found the model for Morgan's wide-brimmed hat, one of the many hats and costumes he wears as he seeks his own identity in the novel.

Morgan's search for identity leads him to pose as various characters throughout the novel. Tyler has admitted a similar lifelong fascination with "the inveterate imposter, who is unable to stop himself from stepping into other people's worlds."[136] As a writer, she also felt a particular affinity with Morgan on this issue: "[M]y interest in imposters has to do with my being a writer. *We* go in and out of other lives all the time." But then she wondered what would happen "if an imposter got into another life and couldn't get out again."[137]

In the novel, Morgan Gower, a 42-year-old man married to a wealthy wife whose family has given him a job managing one of the hardware stores in the family chain, rebels against the restrictiveness of his life by posing as different characters. In his closet he keeps costumes of all kinds that allow him to play roles such as priest, doctor, or mailman. Tyler worried that her readers might "be morally offended" by such a character who consciously deceives others and explained in an interview that "[Morgan is] not a full-fledged con man . . . . He's not out to do harm. He's sort of amoral--but basically a kind man."[138]

As the novel opens, Morgan is watching a puppet show play of Cinderella performed by Leon and Emily Meredith. But the show abruptly stops when Emily goes into labor. Seizing the opportunity to step into another role, Morgan steps up and pretends to be a doctor. Already his identity is in flux. As the father of seven daughters, he feels he has enough experience to deliver the baby and does so without any problems. Then he disappears, leaving the Merediths to wonder who he is.

Over the next few years Morgan watches the couple from a distance, in the same way that the private investigator watches the child in "Pantaleo." Because of his many disguises, however, Morgan finds it easy to observe the Merediths. Eventually, probably because he wants to be discovered, the Merediths notice Morgan watching them, and they learn his real identity. He gradually becomes a part of their lives. Ultimately, he has an affair with Emily, finally replacing Leon as both her husband and as her fellow puppeteer. By the end of the novel, Morgan's transformation is complete. Because the puppet show's original name remains, Morgan even assumes the name of Meredith. Like Elizabeth in *The Clock Winder*, his identity has completely changed.

Two aspects of the novel are important for their relationship to Tyler's life. First, Emily Meredith is strikingly similar to Tyler in both her Quaker heritage and her preference for simple dress. Emily owns only three leotards and a wrap-around skirt to avoid the necessity of having to choose what to wear each day. Like Charlotte Emory in *Earthly Possessions*, she also lives an austere life, desiring to rid herself of the extraneous objects that tie her down to her family. Similarly, Tyler prefers simple clothing and a lifestyle unencumbered by too many material possessions.

The second aspect of *Morgan's Passing* that makes it interesting is its use of the fairy tale as a recurring motif. Tyler returns again and again in her fiction to fairy tales as tropes and as sources for allusions. Perhaps she chooses fairy tales because, in a contemporary society no longer familiar with ancient Greek and Roman mythology and increasingly unversed in biblical stories, the fairy tale provides a convenient mythic framework. It is also possible that Tyler, as a mother, has become so used to telling these stories to her daughters that they have become a part of her own consciousness. In 1976 she reviewed Bruno Bettelheim's *The Uses of Enchantment: The Meaning and Importance of Fairy Tales*. In the review she admitted that the story of Beauty and the Beast "seems to have remained with me and become incorporated into my life in ways I had never imagined."[139] But the real lessons of fairy tales are more practical:

> [What] most fairy tales impart to a child is that there is real value in growing, in struggling and persisting. Yet another message is that "by forming a true interpersonal relation, one escapes the separation anxiety which haunts him." This is the real lesson of "happy ever after"--not the "eternal life" or "marriage-is-unmitigated-bliss" that realists deplore.[140]

Tyler's realistic interpretation of such fairy tales reveals her own practicality and common sense.

Whatever the reason, the story of Cinderella works as a motif in *Morgan's Passing*. The story frames both the beginning and ending of the novel. At the beginning of the novel, Cinderella is the play the puppets are performing when Emily goes into labor. In that crisis, Morgan acts as a prince in saving Emily by delivering her baby. Later, however, we see that Morgan is really no prince in the usual sense of the word. Still, he does rescue Emily from a mundane life by adding his own energetic spark to her otherwise bleak passive existence. From Morgan's perspective, Emily provides his own reason to escape completely into the world of make believe through the puppets. The story of Cinderella is basically a story about the possibility for change. Thus, in the end, both Morgan and Emily have gained something from each other. This mutual gift allows them to change their lives and live, if not "happily ever after," at least a life "rich with possibilities" (*MP* 311).

Tyler's editors and publishers had hoped that *Morgan's Passing* would prove to be Tyler's "breakthrough book." With those expectations, the paperback rights were sold to Playboy Press prior to the novel's publication for a larger-than-normal sum. Unfortunately, their high hopes proved unfounded. *Morgan* sold a disappointing 15,000 hardback copies.

The character of Morgan Gower, larger than life and yet not entirely realized, became the focus of most reviews of *Morgan's Passing*. Critic A. G. Mojtabai posed the essential question, noting how Tyler builds "characterization by enumeration . . . . [with] the accumulation of sharp detail yield[ing] a surface richly encrusted, but remain[ing] a surface nonetheless. The question persists: Who is Morgan Gower?"[141] In creating Morgan, "the Great Imposter" of Thomas M. Disch's review, Tyler seemed like Dickens "alive and well and living in Baltimore."[142] The Dickensian element of Morgan was not lost on Edmund Fuller either, who labeled him "a latter-day Micawber."[143] Paul Gray turned to American counterparts to describe this "hero who is greater than the sum of his neuroses," comparing Morgan to Captain Ahab, Henderson the Rain King, and Major Major.[144] Likewise, David Kubal found Morgan "like Henderson and Herzog, part rogue, part paterfamilias, in search of the pristine,"[145] while James Wolcott characterized him as "a scruffy, king-size Life Force--Henderson the Rain King's slightly retarded brother."[146] Peter Prescott's review in *Newsweek*, "Mr.

Chameleon," summed up the metamorphic Morgan as "one of life's anarchists, a protean figure who, with the help of odd hats and a closetful of costumes, responds to what people require of him."[147]

With *Morgan's Passing*, some critics once again noted the Southern aspects of Tyler's writing. David Evanier placed Tyler as "a sprout of the Southern school, with her preference for eccentrics and dropouts."[148] Paul Binding went further, enumerating Tyler's Southern qualities: 1) "concern with the large, ramified family," 2) "social inclusiveness (reflecting the still comparatively cohesive nature of southern society)," 3) "use of gossip, particularly the 'tall story,' as a way of learning about people and their worlds," 4) "concern with the eccentric, obsessive person," 5) "a joyous, mostly ironic humour," 6) "a remarkable . . . tenderness in her depiction of the relations between men and women," and 7) "a mediumistic sense of place."[149]

Still other reviewers compared Morgan and Emily to Jake and Charlotte from *Earthly Possessions*. James Wolcott called *Morgan's Passing* "a misfit romance" with Morgan and Emily playing the parts of the misfits, just as Charlotte and Jake had in *Earthly Possessions*.[150] To Thomas M. Disch, both Emily and her "kissing cousin," Charlotte Emory, "achieve spiritual freedom in circumstances of poverty and psychological subjection; both are dutiful victims, not of the sexist gargoyles grimacing from the pages of so many recent novels, but of entirely ordinary men of limited competence and probity."[151]

Two reviewers even found connections between the novel's main characters and Tyler herself. "Like [Tyler], [Morgan] is a small-scale imposter who laments having one identity."[152] In "Because I Want More Than One Life," Tyler had admitted to just such a motivation for writing. She wants "a wider selection"[153] of lives to live. Similarly, Clarence E. Olson found Emily "a rare combination of a sensitive individual with a very private self who quietly devotes her life to the demands of those around her."[154] Emily shares those qualities with Tyler.

In the end, reviewers had to decide what to make of Morgan himself, and the reviews were mixed. Eva Hoffman felt that he views life "through a kind of aphasic, derealizing blur," creating "baffling dissonances and misplaced reactions [throughout] . . . the entire novel" because, "for lack of an identity of his own, [Morgan] impersonates a ragtag assortment of selves."[155] Peter Grier condemned *Morgan's Passing* because it "pulses with [Tyler's] talent only in spurts, like a jalopy with a dirty carburetor."[156] Paul Gray, however, disagreed: "though she allows her tale to veer toward farce, Tyler always checks it in time with the tug of an emotion, a twitch of regret. Morgan's responses are outrageous, but his stimuli are natural." In the end he pronounced the book "not another novel about mid-life crisis . . . [but] a buoyant story about a struggle unto death."[157] Marilyn Murray Willison saw Morgan emerging as a "true hero" at the end because he "accepts love and its responsibilities."[158]

Despite its disappointing commercial success, *Morgan's Passing* did gain Tyler additional critical acclaim. The novel received a nomination for the National Book Critics Circle Award. It won the Janet Heidinger Kafka Award presented by the University of Rochester for outstanding achievement in fiction by an American woman. Closer to home, Towson State University awarded Tyler the inaugural Towson State University Prize for Literature, a $1000 award given to a young Maryland writer for the best work of fiction, poetry, drama or nonfiction for that year. William Francis Guess, writing about Tyler in the article that announced her selection for the award, summed up her position in the literary world at this stage of her career:

> Anne Tyler is a somewhat unusual figure on the contemporary fictional scene, a
> writer who . . . has no axes to grind, personal, moral, socio-political or aesthetic.

She doesn't assault the consciences or convictions of her readers nor tease them with technical sleight-of-hand. Rather, she tells them beguiling and provocative stories about people not unlike themselves and their next-door neighbors. If she has a ruling creative passion, it is . . . to render the fascination of the ordinary, to reveal the anomalies of the commonplace.[159]

Characteristically, Tyler asked that there not be a public ceremony for the presentation of the award. Rather she offered her services to speak to a group of the university's writing students in an informal setting. Over the next few years, until her growing fame made such classroom visits major events, Tyler returned several times to speak to students about her favorite subject--writing.

During the 1970s, Anne Tyler had begun to explore in earnest many of the rich possibilities within herself and the world around her. Her imagination was to lead her into even more fertile fields during the 1980s. During that decade she was to produce her most mature novels. With books such as *Dinner at the Homesick Restaurant*, *The Accidental Tourist*, and *Breathing Lessons*, she would no longer be considered a minor writer with a small, but loyal reading audience. Her maturing talent had elevated her to the status of one of the most commercially successful and critically acclaimed novelists in America. During the next decade, therefore, Tyler's narrative journeys were to continue, taking her deeper into the Baltimore of her imagination.

Endnotes

1. Anne Tyler, *Morgan's Passing* (New York: Knopf, 1980): 311. Subsequent references will be cited in the text.

2. Anne Tyler, "Because I Want More than One Life," *Washington Post* (15 Aug. 1976): G1.

3. Tyler G7.

4. Marguerite Michaels, "Anne Tyler, Writer 8:05 to 3:30," *New York Times Book Review* (8 May 1977): 42.

5. Tyler G1.

6. Michaels 42.

7. Richard Wilbur, *New and Collected Poems* (San Diego: Harcourt, Brace, Jovanovich, 1988): 158.

8. Tyler G7.

9. Tyler G7.

10. Jeanne Garland, "Who's Who in the Baltimore Writing Establishment," *Baltimore Magazine* (Dec. 1979): 58.

11. Anne Tyler, Chapter One of her entry to the 1960 Flexner Award competition, The Anne Tyler Papers, Special Collections Library, Duke University: 3.

12. Letter from Anne Tyler to the author, 25 Feb. 1993.

13. Brenda Stone Crowe, "Anne Tyler: Building Her Own 'House of Fiction,'" Diss. U of Alabama, 1993: 25.

14. Laurie L. Brown, "Interviews with Seven Contemporary Authors," *Southern Quarterly* 21 (Summer 1983): 20.

15. Anne Tyler, "Stories within Stories," *New Republic* (4 Apr. 1983): 30.

16. Anne Tyler, Review of *I, etcetera*, by Susan Sontag, *New Republic* (25 Nov. 1978): 29.

17. Anne Tyler, "A Talented Writer and a Novel of Sorts," *Raleigh News and Observer* (10 Aug. 1986): D4.

18. Anne Tyler, "Comic Mourning for a Funky Youth," *San Francisco Chronicle* (13 May 1990): 10.

19. Anne Tyler, "Dreams of Inertia," *Saturday Review* (29 Sept. 1979): 46.

20. Anne Tyler, "South Africa after Revolution," *New York Times Book Review* (7 June 1981): 26.

21. Anne Tyler, "Her Younger Self," *New York Times Book Review* (19 Aug. 1979): 14.

22. Anne Tyler, "Moments Sealed in Glass," *Washington Post Book World* (23 Dec. 1979): 11.

23. Anne Tyler, "Male and Lonely," *New York Times Book Review* (31 July 1983): 22.

24. Anne Tyler, "A Civilized Sensibility," *New Republic* (20 June 1983): 32.

25. Anne Tyler, "Tan's 'Wife' Tells More Tales," *USA Today* (13 June 1991): D2.

26. Anne Tyler, "'Southern Light': Magnificent Disaster," *Raleigh News and Observer* (23 Mar. 1986): D4.

27. Anne Tyler, "John Casey's Yankee Waterman," *Washington Post Book World* (4 June 1989): 3.

28. Anne Tyler, Review of *The Magic Hour*, by Susan Isaacs, *Vogue* (Feb. 1991): 224.

29. Anne Tyler, "Novels of Other Times and Other Places," *New York Times Book Review* (23 Nov. 1980): 45.

30. Anne Tyler, "The Poe Perplex," *Washington Post Book World* (9 July 1978): E3.

31. Anne Tyler, "Meg and Hannah and Elaine," *New York Times Book Review* (31 July 1977): 14.

32. Tyler, "Novels of Other Times" 45.

33. Susan Gilbert, "Private Lives and Public Issues: Anne Tyler's Prize-Winning Novels," in C. Ralph Stephens, ed. *The Fiction of Anne Tyler* (Jackson: UP of Mississippi, 1990): 137.

34. Anne Tyler, "Women Writers: Equal but Separate," *National Observer* (10 Apr. 1976): 21.

35. Anne Tyler, "South Bronx Story," *New Republic* (19 July 1982): 42.

36. Anne Tyler, "Kentucky Housewife's Prose Cooks Up Picture of Mid-19th Century Daily Life," *Baltimore Sun* (21 Apr. 1991): E6.

37. Anne Tyler, "Adventures in a Charmed Universe," *New York Times Book Review* (27 Apr. 1980): 61.

38. Anne Tyler, "Books for Those Awkward, In-Between Years," *National Observer* (25 Dec. 1976): 15.

39. Anne Tyler, *The Clock Winder* (New York: Knopf, 1972): 14. Subsequent references will be cited in the text.

40. Clifford Ridley, "Anne Tyler: A Sense of Reticence Balanced by 'Oh, Well, Why Not?'" *National Observer* (22 July 1972): 23.

41. Anne Tyler, "Olives Out of a Bottle," *Archive* 87 (Spring 1975): 74.

42. Ridley 23.

43. Martin Levin, "New and Novel," *New York Times Book Review* (21 May 1972): 31.

44. *Virginia Quarterly Review* 48 (Autumn 1972): cxx.

45. Elizabeth Easton, *Saturday Review* (17 June 1972): 77.

46. Catharine Mack Smith, "Indian File," *New Statesman* (16 Feb. 1973): 241.

47. George Hill, London *Times* (25 Jan. 1973): 12.

48. Telephone conversation between Judith Jones and the author, 23 June 1993.

49. Anne Tyler, "The Plodding Life: Dispatches from a Writer's Desk," *Baltimore Sun* (17 Sept. 1989): M9.

50. Mary Ellen Brooks, "Anne Tyler," in *The Dictionary of Literary Biography: American Novelists Since World War II*, vol. 6 (Detroit: Gale Research, 1980): 341.

51. Brooks 337.

52. Helene Woizesko and Michael Scott Cain, "Anne Tyler," *Northeast Rising Sun* 1 (June-July 1976): 28.

53. Woizesko and Cain 28.

54. Alice Hall Petry, *Understanding Anne Tyler* (Columbia: U of South Carolina P, 1990): 111.

55. Woizesko and Cain 29.

56. Michaels 42-43.

57. Manuscript of *Celestial Navigation*, The Anne Tyler Papers, Special Collections Library, Duke University.

58. Anne Tyler, *Celestial Navigation* (New York: Knopf, 1974): 100. Subsequent references will be cited in the text.

59. Gail Godwin, "Two Novels," *New York Times Book Review* (28 Apr. 1974): 35.

60. Petry 109.

61. Tyler, "Olives" 73.

62. Tyler 73.

63. Wendy Lamb, "An Interview with Anne Tyler," *Iowa Journal of Literary Studies* 3 (1981): 61.

64. Lamb 62.

65. Woizesko and Cain 29.

66. Lamb 61.

67. Julian Barnes, "Kidding," *New Statesman* (4 Apr. 1975): 457.

68. Pearl K. Bell, "The Artist as Hero," *New Leader* (4 Mar. 1974): 18.

69. Alice Hall Petry, ed., *Critical Essays on Anne Tyler* (New York: G. K. Hall, 1992): 16.

70. Godwin 34.

71. Eileen Kennedy, *Best Sellers* (1 May 1974): 63.

72. Anne Tyler, *Searching for Caleb* (New York: Knopf, 1976): 6. Subsequent references will be cited in the text.

73. Newspaper clipping in the Anne Tyler Papers, Special Collections Library, Duke University.

74. Notes with Manuscript of *Searching for Caleb*, The Anne Tyler Papers, Special Collections Library, Duke University.

75. Robert F. Moss, "How Novels Get Titles," *New York Times Book Review* (7 Nov. 1982): 13.

76. Michaels 42.

77. Lamb 64.

78. Brooks 342.

79. Tyler, "Still Just Writing" 12.

80. Letter from Judith Jones to the author, 28 July 1993.

81. John Updike, "Family Ways," *New Yorker* (29 Mar. 1976): 112.

82. *Choice* (July 1976): 668.

83. Katha Pollitt, "Two Novels," *New York Times Book Review* (18 Jan. 1976): 22.

84. Walter Sullivan, "Gifts, Prophecies, and Prestidigitations: Fictional Frameworks, Fictional Modes," *Sewanee Review* 85 (Winter 1977): 122.

85. Pollitt 22.

86. Walt Chura, *America* (10 Apr. 1976): 319.

87. Pollitt 22.

88. Martha B. Tack, "Pecking Order," *Village Voice* (1 Nov. 1976): 95.

89. Sullivan 121.

90. Philip Howard, London *Times* (13 May 1976): 16.

91. Sullivan 121.

92. Lynn Sharon Schwartz, *Saturday Review* (6 Mar. 1976): 28.

93. Ward Just, "A 'Wonderful' Writer and Her 'Magical' Novel," *Washington Post* (10 Mar. 1976): B9.

94. Pollitt 22.

95. Pollitt 22.

96. Victor Howes, "Freedom: Theme of Pecks' Battle Hymns," *Christian Science Monitor* (14 Jan. 1976): 23.

97. Howard 16.

98. *Homeland: History, Bylaws, Deed & Agreement*. (Baltimore: Homeland Association): 3.

99. Mary Anne Brush, "The Two Worlds of Anne Tyler," *Baltimore Towne Magazine* (Apr. 1989): 34.

100. Brooks 343.

101. Notes on Manuscript of *Earthly Possessions*, The Anne Tyler Papers, Special Collections Library, Duke University.

102. Michael Himowitz, "Marylander Is Wonder Boy of the Demolition Derby," *Baltimore Sun* (6 Jan. 1975): B1.

103. Wanda Dobson, "Some Storefront City Churches Grow Big; Few Seem Stereotype," *Baltimore Sun* (18 Feb. 1974): C1.

104. Dobson C1.

105. Anne Tyler, *Earthly Possessions* (New York: Knopf, 1977): 84. Subsequent references will be cited in the text.

106. Tyler, "Still Just Writing" 15.

107. Tyler, "Because I Want" G7.

108. Michaels 43.

109. Tyler, "Still Just Writing" 9.

110. *Choice* (Sept. 1977): 867.

111. Anatole Broyard, "Tyler, Tracy and Wakefield," *New York Times Book Review* (8 May 1977): 12.

112. John Leonard, "A Loosening of Roots," *New York Times* (3 May 1977): 39.

113. *Choice* 867.

114. Nancy Gail Reed, "Novel Follows Unpredictable Escape Routes," *Christian Science Monitor* (22 June 1977): 23.

115. Gilberto Perez, "Narrative Voices," *Hudson Review* 30 (Winter 1977-78): 611.

116. Perez 612.

117. *Progressive* (July 1977): 44.

118. Angela Wigan, "Wilderness Course," *Time* (9 May 1977): 86.

119. Diane Johnson, "Your Money or Your Life," *Washington Post Book World* (29 May 1977): F1.

120. Bruce Cook, "A Writer--During School Hours," *Detroit News* (6 Apr. 1980): E3.

121. Cook E3.

122. Anne Tyler, "Please Don't Call It Persia," *New York Times Book Review* (18 Feb. 1979): 36.

123. Anne Tyler, "Chile: The Novel as History," *Washington Post Book World* (18 Feb. 1979): E3.

124. Cook E3.

125. Cook E3.

126. Tyler, "Still Just Writing" 5, 8.

127. Anne Tyler, "Pantaleo," Unpublished Manuscript in The Anne Tyler Papers, Special Collections Library, Duke University: 133.

128. Michaels 43.

129. Michaels 43.

130. George Dorner, "Anne Tyler: A Brief Interview With a Brilliant Author from Baltimore," *The Rambler* 2 (1974): 22.

131. Dorner 22.

132. Garland 58.

133. Anne Tyler, "My Summer," *New York Times Book Review* (4 June 1978): 35.

134. Tyler 35-36.

135. Cook E3.

136. Brooks 344.

137. Cook E3.

138. Cook E3.

139. Anne Tyler, "Fairy Tales: More Than Meets the Ear," *National Observer* (8 May 1976): 21.

140. Tyler 21.

141. A. G. Mojtabai, "A State of Continual Crisis," *New York Times Book Review* (23 Mar. 1980): 14.

142. Thomas M. Disch, "The Great Imposter," *Washington Post Book World* (16 Mar. 1980): 5.

143. Edmund Fuller, "Micawber as a Hardware Store Manager," *Wall Street Journal* (21 Apr. 1980): 26.

144. Paul Gray, "The Rich Are Different," *Time* (17 Mar. 1980): 91.

145. David Kubal, "Fiction Chronicle," *Hudson Review* 33 (Autumn 1980): 444.

146. James Wolcott, "Some Fun," *New York Review of Books* (3 Apr. 1980): 34.

147. Peter S. Prescott, "Mr. Chameleon," *Newsweek* (24 Mar. 1980): 83.

148. David Evanier, "Song of Baltimore," *National Review* (8 Aug. 1980): 973.

149. Paul Binding, "North of South," *New Statesman* (5 Dec. 1980): 25.

150. Wolcott 34.

151. Disch 5.

152. Stella Nesanovich, "Anne Tyler's Morgan's Passing," *Southern Review* 17 (Summer 1981): 621.

153. Tyler, "Because I Want" G7.

154. Clarence E. Olson, "Many Acts to a Life," St. Louis Post-Dispatch (18 May 1980): D4.

155. Eva Hoffman, "When the Fog Never Lifts," *Saturday Review* (15 Mar. 1980): 38.

156. Peter Grier, "Bright Novel That Overstretches Credibility," *Christian Science Monitor* (14 Apr. 1980): B9.

157. Gray 91.

158. Marilyn Murray Willison, "The Warp and Woof of Contrasting Life Styles," *Los Angeles Times Book Review* (30 Mar. 1980): 8.

159. William Francis Guess, "'Morgan's Passing': The Fascination of the Ordinary by a Master Storyteller," *Towson State University* (Nov. 1980): 1.

"A Border Crossing"

During the 1980s, Anne Tyler's writing attained a level of maturity only hinted at in her earlier novels. Given her age and her prolific literary output, she might produce another five to ten novels. Yet, whatever novels she produces in the future will certainly be judged in comparison to the novels written during this period of her life. One critic has even labeled this dramatic improvement in her writing "a border crossing."[1] Indeed, in these later novels Tyler does seem finally to have gained an understanding of that most crucial element of life: the passage of time. She once noted that "in books about families, the mere passage of time is often the most poignant event of all.[2] In her next four novels she demonstrated her ability to present her highly individual vision of life.

One short story, "Laps," published in 1981, the year before *Dinner at the Homesick Restaurant*, suggests that the issue of time was clearly on Tyler's mind. Perhaps her own daughters' growth from infants into children and then into teenagers prompted the change in Tyler's thinking about time. In this story a woman in her thirties spends the day at the neighborhood pool with a friend of hers and their children. While refereeing fights among their children, the two friends discuss their lives. At different times during the day, the woman sees people that remind her of the past and, through her memory, recollects past events from her life. At the end of the day when it is time to leave, the mother calls to her oldest daughter to get out of the pool. Ignoring her mother, the daughter continues to swim laps, back and forth, in the pool. As the mother watches her daughter, she remembers her own youth when she had been a lifeguard and thinks, "Her stroke is beautiful--slow and effortless. It's clear she has no idea she will ever have to leave the water."[3] Like the laps the daughter swims, time seems to fold back upon itself. Only in brief moments of insight such as the mother's, however, do people stop long enough to notice the passage of time. Even less frequently do they ever understand it or the changes that it brings.

DINNER AT THE HOMESICK RESTAURANT

John Updike, who had been reviewing Tyler's novels for the *New Yorker* ever since *Searching for Caleb* and who had praised her as "wickedly good," also sensed a change in Tyler's writing abilities with the publication of *Dinner at the Homesick Restaurant* in 1982. He wrote, [I]n her ninth novel [Anne Tyler] has arrived . . . at a new level of power, and gives us a lucid and delightful yet complex and somber improvisation on her favorite theme, family life."[4]

As Updike noted, with *Dinner at the Homesick Restaurant* Tyler had finally directly addressed the topic that had intrigued her from the earliest days of her career: family. She seemed to realize that the book was her most serious attempt yet to get to the heart of that complex subject when in a 1983 interview she confessed her motivation for choosing the book's focus: "Well, all right, I've joked around about families long enough; let me tell you now what I really believe about them."[5] A few years earlier, in 1979, Tyler admitted that families also provide a convenient means of investigating one of her main thematic interests, endurance: "My interest in families is a result of my curiosity about how people endure together--adapt, adjust, grate against each other, give up, and then start over again in the morning--and families are simply the most convenient vehicle for studying this."[6]

The family in *Dinner at the Homesick Restaurant* is the Tull family of Baltimore. At the beginning of the novel, Pearl Tull, the eighty-five-year-old mother of the family, lies dying. She begins to remember her life: first, her early years growing up in North Carolina, then her marriage at the age of thirty to a traveling salesman named Beck Tull, and finally, the birth of her three children--Cody, Ezra, and Jenny. The retrospective, deathbed viewpoint of chapter one, superficially reminiscent of William Faulkner's *As I Lay Dying*, is Tyler's vehicle for investigating time. For her, memory (not only Pearl's but the other characters' as well) is a way to gain control over time. Memory provides a manageable structure for presenting the events of a character's life.

Through Pearl's memory, the reader experiences both the immediacy of the events in her life as well as the longer perspective of how these events have affected her and her family over the years. One of Pearl's first memories, the one that colors all the others, is the unexpected turn her marriage takes one Sunday night in 1944 when Beck announces that he no longer wishes to stay married. Despite his having been away travelling most of the time during the first fifteen years of their marriage, Pearl is shocked when he leaves the next day on a permanent business trip.

Shamed by her husband's desertion, the intensely private Pearl decides that she must keep Beck's absence a secret both from her neighbors and her children, who at the time of their father's departure are fourteen, eleven, and nine. She finds a modest job working at a grocery store to provide for her children, but the burden of supporting them turns her into "an angry sort of mother,"[7] overwhelmed by the weight of her responsibilities. Pearl, symbolically, spends much of her spare time repairing the shabby row house on Calvert Street in which her family lives. Yet her feeling that the "whole, entire house is resting on [her] shoulders" (*DHR* 16) illustrates the negative effects of such heavy familial responsibility. Her obsession with keeping the house in repair reveals more than her desperation. The physical condition of the house is the one area of her chaotic life over which she can exercise some control. Pearl's personality becomes overly serious and pessimistic because of her heavy burdens. Only later, when these responsibilities ease as the children grow up and move away, does her character become less tense.

The three Tull children are all affected differently by their father's desertion and their mother's transformation into the "witch of Calvert Street" (*DHR* 16). In the novel's second chapter, Tyler expands her perspective to capture the variety of these responses. In each successive chapter, the perspective shifts to another character, creating a multiple perspective that more accurately portrays "what really happened," to paraphrase the title of chapter eight. Because of the multiple perspectives, each chapter can actually be considered a separate short story, complete with its own title. In fact, the fifth chapter, "The Country Cook," which uses Cody's viewpoint to relate his successful campaign to steal Ezra's fiancee, Ruth Spivey, away from him, was published, in slightly abridged form, as a short story in *Harper's*.

Cody's perspective in that story, as well as in chapters two and ten, presents a young boy and then a grown man deeply affected by his father's "absent presence" (*DHR* 20). Fourteen at the time of Beck's departure, Cody spends the rest of his life trying to gain his father's acceptance through his success in the business world, which is measured by the car he drives, first a Pontiac, then a Cadillac, and finally a Mercedes. Cody feels this need to impress his absent father all the more keenly because he does not receive special treatment from his mother. In fact, Pearl rather openly favors Ezra. Consequently, an intense rivalry develops between the two brothers. As a child, Cody wages a calculated campaign to discredit Ezra in his mother's eyes. He plays a series of cruel yet hilarious practical jokes on the unsuspecting Ezra, such as turning on all the hot water while Ezra is in the shower, sending in a response card in Ezra's name asking for information about cemetery plots, fixing Ezra's bed so that it comes crashing down when he sits on it, and setting Ezra up for a compromising picture that makes him look like a drunk and a pervert. None of these ruses sway Pearl, however. She sees through Cody's tricks and, after such incidents, merely flies into a rage at all her children, calling them "parasites" (*DHR* 53).

As the title of the novel suggests, food is especially important in *Dinner at the Homesick Restaurant*. Tyler, a fine cook herself, exhibits a keen interest in food in all her novels, but here it becomes a central metaphor for the emotional status of the entire family. Pearl's responsibilities and stress leave her little energy to prepare elaborate meals for her children. They have to settle for warmed-over canned food. Pearl is also limited in the emotional support that she is able to give her children. Consequently, each child suffers from emotional starvation. Cody becomes emotionally stunted like his mother, concentrating on business success until he is "starved for work" (*DHR* 223). Jenny, always thin, has Hansel and Gretel-like nightmares that her mother is raising her to eat her. Ezra, of course, responds to the lack of emotional nourishment most directly by opening a restaurant in which he serves foods prepared with love, such as "consoling" pot roasts (*DHR* 136).

Cody's jealousy grows deeper as he ages. He becomes increasingly competitive, relishing his victories in Monopoly games and even resorting to cheating in order to win. The ultimate competition, however, occurs when Cody and Ezra are adults. In a letter, Jenny happens to mention the possibility that Ezra might be getting married. Cody, who has plenty of girlfriends himself, nevertheless, becomes obsessed with Ezra's fiancee, Ruth Spivey, and wages a deliberate campaign to steal her away just a few months before the wedding. Even when he succeeds in getting Ruth to elope with him, he cannot end the competition. He becomes increasingly jealous of Ezra, refusing to live in Baltimore despite having bought a farmhouse outside of town. Instead he drags Ruth (and eventually their son Luke) around with him as his job takes him from city to city; consequently, he never establishes a home for them.

In some ways, Cody is re-enacting the traveling life of his father. Ironically, though he has sworn that he would never desert his family as his father did, he inadvertently condemns Ruth and Luke to the same type of isolation that he suffered as a child. Because of Cody's job, his family never lives anywhere long enough to buy a house. Instead, they always rent cold, impersonal modern houses with no personality or warmth. They never make friends either and are forced to depend on themselves alone for companionship. Even though Cody helps support his mother and comes home for occasional visits, the visits are short because Cody suspects Ezra of harboring feelings for Ruth, and at one point even accuses Ruth of still loving him.

In one incident, fourteen-year-old Luke runs away from home and hitchhikes to Baltimore to see his grandmother and uncle. Although Ezra immediately calls Cody to let him know that Luke is all right, Cody refuses to allow his son to stay in Baltimore. Instead he drives straight through to Baltimore and picks Luke up that night. The rivalry Cody sustains stunts both his own and his son's emotional maturation.

Although Ezra's quiet presence is felt throughout the novel, Tyler devotes only chapters four and nine to his perspective. As a child, he is Pearl's favorite because of his vulnerability. He is a sensitive boy, blue-eyed, a little pudgy, and musically inclined. He is forever playing "Greensleeves" on his recorder, symbolic of his airy, passive personality. His childhood in the Tull house, nourished only by Pearl's hastily heated quick suppers, creates in him a need to nurture others. He begins to work in a fancy Italian restaurant owned by an elegant, older woman, Mrs. Scarlatti, whose only son had died in the Korean War. Over the years, Mrs. Scarlatti expands Ezra's role in the running of the restaurant, first making him a full partner and then willing him the restaurant upon her death.

Once he takes control of Scarlatti's, Ezra makes several changes in the restaurant. The changes range from the menu selections to the people who serve the food. Most significantly, he changes the restaurant's name to the Homesick Restaurant. The name of the restaurant is central to Tyler's view of the contradictory effects of family. On the one hand, family members seek to maintain links with their relatives because the family unit defines an individual's identity, provides security, and creates a vehicle for giving and receiving love. Anyone who stays away from this central core of the family long enough eventually becomes homesick. At the same time, however, members of a family often experience the exact opposite feeling about family. The longer a person stays with a family, the more likely he or she is to rebel against its restrictiveness and its constant demands. Thus, one becomes sick of home. Often neither of these two contradictory feelings predominates. Instead the family member experiences a conflicting (and confusing) mixture of the two feelings. Cody, Ezra, and Jenny all feel this inner conflict and work to resolve it as best they can.

Ezra attempts to reconcile his opposing views of home in a series of family dinners at his restaurant. Paradoxically, he tries to recreate the homelike atmosphere that was missing in his own childhood home. His ulterior motive is to reunite the members of his family, who have grown distant in miles and in emotional connections. But such misconnections are ultimately the cause of these dinners never quite coming off. Inevitably, some argument, usually stemming from a misunderstanding, breaks out before the last course is finished. Ezra seems baffled by his family's inability to get through a single meal, yet he keeps trying. Finally, at the end of the novel, he almost achieves success, although by that time Pearl has died and Beck has returned for her funeral.

Jenny, whose perspective is presented in chapters three and seven, perhaps suffers the most from Pearl's lack of mothering. After the boys leave (Cody for college and Ezra for the army), Jenny is left alone with Pearl. She becomes thin, almost anorexic. Although she is intelligent and attends college, she chooses to involve herself in two unsatisfying marriages. These marriages are her misguided attempts to find the emotional support she missed as a child. First she marries Harley Baines, an obsessive genius and geneticist, who arranges his books according to height and color. Then she quickly moves to another equally unsatisfying marriage with Sam Wiley, an unfaithful artist, who abandons her three months before their daughter Becky is born.

Under the stress of raising a child on her own and the rigors of medical school, Jenny almost cracks. She even begins to repeat the pattern of abuse that her mother once inflicted upon her. At one point, she yells at her daughter and smashes Becky's head into her cereal. Her behavior causes her to wonder if such cycles of abuse are "doomed to continue, generation after generation" (*DHR* 209). Tyler's view of the effect of heredity and environment here borders on the fatalistic. Jenny seems to be repeating her mother's mistakes.

The effects of heredity also surface in the next generation of the family. Jenny's daughter Becky suffers from an even more severe case of anorexia nervosa than her mother. Luke, Cody's son, seems to Cody to look and act just like Ezra: blond, musical, passive. Ezra, on the other hand, thinks Luke resembles Cody. When the boy runs away and shows up at his restaurant, Ezra recognizes him by the set of his shoulders, which is just like Cody's. With the hold of heredity seemingly so strong, one might conclude that Tyler views each character as fated to repeat the mistakes of the past.

Tyler, however, does not believe in fate. Instead she allows her characters to change, adapt, and endure. Even Pearl softens and becomes more pleasant once the responsibilities of raising children ease. She comes to her daughter's rescue when Jenny is about to break, staying for two weeks to nurse her back to health and to comfort Becky. Despite her failures as a mother, Pearl proves to be a loving, caring grandmother. She establishes a strong link with Becky, reading *The Little House* to her, just as she had when Jenny was young. Tyler uses her favorite children's book to reinforce its lesson about the cyclical nature of time. Becky's childhood is, after all, not that different from Jenny's. Both have to endure the loss of a father and the temper tantrums of an overburdened mother.

Ultimately, Jenny recovers, finishes medical school, and moves back to Baltimore. Unlike Cody, who runs away from home, Jenny seems to seek connections with home. She eventually remarries, this time to Joe St. Ambrose, a man whose wife had deserted him, leaving him to care for their six children. Jenny likes Joe because she cannot "resist a man who needs [her]" (*DHR* 189). Likewise, through her pediatric practice, she becomes a surrogate mother to a whole brood of children. Over time, she becomes less edgy and learns to take life as it comes by "mak[ing] it through life on a slant" (*DHR* 212). In focussing on the issues that are important, Jenny changes what she can and does not worry too much about what she cannot change. Her attitude is similar to Tyler's mature passivity, which in her essay "Still Just Writing" she worried had made her "as passive as a piece of wood on a wave."[8]

The novel's final dinner, which reinforces this "slanted" view of life, brings Beck back after a "thirty-five year business trip" (*DHR* 284). At the restaurant following Pearl's funeral, Beck is amazed at the "assemblage" (*DHR* 292) of family members before him: Ezra; Cody, with Ruth and Luke; and Jenny, with Joe and their yours-mine-and-ours conglomeration of children. To Beck, the group looks like "one of those great, big, jolly, noisy, rambling . . . *families*!" (*DHR* 294).

But appearances can be deceiving, as Cody is quick to point out, noting that most of the children are Joe's from his previous marriage and therefore unrelated to Beck. Even Becky, whom Beck at first thinks might have been named for him, is actually short for Rebecca, not a variation of her grandfather's name. To make the moment more awkward, Cody chooses to confront Beck by asking him why he left them with Pearl, "a raving, shrieking, unpredictable witch" (*DHR* 294). Despite Ezra's more balanced view that their mother was not "*always* angry" (*DHR* 295), Cody continues the attack on his father, even implying that Beck has no place in the family. Taking advantage of a distraction, Beck leaves. Once his absence is discovered, the others immediately begin to search for him, but not Cody. It takes him a few minutes to think before he joins the search. Yet, because he thinks like Beck, he is the one to find his father first, even though at first, due to the bright sunlight, he mistakes Beck for his own son Luke. The connection startles Cody, who thinks that he would never abandon his son. Even so,

Cody has also been struggling to establish bonds with Luke, who is about to go off to college. Again, such generational misconnections seem almost hereditary.

In the final scene of the novel, Tyler gives her characters moments of insight that allow them to understand what time is doing to them and those they love. Cody's moment of privacy with his father gives him the opportunity to ask the question he has been wanting to ask for thirty-five years: Why did you leave us? In particular, he wants to know why Beck left them in Pearl's "clutches" (*DHR* 299). Beck explains that he left because Pearl "wore [him] out" (*DHR* 300) and saw right through his faults. More importantly, he could no longer take "the grayness . . . half-right-and-half-wrongness of things" (*DHR* 301). Once, two or three years after he left, he says, he returned to watch the house from a distance. What he saw was Cody, then sixteen or so, come out of the house, pick up the paper, and then toss it up flippantly into the air. Such a gesture told him that his family was getting along fine without him. He gives Pearl the credit for managing and asserts, as Jenny had in the earlier scene with Ezra, that his three children have turned out all right.

Just at that moment, as if to prove Beck's point, the rest of the family rounds the corner. Cody feels drawn to them and also to his father. Helping the reluctant Beck to his feet, Cody convinces him to stay for the remainder of the dinner. Finally, even though Beck insists that he will not stay for the dessert wine, there is at least the possibility that at long last one of Ezra's dinners will succeed.

As Cody walks back to the restaurant with his father, he remembers the past, the family outings from his childhood, especially the archery trip during which he shot his mother with an arrow. In retrospect, that arrow now seems forever suspended in flight. And journeying high above is an airplane droning like a bee. Tyler's perspective on time in this last scene is circular and reflexive. For the first time, if only briefly, Cody sees how time draws all the events in life together. All moments are linked like the path of the arrow. In moments of rare insight, people can view the whole scene, just as the passengers in the plane can view the landscape beneath them. Yet, at the same time, no part of the scene is ever still. The arrow remains in constant motion, and even the plane with its distant perspective vibrates with motion. Such is Tyler's view of time in the novel, ever changing and yet endlessly repeating itself in remarkable circles in the lives of her characters.

Although *Morgan's Passing* had disappointed Knopf's expectations, Tyler's publishers were thrilled by the tremendous sales of *Dinner at the Homesick Restaurant*. Not only did the book sell 71,000 hardcover copies, it prompted a flurry of interest in the paperback rights for Tyler's previous novels. In addition to buying the paperback rights to *Dinner*, Playboy Press brought out new paperback editions of *If Morning Ever Comes* (May 1983), *The Clock Winder* (June 1983), *A Slipping-Down Life* (July 1983), and *The Tin Can Tree* (September 1983). The next year, Berkley Books, which had taken over Playboy Press, published new editions of *Celestial Navigation* and *Earthly Possessions*. Anne Tyler had finally produced her breakthrough novel.

Reviews of *Dinner at the Homesick Restaurant* recognized the maturation of Tyler's artistic talent and vision. For the first time one of Tyler's books was reviewed on page one of the prestigious *New York Times Book Review*. The review by Benjamin de Mott, who had called this quantum leap in Tyler's abilities "a border crossing," noted that "in recent years her narrators have grown bolder and her characters more striking."[9] Commenting on the ultimate message of the book, he wrote: "If we pause too long in contemplation of a former self, we run the risk of forgetting how to take our present selves for granted. And down that road there's a risk of starting to treat life as a mystery instead of the way smart people treat it--as a set of done and undone errands."[10] This emphasis on the ordinary aspect of life must have pleased Tyler.

Tyler's style in *Dinner at the Homesick Restaurant* either charmed or exasperated critics. Julia Ehresmann described it as "a kind of modern pastoral rococo,"[11] while George Kearns considered it too elegiac and sentimental.[12] The book's realism, however, noted Robert Taubman, "has a way of endearing its subject, not just of documenting it."[13] The overall tone of the book was too depressed for some reviewers. Andrea Barnet felt "a disquieting determinism" similar to the "sullen psychic menace" of "Flannery O'Connor's gothic South."[14] This sense of fate struck R. Z. Sheppard as well: Tyler "launches her imagined lives and describes their trajectories with an unpretentious sense of fate."[15] Finally, James Wolcott called the novel "a work of unwavering integrity" but concluded that "[i]t's *conscientiously* dour."[16]

The harshest words for *Dinner at the Homesick Restaurant* concerned a familiar criticism of Tyler's work: her failure to deal openly with sex. James Wolcott quipped, "Sex is always a flimsy rumor in Tyler's novels."[17] Vivian Gornick was much blunter, titling her review for the *Village Voice* "Anne Tyler's Arrested Development." In Gornick's opinion, Tyler failed to recognize that contemporary novels must "dive down into the experience that gives us back to ourselves . . . people . . . struggling to become men and women. The energy that ignites them is sexual in character, not filial."[18] Ignoring the sexual nature of her characters, Tyler was swimming against the tide of "time and place that is stimulated by the idea of the separately maturing self, [instead remaining] relentlessly devoted to the idea of never growing up, never leaving home."[19] As a result, Gornick dismissed Tyler's prose as "sexually anesthetized" and bemoaned her growing critical and popular acclaim as a reward "for making a virtue out of the fear of experience."[20]

Tyler has argued that her reticence to explore the sexual aspects of her characters' lives stems from her respect for them as individuals. In later works, however, she has delved more deeply into the private sexual lives of her characters. In a hilarious scene in *Breathing Lessons* Maggie and Ira begin making out in Serena's bedroom only to be interrupted in mid-grope. In *The Accidental Tourist*, love scenes, although not very torrid ones, occur between Macon and Sarah and between Macon and Muriel. Finally, in *Saint Maybe*, Ian's search for a condom to consummate his relationship with his girlfriend Cicely precipitates the tragedy of Danny's death. Tyler's attempt to enter the closed doors of her characters' sexual lives is apparent in all these scenes. Still her approach to sex is always guarded, never explicit. Often it is downright funny. Sex, she seems to think, should not be taken too seriously. As she explained in a review of Milan Kundera's *Book of Laughter and Forgetting*, she dislikes books which treat sex in "an unpleasantly clinical, almost gruesome" way.[21]

Most critics sensed a complexity and depth in the characters in *Dinner at the Homesick Restaurant* that had been absent in her previous novels. For these critics, Tyler had succeeded in creating a credible little world peopled by believable characters. These fictional creations might have looked like ants to someone looking down at what in her dream Pearl Tull called "such a beautiful green little planet" (*DHR* 277) or from the airplane droning overhead like a bee in the book's final sentence, which Eudora Welty loved so much that she declared, "If I had written that I'd be happy all my life."[22]

FAME

With the publication of *Dinner at the Homesick Restaurant*, Tyler for the first time had to contend with the problem of fame, as well as the demands of a much larger reading audience. She asserts that she "tr[ies] to think as little as possible about critical reception, since the only way I can happily write a book is to pretend that no one but me will ever read it."[23] But the increasing audience brought a price as well. In "Still Just

Writing," she pondered this invasion by "the outside world" and wondered why writers, who have chosen "the most private of professions," would be interested in public performances or magazine interviews.[24]

Dinner at the Homesick Restaurant did nevertheless bring Tyler a much greater audience, both critical and popular. The book received nominations for several prestigious awards, including the National Book Critics Circle Award and a finalist for the Pulitzer Prize for Fiction, which Alice Walker's *The Color Purple* won. The novel did, however, win the Pen\Faulkner Award. As an additional accolade, Tyler was elected to the American Academy and Institute of Arts and Letters that same year.

One major change that Tyler made in her writing during the years following *Dinner* was gradually to give up writing short stories. Whereas earlier the short story form had provided a respite between longer efforts, she eventually stopped writing stories because she found that she does not "get so absorbed in the process as when I spend months and years on a novel."[25] Her deeper and more complete immersion in her novels has since produced her greatest work, so perhaps her decision was a wise one.

The stories she did publish after *Dinner at the Homesick Restaurant*, with just two exceptions ("Teenage Wasteland" and "A Woman Like a Fieldstone House"), were all chapters from novels in progress. Chapter five of *Dinner* became "The Country Cook," published in *Harper's* in a slightly abridged form and refocussed from Cody's viewpoint. More recently, such chapter/stories have needed fewer and fewer revisions for publication as separate short stories. With only slight abridgement, Max Gill's unconventional funeral in *Breathing Lessons* became "Rerun" for the *New Yorker*. Doug Bedloe's chapter in *Saint Maybe*, complete with its same title, "People Who Don't Know the Answers," was published in *Harper's*.

One story Tyler published during this time that is not associated with a novel is "A Woman Like a Fieldstone House," which she wrote as a charitable-donation to *Louder than Words*, a collection of short stories to benefit Share Our Strength, an organization that fights hunger and homelessness. The story focusses on the passage of time as the seventeen-year cycles of the cicada frame the life of a young woman who ages over the fifty-one-year span of the story. Like *The Little House*, the story presents the passage of time with great subtlety. By the end of the story, monumental, life-altering events have drastically changed the woman's life. The reader, like the woman, experiences the flow of time and, in a moment of insight, shares Tyler's awe-filled vision of the passage of time.

By the end of the 1980s, Tyler also began to reduce the number of book reviews she was writing. She had begun writing reviews "just because the various publications asked [her] to" and stopped writing them because she "worried that [she] was gradually using up [her] capacity for enthusiasm."[26]

THE ACCIDENTAL TOURIST

Not since Jeremy Pauling, in *Celestial Navigation*, had Tyler created a hero as much like herself as Macon Leary in *The Accidental Tourist* (1985). Like Tyler, Macon, a writer of travel guides for people who hate to travel, loves catalogues and small travel-sized packages. He suffers from insomnia and believes that time, like the old fashioned watch he insists upon wearing, is "not digital but real time, circular."[27] He also shares her dislike of crowds, considering shopping malls his "notion of hell" (*AT* 49). He loves orderliness and routine. Both of them have days set aside for grocery shopping, Macon on Tuesday and Tyler on Friday. Like Tyler, who repairs the electrical switches at her house, he is handy with tools. Words fascinate them both, and each is nearly obsessed with correct grammar. Both interests reveal a desire to order and thus control the uncertainty of life. Most importantly, Macon shares Tyler's profession, writing. Under the logo of an armchair with wings, he writes guidebooks that allow people to travel without feeling they have ever left home. As a man who sits next to Macon on a plane explains, "Going with the *Accidental Tourist* is like going in a capsule, a cocoon" (*AT* 253).

This encapsulation is Macon's problem. In the novel he insulates himself through a series of systematic devices. From his "Macon Leary Body Bag," a folded sheet stitched together to save him time laundering sheets and making beds, to *Miss MacIntosh*, the 1198-page novel that he carries on trips to ward off overly friendly fellow passengers, to the cast on his leg that "sealed [him] away from himself" (*AT* 60), Macon is in full retreat from the world.

This isolation is precipitated by the sudden death of Macon's only son Ethan a year earlier in a senseless robbery at a fastfood restaurant, and his subsequent separation from Sarah, his wife of twenty years. Ironically, Ethan's death occurs the first time that Macon and Sarah allow him to leave the safety of home. Until that time, Macon had sought to protect his son and had not allowed him to go to camp. Tyler's choice of subject matter, overcoming the death of a child, made the book "unusually difficult [for her] to write." With children of her own, she superstitiously made Ethan younger than her daughters so that she "could take comfort that they were already past that danger."[28] The loss of his son affects Macon deeply, but he internalizes his grief rather than expressing it. In fact, the word *communicate* is his least favorite word (*AT* 137).

By contrast, Sarah wants to talk about her grief but finds no emotional support from Macon, whom she labels "ossified" and "muffled," and whom she accuses of trying to "slip through life unchanged" (*AT* 142). To Sarah, the world is incomprehensible and evil now that Ethan is gone. She cannot understand how Macon can go on living as if nothing had happened to their son. Even the night Ethan died, Macon still flossed his teeth, and within a week he was mowing the grass in their yard. Sarah believes that the trouble with Macon is that he thinks "people should stay in their own sealed packages" (*AT* 321). She compares him to Harpo Marx's famous telegram: "No message. Harpo" (*AT* 321). Macon, however, does recognize that something is wrong with his relationship with Sarah. He feels that they are "like people who run to meet, holding out their arms, but their aim is wrong; they pass each other and keep running" (*AT* 10). They are definitely not communicating, if they ever did. Perhaps Ethan's death just makes them realize what was missing all along.

Sarah (and perhaps Tyler as well) expresses her feelings of anger and helplessness about the growing violence of American society. Sarah imagines confronting her son's killer and explaining to him that he killed more than just one person; he killed everyone connected to Ethan. Apparent is Tyler's belief in the interconnectedness of all individuals. Violence, she seems to be saying, harms everyone in a society.

In his grief, Macon tries to remain apart from other people. In denial himself, he cannot bring himself to feel even Sarah's blind anger. He retreats further into himself, finally winding up back at his childhood home where his family has actually stopped answering the telephone. Characteristically, he tells no one of his move because he enjoys being "so unconnected" (*AT* 67).

The whole Leary family suffers the same problem. If the effects of heredity were strong in *Dinner at the Homesick Restaurant* and *Searching for Caleb*, they seem still more apparent in the lives of the Learys, whose name perfectly captures their attitude towards contact with the outside world. Both of Macon's brothers, Charles and Porter, are divorced and have returned to the home where they grew up with their grandparents to live with their unmarried sister Rose. After Macon breaks his leg in an accident caused by one of his timesaving systems, he too returns to his old home. Once there the four siblings play Vaccination, a card game they invented over the years with rules so arcane and complicated that no one outside the immediate family can ever learn to play. They also eat dinners of ritual baked potatoes prepared by Rose, whose sole job is to look after "the boys." They even alphabetize their groceries with "allspice next to ant poisoning" (*AT* 14), proof, if one ever needed it, that absolutely rigid order is not always necessarily best. In the face of the chaos of the outside world, however, such an orderly, predictable, unchanging world appeals to Macon and the rest of the Learys. Soon after he settles back into the family's routine, he wonders if he had not "by some devious subconscious means . . . engineered this injury . . . so he could settle down safe among the people he'd started out with" (*AT* 63).

One living connection to his son remains--Ethan's dog, Edward. Since Ethan's death, Edward, a Corgi similar to the dog Tyler had at the time she was writing the novel, has been misbehaving. His increasingly serious misconduct finally prompts Macon to call in outside help. The help that comes is not for Edward alone, though. Muriel Pritchett, an outspoken dog trainer, whom Rose says looks like "a flamenco dancer with galloping consumption" (*AT* 103), appears on the scene to set both Edward's and Macon's lives in order.

Edward desperately needs training, for he has begun to tree strangers and corner family members. Finally, he even bites Macon, who tries to excuse his behavior by telling Muriel that the dog is just protecting him. Muriel's response applies to both the dog and its owner: "You can take protection too far" (*AT* 97). Despite a few setbacks, Edward begins to respond to Muriel's training. When Muriel is too rough on the dog, however, Macon intervenes and fires her. She tells him that he must want a dog "that hates the entire world" (*AT* 123), again summing up Macon's problem more aptly than the dog's. Muriel senses his isolation and tries to draw him out of it.

Matters with Edward (and Macon) only get worse. Left alone to cope with the dog and his loneliness, Macon cannot survive. On a trip to New York, he has a panic attack in a restaurant at the top of a skyscraper. Looking out from that height, he feels "completely isolated from everyone else in the universe" (*AT* 160). First he calls his family for help, but Rose, Sarah, and Porter are out, and Edward has Charles penned up in the pantry. As a last resort, Macon calls Muriel, who takes charge of Edward. Once Muriel takes over, Macon immediately feels calmer and is able to finish his dinner. From this point on Muriel becomes an integral part of his life. Deny it though he tries, he needs her.

What draws Macon to Muriel? She seems too different from him, too much an outsider. She lives on Singleton Street, in a rough section of downtown Baltimore, where she manages to survive quite well through shrewdness and ingenuity. She works a variety of jobs, everything from dog trainer to errand runner, and has raised her seven-year-old son, Alexander, by herself since his father left them. The first time Macon goes to her house to try to slip a note under her door explaining that he cannot come to dinner because he has not yet gotten over Ethan's death, she hears him and, thinking he is a burglar, threatens him with a shotgun. When he speaks up, she lets him in and he collapses into her arms, telling her about Ethan's death, the first time he has talked about it with anyone. Later that night he and Muriel make love for the first time. Afterwards he notices the Caesarean scar on her stomach and realizes that he is not the only person who has suffered pain or loss.

Macon becomes increasingly connected to Muriel and her son, although he is reticent to make a firm commitment. Still he enjoys his new identity in "the foreign country that was Singleton Street" (*AT* 212). In particular, he is drawn to Alexander, a scrawny boy with allergies. Macon teaches him to fix a leaky faucet and gives him a child-sized tool set for Christmas. Eventually, Macon moves in with Muriel and takes on a fatherly role to Alexander. In one scene, Macon sets Edward on some children who are picking on the young boy. In gratitude, Alexander takes Macon's hand as they are walking back to the house. At that moment Macon realizes that "his life had regained all its old perils," for with someone to care about (and to worry about) he "can never be completely happy" again (*AT* 258).

Tyler uses dreams to reveal Macon's changing emotional status throughout the novel. At first, in his grief, he dreams about Ethan and continues to worry about him. Later he begins to dream about Muriel, surprising himself that he can feel anything for another person, especially one so different from himself. Critical interpretations of Macon's emotional growth in the novel vary widely. Some critics see his passive attempt to make sense of the world as inherently feminine,[29] while others view it in more psychological terms as an embracing of life's complexity,[30] a "journey through psychic despair to rebirth,"[31] or the "intrapsychic change" necessary to overcome his grief.[32] One critic even likens Macon's psychological development to Odysseus's quest in *The Odyssey*.[33]

Tyler also continues to display her interest in language in the novel. In *The Accidental Tourist*, she uses correctness of grammar to make distinctions between her characters. Muriel Pritchett's lower class status is reinforced by her poor grammar. Rose Queillo suggests that Muriel, "relegated to the margins of social existence, . . . often cannot find the 'correct' language she needs to convey the intensity of her feelings behind the words," yet "she does not reject language entirely (by remaining silent) but deconstructs it in order to reconstruct it."[34] So when Muriel says "speciality," Macon is quick to correct her. Yet, despite her incorrect grammar, Muriel continues talking and attempting to open lines of communication with Macon. She knows that she has lessons, perhaps more important than grammatical ones, to teach him as well.

Nevertheless, Macon's reticence to commit to Muriel ultimately causes conflict. Muriel begins to allude to marriage, but Macon simply ignores her increasingly overt hints. Meanwhile, to complicate matters still further, Sarah also expresses an interest in resuming her marriage to Macon. Faced with the choice between an old, familiar relationship and a new, yet unpredictable one, Macon chooses to return to his old home and to Sarah. Change is hard for anyone, but especially so for someone as afraid of it as Macon.

The Accidental Tourist marks one of the few times in her later novels when Tyler uses a setting outside Baltimore. In the final chapter Macon boards his flight to Paris, only to discover that Muriel has followed him. Once in Paris, however, he virtually ignores her. When he injures his back, it is Sarah who flies over to care for him and take over his business trips. Sarah offers him her limited view of a life stuck in the past. After their reconciliation she had said, "After a certain age people just don't have a choice" and "You can only choose what to lose" (*AT* 310). After his experience with Muriel, though, such a limited view of life no longer appeals to Macon. For a few days he obediently takes the pain pills Sarah offers him, although they completely knock him out. But then he makes a decision to face life on new terms. In a very significant action, he "open[s] his hand and let[s] the pill fall" (*AT* 351), symbolizing the rejection of his anesthetized relationship with Sarah and his acceptance of an uncertain, and possibly painful, future relationship with Muriel. In accepting such a relationship, he joins "the real adventure . . . the flow of time" (*AT* 354).

Macon's choice at the end of the novel resembles choices made by many of Tyler's earlier characters who choose to accept change and move on with their lives rather than remain stuck in the past. Like Justine Peck in *Searching for Caleb*, Evie Decker in *A Slipping-Down Life*, and Cody Tull in *Dinner at the Homesick Restaurant*, Macon overcomes the hold that the past has on him and endures. Tyler ends the novel with a celebration of Macon's successful escape from the past, complete with a description of the confetti-like sunlight reflecting off the window of the cab as it turns around to pick up Muriel.

Reviews of *The Accidental Tourist* reflected Tyler's growing critical acclaim. Jonathan Yardley ended his review in the *Washington Post Book World* with outright adulation: "Words fail me: one cannot reasonably expect fiction to be much better than this."[35]   Richard Eder, in the *Los Angeles Times Book Review*, echoed Yardley's sentiments by wondering: "I don't know if there is a better American writer going."[36] Writing for the *Chicago Tribune BookWorld*, John Blades called Tyler a "cockeyed humanist," "the voice of sweet reason, the heiress apparent to Eudora Welty as the earth mother of American writers," whose "warm but mildly disquieting vision of family life, . . . lovably neurotic characters, [and] . . . quiet but reverberant prose . . . [have] managed to disarm all but the most calloused readers."[37]   One such callous reader was Jessica Sitton, who felt that "Tyler's characters often seem wrapped in cellophane: they rustle through their world, observe their surroundings, yet remain insulated, yearning to be touched even as they shrink away."[38]

In particular, the issue of family continued to dominate critical comment. Noting that Tyler is "an archeologist of manners" writing about a Baltimore that is "a veritable Troy," Larry McMurtry wrote in the *New York Times Book Review* that "in Anne Tyler's fiction, family is destiny."[39]   In his review in the *New York Times*, Michiko Kakutani observed that Tyler uses the family as a symbol for "those two imperatives in American life: the need for community, definition and safety, and the desire for flight, adventure, independence."[40]

Writing for the *Times Literary Supplement*, Adam Mars-Jones noted that Macon continues the line of artist heroes in Tyler's fiction and commented on the narrative efficacy of Macon's job writing travel guidebooks. Such a job "gives Tyler all the advantages of having an artist hero (not having, for instance, to invent a working life to counterbalance a private drama), and none of the disadvantages. Macon Leary's job is perfectly expressive of him, and involves little or no distorting feedback, since he is represented on the cover of his books not by a name but by a logo: a winged armchair."[41]

Critical approval was seconded by the selection of *The Accidental Tourist* as the National Book Critic Circle's most distinguished work of fiction published in 1985. In addition, the novel was among the finalists for the Pulitzer Prize for Fiction in 1986, which was awarded to Larry McMurtry for *Lonesome Dove*.

From a commercial standpoint, *The Accidental Tourist* continued Tyler's rise to prominence. The book sold 114,000 hardback copies. It was also chosen as the fall main selection of the Book of the Month Club (along with Garrison Keillor's *Lake Wobegon Days*). The *Book of the Month Club News* called it "by far her funniest book: which means, in some ways, her most compassionate."[42] The Berkley paperback edition, published in September 1986, sold nearly two million copies within five years.

To make Tyler's financial success even sweeter, the movie rights to the book were purchased for a six-figure sum, assuring her financial security for years to come. Even more important for her literary reputation, the release of the movie starring William Hurt (as Macon Leary), Geena Davis (as Muriel Pritchett), and Kathleen Turner (as Sarah Leary) brought Tyler to the attention of a much larger and more diverse audience than she had previously enjoyed.

The movie premiered in Washington, D.C. on December 12, 1988, with all the movie's stars in attendance. It went on to win four Academy Award nominations: best picture; best screenplay based on material from another medium (Frank Galati and director Lawrence Kasdan wrote the screenplay after Tyler declined); best original score

(John Williams); and best supporting actress (Geena Davis), who won the Oscar for her portrayal of Muriel. Tyler, however, remained aloof from the publicity. She was not present at the Washington premiere, but agreed to attend a Baltimore premiere on January 6, 1989, on the condition that the occasion be informal and that it benefit a worthy cause, the Juvenile Diabetes Foundation of Central Maryland. As a result, the affair turned into "a real home-grown premiere--just everyday people going to catch a film in their cozy hometown"--and raised $20,000 for the charity.[43] Tyler, who paid for her own tickets, attended with Taghi. She wore her hair up in a bun and sat in a reserved section. At the reception, asked for a comment by a reporter, Tyler demurred, "'I can't. I'm sorry.'"[44]

Tyler's noncommittal response to the reporter's question was prompted by the very public atmosphere in which the question was posed. It did not mean that she had no opinion about the movie. In fact, on the whole, she was pleased with the film, considering it faithful to the book's overall spirit and theme, even though she had declined the opportunity to write the screenplay. She was, by one friend's account, especially happy with the performance of William Hurt as Macon Leary.[45]

BREATHING LESSONS

In her next novel, *Breathing Lessons* (1988), Tyler decided to treat the subject of marriage in greater depth than she had in any of her previous novels. In fact, she used a marriage similar to her own. The novel's main characters, Maggie and Ira Moran, have been married twenty-eight years. Maggie is also about the same age as Tyler was when she wrote the novel. Tyler's choice of marriage for the subject of the novel reflects her continuing fascination with ordinary relationships and the way in which people manage to endure. In a book review of *Intimate Partners: Patterns in Love and Marriage*, which she wrote while working on *Breathing Lessons*, Tyler questions whether any marriage is average and asserts that "an ordinary, run-of-the-mill marriage has in many ways a more dramatic plot than any thriller ever written."[46]

As *Breathing Lessons* opens, Maggie and Ira are preparing for their trip to the funeral of Max Gill, the husband of Serena, an old friend of Maggie's. As Maggie drives home from the Harbor Body and Fender Shop where the Morans' car has been being repaired following one of her frequent accidents, she listens to a radio talk show where the question of the day is "What Makes an Ideal Marriage?"[47] This question presents the theme of the novel. Over the course of the day, and, through Maggie's and Ira's memories, Tyler explores the ups and downs of their twenty-eight-year marriage.

The structure of the novel is a departure for Tyler. Instead of a plot covering several years, she experiments with an Aristotelian time frame, setting the entire novel on the September Saturday of Max Gill's funeral. Tyler's treatment of extended time periods in her previous novels is here reversed and encapsulized. Through memory, Tyler is able to recreate the past in its entirety, although, as Maggie and Ira discover, their memories of the past do not always coincide; instead they "dovetail" (*BL* 289), with Maggie remembering some details and Ira others.

Maggie and Ira's marriage is a good one. Yet no marriage is perfect, and neither is the Morans'. The conflict between them starts at the very beginning of the novel when they wake up late because Maggie has forgotten to set the alarm clock. Due to Maggie's mistake, it is she who must retrieve the car from the repair shop. As Maggie leaves the shop, she hears a woman on the radio whose voice she thinks sounds like Fiona, her ex-daughter-in-law and mother of Leroy--Maggie and Ira's only grandchild. The woman says she is remarrying, this time for security, not love. This news startles Maggie so much that she hits the gas pedal instead of the brake as she drives off from the repair shop. Unfortunately, but typically for the accident-prone Maggie, she runs right into a Pepsi truck, which hits the only part of the car that has not been previously dented. The Morans' battered, yet still serviceable, old car is Tyler's metaphor for life. No part of it escapes injury forever. Eventually everything and everyone are involved. The one variable is the way that people react to the conditions life sets for them. The ever resourceful Maggie drives on, turns the corner, pulls over so she can pull the fender out to keep it from scraping the tire, and picks up an incredulous Ira to whom she explains, "There was an unexpected situation" (*BL* 7).

Thus begins the first in a series of "breathing lessons" that Tyler introduces in the novel. The term ostensibly refers to the Lamaze breathing exercises Maggie practiced with Fiona in preparation for Leroy's birth. Actually, the term is a metaphor for the give and take of marriage. To emphasize this dynamic flow, the two words of the title appear on alternating pages in the book. The picture on the front of the book's dust jacket also reinforces this aspect of married life. The picture shows a flock of birds flying in the air, forming two interlocking circles that symbolize the way in which two lives are joined and yet remain separate and distinct in a marriage.

One of Maggie's breathing lessons has been learning to cope with her separation from her six-year-old granddaughter Leroy following her son Jesse's divorce from Fiona. Consequently, she has an ulterior motive for the trip to Max Gill's funeral in Deer Lick, Pennsylvania. Cartwheel, Pennsylvania, where Fiona now lives with her mother, is close to Deer Lick. From the moment Maggie hears about Max's death, she begins scheming to reconcile Fiona and Jesse so that Leroy will be able to live in Baltimore again and be near her grandparents.

This is not the first instance of Maggie's scheming. Thinking back, she remembers having rescued Leroy as a baby. Fiona had gotten pregnant while she and Jesse were dating. Jesse wanted to marry her, but Fiona thought he was doing it only for the baby, so she planned an abortion. Jesse, who does not communicate well with Fiona, begged Maggie to go to the abortion clinic and convince Fiona not to go through with the procedure.

The scene at the abortion clinic is one of the few instances in Tyler's fiction in which her views on a social issue are suggested. The abortion clinic is being picketed by protesters who confront arriving clients. Maggie, whose purpose is paradoxically the same as theirs--to prevent Fiona from going through with the abortion--nevertheless shouts them down, mentioning "constitutional permission" (*BL* 242). At the same time, she tries desperately to change Fiona's mind, finally inventing a lie about a cradle Jesse was supposedly building for the baby. This information convinces Fiona that Jesse cares for her, so she decides not to have the abortion. Instead she comes home with Maggie, marries Jesse, and Leroy is born.

As suggested by Maggie's actions in this scene, Tyler's views on abortion seem moderate. Characteristically, she does not assume the authority to make the choice for someone else. In fact, Maggie tells Jesse when he first asks her to go to the clinic and change Fiona's mind that "this really has to be the girl's decision" (*BL* 233). Yet, Maggie does convince Fiona not to terminate her pregnancy, and that nearly aborted fetus turns up in full life and six years old in the last half of the book--a living human being whose life would never have been if Fiona had made a different choice. Tyler, personally, apparently does not favor abortion if it would cost the life of an individual such as Leroy, yet she nevertheless seems to uphold a woman's right to make the decision.

The major breathing lesson Maggie and Ira have to master is marriage itself. Throughout the novel, Maggie often wonders about marriages and how they succeed or fail. Her friend Serena had married Max Gill the year before Maggie married Ira. She had thus been able to give Maggie a more realistic view of married life and motherhood: the former is "no Rock Hudson Doris Day movie" and the latter is "much too hard and . . . perhaps not worth the effort" (*BL* 54). For Serena, with Max's death, life has become a casting off of burdens and responsibilities. Much like Pearl in *Dinner at the Homesick Restaurant*, Serena feels that she has always been the one who had "to carry the household" (*BL* 68). In the end this cessation of responsibility is a relief to her. She urges Maggie to forget about Leroy and "Let it all go" (*BL* 80).

That message is reinforced by the last song sung at Max's unconventional funeral, at which Serena re-enacts her marriage ceremony, complete with all the old songs her friends sang on her wedding day nearly thirty years earlier. The music is Tyler's trope for bringing the two time periods together and simulating the feel of the late 1950s for Maggie and for the reader. After Maggie's rendition of "Love Is a Many Splendored Thing," an old classmate, Sugar Tilghman, rises to sing the song most perfectly expressive of Tyler's attitude about time: "Que Sera, Sera."

Maggie, however, is incapable of letting things be. Even though she professes a view of life permitting little change, believing that everyone is trapped by the centrifugal force of the earth like people riding in those little spinning teacup rides at amusement parks (*BL* 46), she continuously dreams of changing both her life and the lives of the people around her. This tendency often gets her into trouble with Ira. She thinks that Ira's most serious flaw is his being "a closed-in, isolated man" (*BL* 13). For his part, Ira feels that Maggie does not take her life seriously enough and that she considers it instead a "practice life" (*BL* 125). He is continuously having to deal with some mishap she has caused, whether it is something simple like a botched answering machine message or something more serious like her interference in Jesse and Fiona's marriage.

Even so, it was one of Maggie's errors that brought her and Ira together in the first place. She attended the same church as Ira and had mistakenly heard that he had been killed in an army training accident. Maggie sent a sympathy note to Ira's father only to be embarrassed when Ira showed up, unharmed, the next week at choir practice. Because he must take care of his invalid father and two unmarried sisters, Ira has to abandon his plans for medical school. Therefore, his subsequent marriage to Maggie, who had "dropp[ed] into his lap like a wonderful gift out of nowhere" (*BL* 160), becomes his only escape from the dullness and loneliness of caring for his family. As a result, he believes that his marriage to Maggie, despite its setbacks, is "as steady as a tree . . . [and that] not even he could tell how wide and deep the roots went" (*BL* 157).

On the way to pick up Fiona and Leroy, Ira and Maggie catch a glimpse of yet another marriage. They pass an old black man, Daniel Otis, whose car Maggie notices has a wobbly wheel. Maggie insists that they take him to get help and refuses to leave him at the service station until his nephew Lamont returns. Like Tyler, who will not stop writing a novel until she knows what is going to happen, Maggie will not leave Mr. Otis because she "wouldn't know how it came out" (*BL* 150). While they wait, Mr. Otis relates the story of his rocky marriage of over fifty years. His wife had kicked him out because she had dreamed that he had stepped on her needlepoint chair. Despite many such incidents during their marriage, they have still managed to remain married, unlike Lamont or Jesse. Mr. Otis's advice for a successful life (and marriage) is simply to "spill it all" (*BL* 170), giving one's all to the venture and not holding back anything. Ira realizes that Mr. Otis's philosophy more closely resembles Maggie's than his own. After this encounter, he finally relents and agrees to take Maggie to see Fiona and Leroy in Cartwheel.

Like Daniel and Duluth Otis, Ira and Maggie also struggle to maintain the balance of their marriage. During this one day they run the emotional gamut of marriage. On the way to the funeral they argue often, sometimes over the song Ira is whistling because, unknown to him, Maggie has learned that his songs reveal his thoughts. At one point Maggie becomes so angry that she actually gets out of the car and leaves Ira. She even begins to plan a life without him. But then he returns for her, allowing them to continue their journey, and, metaphorically, their marriage. On the opposite end of the scale, at the totally inappropriate occasion of Max's wake, they find themselves embroiled in a passionate scene in Serena's bedroom. Serena is incensed when she catches them, and they leave her house in shame. As they walk back to their car, they hold hands for a while, basking in their solidarity. Eventually, however, they resume their more typical stance and walk "slightly apart, not touching. They were back to their normal selves" (*BL* 121).

In the midst of the many ordinary moments of their mundane marriage, however, a few moments of insight allow them to understand how deeply they are bound to each other. Maggie's epiphany comes several days after Jesse and Fiona's marriage breaks up and Fiona moves out, taking Leroy with her. Upset, Maggie is sitting at the kitchen table crying. Ira walks in and sits down and puts his head in his hands. At that moment Maggie realizes that she is not the only person in pain: "He was just as sad as Maggie was, and for just the same reasons. He was lonely and tired and lacking in hope and his son had not turned out well and his daughter didn't think much of him, and he still couldn't figure where he had gone wrong" (*BL* 280). Maggie's response is simply to hug him and reassure him, "It will be all right. It will be all right" (*BL* 281). This moment with Ira gives her the security and reassurance that she needs to endure the crisis of Jesse's failed marriage. The incident remains an unspoken understanding between the two of them, and "life continued just the same as always" (*BL* 281).

After their detour with Mr. Otis, Maggie and Ira finally arrive in Cartwheel. Once there Maggie convinces Fiona to come for a visit to Baltimore by lying to her about Jesse's feelings, just as she had earlier about the cradle. Consequently, Maggie should not have been surprised when her elaborate plan falls on its face. Back in Baltimore, when Jesse and Fiona finally meet, they quarrel and Fiona leaves, taking only her purse and Leroy's baseball glove. Thus, the best-laid plans of mice and Maggie have once again come to naught. At the end of the day (and the novel), Maggie and Ira are once again in bed. Ira is playing solitaire, a game that symbolizes his isolation, but which also serves as a metaphor for the stage of marriage he and Maggie are in. She wonders what they are "going to live for, all the rest of our lives" (*BL* 326). Ira puts his arm around her to comfort her but continues his game. The game, like their lives and their marriage, Maggie notices, has "passed that early, superficial stage when any number of moves seemed possible, and now his choices were narrower and he had to show real skill and judgment" (*BL* 327). This knowledge lifts Maggie. She moves over to her side of the bed and goes to sleep because she realizes that she will need her energy tomorrow to resume her campaign to return Leroy to Baltimore. The final image of the novel depicts Maggie and Ira's endurance, as well as Maggie's intrinsic determination.

The third time around proved a charm for Tyler with the selection of *Breathing Lessons* for the 1989 Pulitzer Prize for fiction. She was characteristically nonchalant over the award, issuing the following statement through her publisher: "I consider it a great honor, and I am so happy to hear about it and I'm wonderfully pleased and stupefied."[48] A resourceful *Baltimore Sun* reporter, who arrived at her door hoping for a comment the day of the announcement, went away empty-handed. Tyler herself answered the door but, after being asked for a comment, apologized, "I'm in the middle of writing a sentence so I can't be interrupted, but I'm very pleased."[49] Additional accolades came when the book was also nominated for the National Book Award, which was given that year to Pete Dexter's *Paris Trout*.

Like *The Accidental Tourist* before it, *Breathing Lessons* became a bestseller. *Time* named it one of the best fiction books of 1988 and the next year cited it as one of the ten best fiction books of the decade. Hardcover sales of the novel nearly doubled those of *The Accidental Tourist* (222,000), while paperback sales of the Berkley edition had topped 1,000,000 within two years of its October 1989 release. Sales figures for her earlier books continued to climb as well. By September 1991, each of her previous novels had sold more than ten times its original hardcover sales in their Berkley paperback editions: *If Morning Ever Comes* (153,000), *The Tin Can Tree* (95,000), *A Slipping-Down Life* (89,000), *The Clock Winder* (125,000), *Celestial Navigation* (122,000), *Searching for Caleb* (180,000), *Earthly Possessions* (137,000), *Morgan's Passing* (257,000), *Dinner at the Homesick Restaurant* (885,000), and *The Accidental Tourist* (1,500,000).[50]

On February 6, 1994, *Breathing Lessons* premiered as a "Hallmark Hall of Fame" television production. Joanne Woodward played Maggie, and James Garner was Ira. The production captured the overall tone of the novel, but changed the ending slightly. In the movie version, Woodward's Maggie is presented as somewhat more accepting of her lot in life than the novel's Maggie, who goes to sleep so that she'll be rested to begin anew her struggle to change the lives of everyone in her family.

As additional fame and recognition came to Tyler, however, she did not allow them to change her life or her work schedule any more than she could help. That is not to say that she was not pleased with the growing audience for her work. The type of response that pleases her most is a personal letter from a reader who has enjoyed one of her novels: "I see that they in their solitude, and I in mine, have somehow managed to touch without either of us feeling intruded upon. We've spent some time on neutral territory, sharing a life that belongs to neither of us."[51]

Tyler's portrayal of a daughter going away to college in *Breathing Lessons* mirrors her own life as Mitra and Tezh left home to enroll at the Rhode Island School of Design to study, as Taghi put it, "art for art's sake."[52] Her daughters' choice of art must have been particularly satisfying to Tyler, whose own aspirations in that field had never been fully realized. At the same time, the understated way in which she presented Daisy's departure in the novel hints at deeper feelings about the loss of her own daughters.

Critics were appreciative of the humor and characterizations in *Breathing Lessons*, but few found it to be Tyler's best work. Richard Eder, writing for the *Los Angeles Times Book Review*, praised it as possibly "her funniest book" but not her best.[53] Marita Golden noted that "much like the enduring marriage it describes, *Breathing Lessons* possesses an unevenness, periodically radiant with moments of glorious near-perfection, yet falling too often into the vaguely predictable."[54]

As always the reviewers touched on familiar themes of family and character. Nigel Andrew called the book "another tour of the emotional force-fields which hold together the ordinarily extraordinary American family."[55] Despite Tyler's focus on the ordinary, Hope Hale Davis pointed out Tyler's "sympathetic, funny, disclosing way of showing people who are typical and yet wildly individual."[56] Wallace Stegner, writing for the *Washington Post Book World*, considered the book's characters "ordinary people going about their ordinary affairs in ordinary cities such as Baltimore . . . . First they surprise us, then we recognize them, then we acknowledge how much they tell us about ourselves."[57]

Most particularly, according to the reviewers, in *Breathing Lessons* Tyler concerns herself with the issue of marriage. Edward Hoagland, in the *New York Times Book Review*, described Tyler as "a domestic novelist" in "that great line descending from Jane Austen . . . interested not in divorce or infidelity, but in marriage--not very much in isolation, estrangement, alienation and other fashionable concerns, but in courtship, child raising and filial responsibility."[58] Reviewing for *Time*, R. Z. Sheppard was impressed by Tyler's treatment of marriage "as fate and mystery, something that grows, for better or for worse, in flood and drought."[59] Likewise, Carole Angier connected the subject of marriage to life itself and to Tyler's prevailing themes of the flux and flow of life, love, and enduring relationships in the "circularity and absurdity [of] the endless desire to come together, the endless fact of being apart."[60]

The central critical debate, however, focused on the character of Maggie herself. Critics wondered whether she is too optimistic for her own good and whether she should stop meddling in other people's lives and pay more attention to her own. Most reviewers found something to praise as well as to criticize in Maggie, describing her as one of those complex, fully human and flawed, well-rounded characters, neither all good or all bad--in other words, the type of character Tyler loves best. Marianne Brace called Maggie "a well-meaning optimist whose acts of kindness are infuriating at best, at worst dangerous,"[61] while Dean Flower found her "the inveterate maternal do-gooder doomed to fail, probably, but undeterred, a species of comic existentialist."[62] Writing in the *National Review*, David Klinghoffer labeled her a "bored housewife [turned] into a kind of domestic Sisyphus,"[63] whereas Marita Golden was put off by Maggie's "Lucy Ricardo quality."[64]

In the end, Maggie remained an enigma to reviewers, as she must have to Tyler. Elizabeth Beverly, writing for *Commonweal*, observed that Maggie "has more faith in herself and in the world than Tyler herself does."[65] Tyler's depiction of Maggie does seem at odds with Tyler's warier, more skeptical view of life. *Breathing Lessons*, though reaffirming that "Tyler clearly is not feminist,"[66] actually presents a picture of endurance and active pursuit of a better world.

Tyler's depiction of Ira and Maggie's married life reveals her own idealistic philosophy being tempered by realism. After all, although Maggie Moran advises her family to place their bets on Infinite Mercy at Pimlico, in the end, "Maggie must also more fully grasp what the author who created her has always . . . known: loving, understanding relationships between men and women are difficult to achieve, but they are possible; romance, however, is always an illusion."[67]

In an effort to maintain her privacy and to preserve time for her writing, Tyler has become increasingly sparing of herself to the public. She no longer makes public appearances, such as her 1974 panel discussion at Duke on which the article "Olives from a Bottle" is based. She no longer speaks to writing classes at Towson State University because the crowds eventually grew too large. She no longer grants interviews, although she does answer selected questions by mail. Despite these self-imposed restrictions, she is not a recluse. In fact, she loves to recount the story of a newspaper announcement of an award given to "Cynthia Somebody, poet, and Anne Tyler, recluse."[68] Instead, she is simply a strong-willed, highly disciplined person who chooses what she will and will not do. As she noted in "Still Just Writing," her focus is "narrow,"[69] but that allows her more control over her world and her art. Such insulation from the outside world has proven increasingly pleasing to her: "As I get older, I've learned to say 'no' more and more--and I get happier and happier."[70] This narrowness provides an added benefit to her writing: "As the outside world grows less dependable, I keep buttressing my inside world, where people go one meaning well and surprising other people with little touches of grace."[71]

SAINT MAYBE

In *Saint Maybe* Tyler turned to the topic of religion. Although her aim seems less direct here than when she wrote about families in *Dinner at the Homesick Restaurant*, she nonetheless does seem finally to want to "tell us what she really thinks" about religion. Earlier novels had dealt with religion only tangentially, and many of her novels treated ministers in particular with skepticism. From James Green's unforgiving fundamentalist father in *The Tin Can Tree*, to Elizabeth Abbott's strict Baptist father in *The Clock Winder*, to Charlotte Emory's preacher husband Saul in *Earthly Possessions*, Tyler had consistently presented ministers as rigid and insensitive. Yet Tyler herself claims to have nothing against clergymen. Rather she is "particularly concerned with how much right anyone has to change someone, and ministers are people who feel they have that right."[72]

From the very beginning, Tyler seemed aware of the extreme sensitivity of her subject. In choosing a religion for Ian, she did not research any particular religions because "research of that sort cramps and stunts a novel"; additionally, she was concerned about giving offense, so, in the end, to "avoid offending any particular religion, I figured it was best to just think up my own imaginary one."[73]

Tyler's hesitation to offend others parallels Ian's dilemma in *Saint Maybe*. Throughout the novel he struggles with the question of "how much right" one person has to intrude upon another's life. In starting this novel, Tyler had "wondered what it must feel like to be a born-again Christian, since that is a kind of life very different from mine."[74] The character she eventually imagined is Ian Bedloe, a typical seventeen-year-old boy living with his family in Baltimore in 1965. But Ian's life does not remain typical for long. He makes a mistake that alters the course of his life. This mistake is to tell his brother Danny that he suspects that his wife Lucy has been unfaithful and that their child, Daphne, is not really his.

The consequences of Ian's mistake are dire. First Danny kills himself. Then Lucy, struggling to raise her children--the baby Daphne and two older children by a previous marriage, Agatha and Thomas--takes an overdose of sleeping pills. The orphaned children have to move in with Ian's parents, Doug and Bee. As the tragedy mounts, so does Ian's guilt. He wonders how such a momentary error in judgment could lead to such tragic consequences. But in Tyler's world, there are no disconnected events. Everything and everyone affect everyone else.

In *Saint Maybe* Tyler uses a technique she used earlier in *The Accidental Tourist*. To portray Ian's struggle to come to grips with his guilt, she incorporates his dreams into the narrative structure. At first Ian's dreams are guilt-ridden. In one dream, Danny tries to pay Ian for babysitting the children on the night he was killed. In another, Lucy complains to Danny, who works as a postman, that Ian has called her "not a bit first-class" (*SM* 106). After Ian decides to accept the responsibility for raising the children, he dreams that he is working for a moving company and struggling to move a heavy carton. Danny suddenly appears and helps him lift the heavy box, all the while smiling at him. Significantly, this is the last dream Ian has about Danny. It reveals how Ian's guilt has finally been eased.

The main reason for Ian's change of heart is his involvement with the Church of the Second Chance, an odd, storefront church run by Reverend Emmett. Many of the church's beliefs come from Tyler's own Quaker heritage. Joseph Voelker notes several similarities between the two faiths: "Members of Reverend Emmett's congregation remain silent during 'Amending' until someone is moved to speak. They eschew all iconography and most ritual and dogma. They are extremely democratic. And finally, they find real discomfort with the necessity of authority."[75] There are other links as well. For example, while Tyler was living at Celo, she participated in the community's Saturday Works programs, a possible source for the novel's Good Works program.[76]

The doctrine of the Church of the Second Chance is a mixture of Calvinistic salvation by works and benign social gospel. On the one hand, Rev. Emmett tells Ian that he will not be forgiven for his part in his brother's death unless he "see[s] to those children" (*SM* 123). Furthermore, the church rules are strict and rather quirky: No sugar, No alcohol, No sex before marriage. Despite the rules, however, the church is very personal and sympathetic to individual needs, as evidenced by the Saturday Good Works program and the Christian Fellowship picnic.

Rev. Emmett, therefore, differs markedly from Tyler's previous ministers. She presents him as both caring and open-minded. By the end of the novel, pastoring for twenty years has taught Rev. Emmett that his original idealistic expectations are not attainable. He gradually accepts his parishioners' foibles and failings. Eventually, he even breaks one of his own rules when he shares a drink with a man whose wife had died before they could open a bottle of wine they had been saving for their fiftieth anniversary. Rev. Emmett breaks the Alcohol Rule in this instance because "drinking that glass of wine was a gift to another human being" (*SM* 303). Rev. Emmett's action humanizes him and makes him for Ian one of those "people . . . who simply never [come] clear" (*SM* 334). No dogmatist, Rev. Emmett becomes another of Tyler's multifaceted, fully human characters.

As for Ian's response to the church, Tyler has written that she "certainly never intended to satirize Ian's religious beliefs," thinking "of his faith as, literally, his Second Chance at a moment when he had given up hope."[77] Throughout the novel, Ian's religious faith hardly ever wavers. He becomes increasingly closer to God and begins to view himself resting in the hands of God. After he forgives Danny and Lucy for burdening him with the responsibility for raising the children, Ian sees himself as "an arrow--not an arrow shot by God but an arrow heading toward God," certain that if it takes his "only life" he will prevail (*SM* 225). His faith allows him to meet the challenges placed in his path and overcome each of them.

In *Saint Maybe* Tyler again chose a structure utilizing multiple narrative perspectives. In several chapters, this approach allowed her to concentrate on the viewpoint of the children. Each child is therefore presented as an individual whose character and personality are fully formed, seemingly almost from birth. Agatha, who first appears at the age of seven, is already the serious, responsible adult who will grow up to be an oncologist. Tyler presents her as a caregiver to the other children, taking on the role of parent because of Lucy's incompetence and irresponsibility. Thomas, on the other hand, from the beginning is childlike in his passive personality and underdeveloped emotional maturity. He needs mothering, misses Lucy terribly, and gravitates towards Bee, preferring her softness to Ian's rough edges, although like the other children he loves Ian deeply. Unlike Agatha, Thomas enjoys popularity among his peers, yet he is always seeking approval and attention. Unfortunately, he never quite grows up. As an adult, he works designing software for children's computer games and chooses a domineering woman for a wife. Daphne, the "child of [Ian's] life" (*SM* 254), grows up a difficult and independent individual, who is always in search of her identity. That search begins with her crawling around the crowded Bedloe living room until she finds Ian. Her search continues as she grows older and experiences trouble in school. Finally, as a young adult she moves from job to job. Of all the children, she causes Ian the most worry, yet, much to his surprise and relief, she somehow manages to maneuver through life unscathed. At the end of the novel, she remains as much an enigma as she ever was.

Tyler's depiction of each child illustrates her belief in the unchanging self. She has written that she believes "each person has a fairly immutable self, issued before birth, and heavily influenced by various earnest decisions made during early childhood. Not that change beyond that isn't possible . . . but I tend to be skeptical about wholesale transformation of the self much beyond childhood."[78] Ian's "conversion," in her view, therefore, is "not a personality change," but rather "a *course of action,*"[79] for his character too is set early in his life. His decision to take care of the children is therefore a conscious choice on his part.

Tyler's continuing interest in the ordinary is also apparent in *Saint Maybe*. The novel begins by describing the Bedloes as an average family, almost stereotypical: "Waverly Street's version of the ideal, apple-pie household" (*SM* 4). Yet before the novel is over Tyler has managed to demonstrate that the "ordinary" lives of her characters are actually filled with significance and meaning. After Danny's death and several years of caring for the three children have taken their toll on Bee, she bemoans the family's fate: "We've had such extraordinary troubles . . . and somehow they've turned us ordinary" (*SM* 181). Actually, the opposite has occurred. By capturing the ordinary life of this family in her novel, Tyler proves that the common is really full of significance. With such a view, even ordinary objects, such as Bee's flooded sewing basket, become important. When Daphne and Agatha find the basket in the closet, they realize that it captures and holds all their memories of their grandmother better than any monument, and wordlessly put it back in its place, even though it is wet. This inanimate object teaches them a lesson that Tyler instinctively already knows: what people live day in and day out is the real truth about life, not Andy Warhol's infamous fifteen minutes of fame.

Ian, likewise, grapples with the ostensibly disappointing turn his life seems to have taken after a few years of "seeing to" the children. He fantasizes about a beautiful Church Maiden, who simultaneously fulfills his suppressed sexual desires and relieves him of the burden of caring for the children. Ultimately, though, no maiden appears, and Ian must bear the burden alone. He finally realizes, however, that the burden is not without its rewards, for he comes to love the children as his own. Yet one aspect of his life is incomplete. He still seems determined to avoid intruding in the lives of others. He is afraid to risk taking responsibility for changing someone else's life, as he had Danny's. His attitude is summed up in the kind of furniture he likes to build, pieces with straight lines that can be measured out carefully beforehand, and which can be fixed easily if he makes any mistakes. Following the path of other Tyler characters before him, he retreats into emotional isolation.

Like Macon Leary in *The Accidental Tourist*, however, Ian receives some outside help. Rita di Carlo, whose job as "Clutter Counselor" requires her to set the Bedloe house in order following Bee's death, appears on the scene. Although an improbable mate for Ian, she serves as a catalyst for his final step toward redemption. Through his connection to Rita, Ian finally risks committing himself to another person. Rita's almost immediate, albeit unexpected, pregnancy reinforces the forward movement of Ian's spiritual odyssey. His change in attitude is again reflected in the furniture he builds, for he chooses to build a cradle for the new baby. Whereas before he had stuck with straight lines, he now delights in the cradle's curves, taking "special pride" in its "nearly seamless joints, which would expand and contract in harmony and continue to stay tight through a hundred steamy summers and parched winters" (*SM* 315).

What Ian has learned is a lesson about time and his place in life. Prior to his marriage and the birth of his son Joshua, named perhaps for the man who led the children of Israel into the Promised Land, Ian had been afraid to assume his rightful place in the flow of time. By the end of the novel, however, he has assumed his proper role as father and husband and joined the march of time. Through faith in God, in others, and in himself, he has re-entered the mainstream of life.

Perhaps due to Tyler's growing critical stature, her increasing popularity, or the novel's treatment of religious themes, *Saint Maybe* was reviewed more widely than any of Tyler's previous novels. Because of this religious focus, an unusual theme for a contemporary novel, *Saint Maybe* was reviewed in a number of religious publications, such as *Christianity Today* and *Christian Century*. Religion remained the focus of criticism in other secular periodicals as well. Bruce Bawer, writing for the *Washington Post Book World*, observed that "Tyler has always . . . manifested what might be called a Christian perspective."[80] Playing on the title of Tyler's earlier novel, Jay Parini entitled his review in the *New York Times Book Review* "The Accidental Convert."[81]

Some reviewers, however, criticized Tyler's religious focus, as well as her depiction of the Church of the Second Chance. John C. Hawley found *Saint Maybe* a "rather treacly tale of conversion," "the result of [Tyler's] investigation of the role of faith . . . Norman Rockwell, with religion."[82] The Church of the Second Chance reminded Hawley of Flannery O'Connor's "Church of Christ Without Christ, minus the grit."[83] Crystal Gromer, on the other hand, saw little of O'Connor's church from *Wiseblood* in Tyler's "pale, beige, drab, flat" institution.[84] Marilyn Gardner felt Ian "derive[s] more comfort than meaning from the Church of the Second Chance, and slides too quickly over his easy acceptance of Brother Emmett's strictures, from no sex to no sugar."[85]

Even so, other critics found much to praise in Tyler's attempt to tackle such a morally complex topic. Linnea Lannon wrote, Tyler "has chosen an extremely unfashionable topic for her [twelfth] novel. Atonement is not something Americans seem to hold much stock in lately."[86] Writing for the *Los Angeles Times Book Review*, Richard Eder noted that *Saint Maybe* "takes an extra risk by being more overtly serious than its predecessors."[87] As for the Church of the Second Chance itself, Robert Wilson considered Tyler's portrayal as "neither patronizing nor mocking."[88] Katie Andraski, even more forcefully, asserted, "Tyler draws a picture of righteousness--not the flashy, ecstatic kind, but the gritty, day-to-day tedium of loving."[89]

Still other reviewers treated the dilemma presented in the novel as more moral than strictly religious. Kelly Cherry wrote in the *Southern Review*, "It is as if Anne Tyler has held a mirror to our mortal fallibility, our inability to love one another perfectly. We gaze into this mirror, like Ian gazes into the bathroom mirror on 'the biggest night of his life,' and what we see of ourselves is so pathetic and incomplete that our strongest desire is to save the world from ourselves."[90] Bruce Bawer contended that "Tyler's aim is to suggest that one find joy not by seeking fixed truths but by abandoning oneself to life's flux and accepting the limitations of one's knowledge."[91] In a similar vein, Linnea Lannon asserted that Tyler had "crafted . . . a novel that is old-fashioned in its moralism . . . . [but] completely convincing and refreshing."[92]

Other reviewers debated the effectiveness of Tyler's narrative technique. Lorna Sage liked Tyler's extensive use of dialogue and the story's being "mediated through someone's point of view, so that there is no separate or superior voice doing the telling. Hence the effect of lucidity and intimacy."[93] John Sutherland enjoyed Tyler's "artfully off-hand way" of storytelling "which teases the reader into close engagement while suggesting that Tyler herself is only just this side of sarcasm," but he also felt that Tyler's "technique gives the impression of a narrator dipping into the primary narrative pudding, almost absentmindedly, yet always coming up with a plum."[94] Such a seemingly random selection of the events Tyler records makes her, according to Joseph Voelker, "less historian than chronicler."[95] He finds that she produces two effects: "First, she gets to hand the enterprise of reconstructing 'what really happened' over to her characters, abdicating the role of judge. Second, she achieves the magical illusion of being able to record in prose the slow passage of moments, months, and years."[96]

Of course, criticism also centered on the character of Ian himself. Many reviewers considered Ian a fully imagined creation, "sit[ting] near the top of Ms. Tyler's fine list of heroes," according to Jay Parini, who went so far as to argue, contrary to earlier critics, that Tyler "charges Ian Bedloe with a wonderfully subtle sexual presence."[97] Yet even Parini conceded that Tyler fails to foreshadow adequately Ian's sacrifice. Most other critics, such as Richard Eder, were harsher, finding the newly converted Ian heroic but dull.[98] Crystal Gromer lamented, "In giving up his soul to God, or at least to the church, Ian abandons his personality. He may be a saint, but he's awfully boring."[99]

As for the book's other characters, reviews were mixed as well. Several critics praised Tyler's portrayal of children: "No one accords to children the seriousness and fullness of treatment, the complexity and the humor, that Anne Tyler does."[100] Jay Parini singled Tyler out as "one of the few contemporary writers who can really 'do' children."[101] On the other hand, the foreigners, whose hilarious fascination with Western technology Tyler had modeled after an Iranian cousin-in-law,[102] struck Anita Brookner as "oddly undeveloped."[103] To Richard Eder, Rita seemed too much "a dead-ringer for Muriel, the dog-trainer in '[The Accidental] Tourist,'"[104] and John C. Hawley pronounced Bee "a self-blinded Polyanna who transforms every crisis into an apparent opportunity for welcome change."[105]

Ultimately, though, the characters of *Saint Maybe* all reflect Tyler's interest in the ordinary aspects of life. Robert Wilson noted that Tyler's people are "characters of resolute ordinariness."[106] They remain quintessentially Tylerian, creations of the imagination of a writer who "plays the sort of God who's not, in the end, very interested in sitting in judgment."[107] Ian, in particular, seems "a character who implicitly upbraids his creator for making so much fuss about him."[108]

This last comment could very well apply to Tyler herself. She simply observes her world and writes about it. From her viewpoint that does not make her anything but an ordinary person. As such she does not want any special attention. Ian's last thoughts at the end of *Saint Maybe* characterize Tyler's viewpoint exactly: "After all, she might have said, this [life] was an ordinary occurrence. People changed other people's lives every day of the year. There was no call to make such a fuss about it" (*SM* 337).

THE TUMBLE TOWER

In 1993, in collaboration with her daughter Mitra, who drew the pictures for the book, Tyler wrote a children's book entitled *The Tumble Tower*. The book is dedicated to Tezh and Taghi. It tells the story of a royal family consisting of two very neat parents, King Clement the Clean and Queen Nellie the Neat; their son, Prince Thomas the Tidy; and their daughter, Princess Molly the Messy, who lives in a tower so untidy that her father dubs it "Sloppy City," "the Den of Disorder," and the "Tumble Tower."[109]

The tension between the members of the family revolves around Molly's insistence on keeping the tower a mess. She does not mind books and clothes lying everywhere or leftover bits of food because these are eventually useful to her. She asserts, "It's my own private room, and I like it just the way it is" (*TT* n.p.).

The family finally comes to accept Molly's messiness when their castle floods one night, forcing them to seek refuge in Molly's messy tower. There they find dry clothes to replace their wet ones, spare food to curb their hunger, and a warm bed to keep them cozy. After this experience, they learn a new respect for Molly and her untidiness.

Though they straighten their own rooms after the flood, they do not insist on keeping them quite so neat.

Many of the themes of Tyler's earlier work are summarized in this short children's book. First, she loves the interplay between order and chaos, finding neither condition acceptable and insisting on a merging of the two. Second, she stresses the importance of the individual and demands a respect for each person's uniqueness. Finally, she explores the way in which members of a family manage to live together despite their differences, learning to accommodate each other's foibles and even allowing the other members to change them a little.

These are the credos of Anne Tyler, a novelist who will, hopefully, be adding to her already significant body of work in the years to come. To Tyler, all her characters, despite their ordinariness, are unique and important. In asserting their worth, she makes a strong statement about the value of all individuals. Her vision is a wonderfully humanistic one in a world that all too often overlooks the individual human beings that inhabit it.

Endnotes

1. Benjamin de Mott, "Funny, Wise and True," *New York Times Book Review* (14 Mar. 1982): 1.

2. Anne Tyler, "A Photo Album of Snips and Surprises," *National Observer* (18 Oct. 1975: 21.

3. Anne Tyler, "Laps," *Parents* (Aug. 1981): 130.

4. John Updike, "On Such a Beautiful Green Little Planet," in *Hugging the Shore: Essays and Criticism* (New York: Knopf, 1983): 296.

5. Sarah English, "An Interview with Anne Tyler," in *The Dictionary of Literary Biography Yearbook: 1982* (Detroit: Gale Research, 1983): 194.

6. George Dorner, "A Brief Interview with a Brilliant Author from Baltimore," *The Rambler* 2 (1979): 22.

7. Anne Tyler, *Dinner at the Homesick Restaurant* (New York: Knopf, 1982): 19. Subsequent references will be cited in the text.

8. Anne Tyler, "Still Just Writing," in Janet Sternberg, ed., *The Writer on Her Work* (New York: Norton, 1980): 11.

9. de Mott 1.

10. de Mott 14.

11. Julia M. Ehresmann, *Booklist* (15 Dec. 1981): 522.

12. George Kearns, "Fiction Chronicle," *Hudson Review* 35 (Autumn 1982): 509.

13. Robert Taubman, "Beckett's Buttonholes," *London Review of Books* (21 Oct.-3 Nov. 1982): 17.

14. Andrea Barnet, *Saturday Review* (Mar. 1982): 62.

15. R. Z. Sheppard, "Eat and Run," *Time* (5 Apr. 1982): 77.

16. James Wolcott, "Strange New World," *Esquire* (Apr. 1982): 124.

17. Wolcott 124.

18. Vivian Gornick, "Anne Tyler's Arrested Development," *Village Voice* (30 Mar. 1982): 41.

19. Gornick 40.

20. Gornick 41.

21. Anne Tyler, "A Czech in Mourning for His Country," *Chicago Sun-Times Book Week* (2 Nov. 1980): 12.

22. Barbara Lazear Ascher, "A Visit with Eudora Welty," *Yale Review* 74 (Autumn 1984): 149.

23. English 194.

24. Tyler, "Still Just Writing" 15.

25. Letter from Anne Tyler to the author, 25 Feb. 1993.

26. Letter from Anne Tyler to the author, 25 Feb. 1993.

27. Anne Tyler, *The Accidental Tourist* (New York: Knopf, 1985): 34. Subsequent references will be cited in the text.

28. Patricia Rowe Willrich, "Watching through Windows: A Perspective on Anne Tyler," *Virginia Quarterly Review* 68 (Summer 1992): 508.

29. Rosalie Murphy Baum, "Boredom and the Land of Impossibilities in Dickey and Tyler," *James Dickey Newsletter* 6 (Fall 1989): 12-20; and Alice Bloom, "George Dennison, *Luisa Domic*, Bobbie Ann Mason, *In Country*, Anne Tyler, *The Accidental Tourist*," *New England Review and Bread Loaf Quarterly* 8 (Summer 1986): 513-25.

30. Barbara Harrell Carson, "Complicate, Complicate: Anne Tyler's Moral Imperative," *Southern Quarterly* 31 (Fall 1992): 24-34.

31. Anne Ricketson Zahlan, "Traveling Towards the Self: The Psychic Drama of Anne Tyler's *The Accidental Tourist*," in C. Ralph Stephens, ed., *The Fiction of Anne Tyler* (Jackson: UP of Mississippi, 1990): 86.

32. Barbara R. Almond, "The Accidental Therapist: Intrapsychic Change in a Novel," *Literature and Psychology* 38 (Spring-Summer 1992): 84.

33. William K. Freiert, "Anne Tyler's Accidental Ulysses," *Classical and Modern Literature* 10 (Fall 1989): 71-79.

34. Rose Maria Quiello, "Breakdowns and Breakthroughs: The Figure of the Hysteric in Contemporary Novels by Women," Diss.. U of Connecticut, 1991: 145.

35. Jonathan Yardley, "Anne Tyler's Family Circles," *Washington Post Book World* (25 Aug. 1985): 3.

36. Richard Eder, *Los Angeles Times Book Review* (15 Sept. 1985): 3.

37. John Blades, "For NutraSweet Fiction, Tyler Takes the Cake," *Chicago Tribune BookWorld* (20 July 1986): 37.

38. Jessica Sitton, *San Francisco Review of Books* 11 (Spring 1986): 12.

39. Larry McMurtry, "Life Is a Foreign Country," *New York Times Book Review* (8 Sept. 1985): 1.

40. Michiko Kakutani, "Books of the Times," *New York Times* (28 Aug. 1985): C21.

41. Adam Mars-Jones, "Despairs of a Time-and-Motion Man," *Times Literary Supplement* (4 Oct. 1985): 1096.

42. *Book of the Month Club News* (Fall 1985): 2.

43. Nora Frenkiel, "'Tourist' Arrives," *Baltimore Sun* (6 Jan. 1989): E1.

44. Frenkiel E5.

45. Letter from Clarinda Harriss Raymond to the author, 19 June 1993.

46. Anne Tyler, "Marriage and the Ties that Bind," *Washington Post Book World* (15 Feb. 1987): 6.

47. Anne Tyler, *Breathing Lessons* (New York: Knopf, 1988): 5. Subsequent references will be cited in the text.

48. "The Pulitzer Prize Winners: Excellence in Journalism, Letters and the Arts," *New York Times* (31 Mar. 1989): B4.

49. Tim Warren, "Baltimore's Tyler, Branch Win Pulitzers," *Baltimore Sun* (31 Mar. 1989): A1, 16.

50. Sales figures constitute sales as of Sept. 1991, according to Toinette Lippy, head of paperback rights for Knopf.

51. Anne Tyler, "Because I Want More than One Life," *Washington Post* (15 Aug. 1976): G7.

52. Nora Frenkiel, "Writing to Find 'Absent People' and Himself," *Baltimore Sun* (25 Feb. 1986): B3.

53. Richard Eder, "Crazy for Sighing and Crazy for Loving You," *Los Angeles Times Book Review* (11 Sept. 1988): 3.

54. Marita Golden, "New Wives' Tales," *Ms.* (Sept. 1988): 86.

55. Nigel Andrew, "Que Sera Sera," *Listener* (19 Jan. 1989): 50.

56. Hope Hale Davis, "Watching the Ordinary People," *New Leader* (28 Nov. 1988): 19.

57. Wallace Stegner, "The Meddler's Progress," *Washington Post Book World* (4 Sept. 1988): 1.

58. Edward Hoagland, "About Maggie, Who Tried Too Hard," *New York Times Book Review* (11 Sept. 1988): 1.

59. R. Z. Sheppard, "In Praise of Lives Without Life-Styles," *Time* (5 Sept. 1988): 75.

60. Carole Angier, "Small City America," *New Statesman & Society* (20 Jan. 1989): 34.

61. Marianne Brace, "Keeping Off the Straight and Narrow," *Books* (Feb. 1989): 17.

62. Dean Flower, "Barbaric Yawps and Breathing Lessons," *Hudson Review* 42 (Spring 1989): 134.

63. David Klinghoffer, "Ordinary People," *National Review* (30 Dec. 1988): 48.

64. Golden 86.

65. Elizabeth Beverly, "The Tidy Plans that Crumbled," *Commonweal* (24 Feb. 1989): 121.

66. Davis 20.

67. Koppell 284.

68. Wendy Lamb, "An Interview with Anne Tyler," *Iowa Journal of Literary Studies* 3 (1981): 62.

69. Tyler, "Still Just Writing" 15.

70. English 193.

71. Tyler, "Still Just Writing" 15.

72. Lamb 61.

73. Willrich 516.

74. Willrich 510.

75. Joseph C. Voelker, "The Semi-Miracle of Time," *World and I* (Feb. 1992): 356.

76. Letter from Peg Neal to the author, 28 July 1993.

77. Letter from Anne Tyler to the author, Oct. 1991.

78. Letter from Anne Tyler to the author, 29 Aug. 1992.

79. Letter from Anne Tyler to the author, 16 Sept. 1992.

80. Bruce Bawer, "Anne Tyler: Gravity and Grace," *Washington Post Book World* (18 Aug. 1991): 1.

81. Jay Parini, "The Accidental Convert," *New York Times Book Review* (25 Aug. 1991): 1+.

82. John C. Hawley, *America* (4-11 Jan. 1992): 18.

83. Hawley 18.

84. Crystal Gromer, "Never Far from Home," *Commonweal* (8 Nov. 1991): 657.

85. Marilyn Gardner, "Ordinariness as Art," *Christian Science Monitor* (25 Sept. 1991): 13.

86. Linnea Lannon, "Days of Atonement," *Detroit News* (25 Aug. 1991): L7.

87. Richard Eder, "Quiescence as Art Form," *Los Angeles Times Book Review* (8 Sept. 1991): 3.

88. Robert Wilson, "'Saint Maybe,' A Sure Thing," *USA Today* (23 Aug. 1991): D1.

89. Katie Andraski, *Christianity Today* (22 June 1992): 43.

90. Kelly Cherry, "The Meaning of Guilt," *Southern Review* 28 (Winter 1992): 173.

91. Bawer 2.

92. Lannon L7.

93. Lorna Sage, "Compassion in Clans," *Times Literary Supplement* (27 Sept. 1991): 24.

94. John Sutherland, "Lucky Brrm," *London Review of Books* (12 Mar. 1992): 23.

95. Voelker 348.

96. Voelker 349.

97. Parini 26.

98. Eder 17.

99. Gromer 657.

100. Gromer 656.

101. Parini 26.

102. Letter from Anne Tyler to the author, 19 Mar. 1993.

103. Anita Brookner, ""The Good, the Drab, and the Tacky," *Spectator* (26 Oct. 1991): 36.

104. Eder 17.

105. Hawley 19.

106. Wilson D1.

107. Sage 24.

108. Sutherland 24.

109. Anne Tyler, *The Tumble Tower* (New York: Orchard Press, 1993): n.p. Subsequent references will be cited in the text.

BIBLIOGRAPHY

Primary Sources

Note: The alpha-numeric code for each bibliographic entry corresponds to the key in the preface and is indexed accordingly.

I. Published Novels

N-1   *If Morning Ever Comes*. New York: Knopf, 1964.

N-2   *The Tin Can Tree*. New York: Knopf, 1965.

N-3   *A Slipping-Down Life*. New York: Knopf, 1970.

N-4   *The Clock Winder*. New York: Knopf, 1972.

N-5   *Celestial Navigation*. New York: Knopf, 1974.

N-6   *Searching for Caleb*. New York: Knopf, 1976.

N-7   *Earthly Possessions*. New York: Knopf, 1977.

N-8   *Morgan's Passing*. New York: Knopf, 1980.

N-9   *Dinner at the Homesick Restaurant*. New York: Knopf, 1982.

N-10   *The Accidental Tourist*. New York: Knopf, 1985.

N-11   *Breathing Lessons*. New York: Knopf, 1988.

N-12   *Saint Maybe*. New York: Knopf, 1991.

II. Short Stories

1959

S-1   "Laura." *Archive* Mar. 1959: 36-37.

S-2   "The Lights on the River." *Archive* Oct. 1959: 5-6.

1960

S-3   "The Bridge." *Archive* Mar. 1960: 10-15.

1961

S-4   "I Never Saw Morning." *Archive* Apr. 1961: 11-14. [Reprinted in *Under Twenty-Five: Duke Narrative and Verse, 1945, 1962*. Ed. William Blackburn. Durham: Duke UP, 1963: 157-66].

S-5   "The Saints in Caesar's Household." *Archive* Apr. 1961: 7-10. [Reprinted in Jessie Rehder. *The Young Writer at Work*. New York: Odyssey, 1962: 75-83; and in *Under Twenty-Five: Duke Narrative and Verse, 1945-1962*. Ed. William Blackburn. Durham: Duke UP, 1963: 146-56].

1963

S-6   "The Baltimore Birth Certificate." *Critic* Feb. 1963: 41-45.

S-7   "I Play Kings." *Seventeen* 1963: 338-41.

S-8   "A Street of Bugles." *Saturday Evening Post* 30 Nov. 1963: 64-66. [Reprinted in *Saturday Evening Post* July-Aug. 1989: 54-57+].

1964

S-9   "Nobody Answers the Door." *Antioch Review* 24 (Fall 1964): 379-86.

1965

S-10   "Dry Water." *Southern Review* NS 1 (Spring 1965): 259-91.

S-11   "I'm Not Going to Ask You Again." *Harper's* Sept. 1965: 88-98.

1966

S-12   "As the Earth Gets Old." *New Yorker* 29 Oct. 1966: 60-64.

S-13   "Two People and a Clock on the Wall." *New Yorker* 19 Nov. 1966: 207-17.

1967

S-14   "The Genuine Fur Eyelashes." *Mademoiselle* Jan. 1967: 102-03+.

S-15   "The Tea-Machine." *Southern Review* NS 3 (Winter 1967): 171-79.

S-16   "The Feather Behind the Rock." *New Yorker* 12 Aug. 1967: 26-30. [Reprinted in *A Duke Miscellany: Narrative and Verse of the Sixties*. Ed. William Blackburn. Durham: Duke UP, 1970: 154-62].

S-17   "A Flaw in the Crust of the Earth." *Reporter* 2 Nov. 1967: 43-46.

1968

S-18   "Who Would Want a Little Boy?" *Ladies Home Journal* May 1968: 132-33+.

S-19   "The Common Courtesies." *McCall's* June 1968: 62-63+. [Reprinted in *Prize Stories 1969: The O. Henry Awards*. Ed. William Abrahams. Garden City: Doubleday, 1969: 121-30].

1971

S-20   "With All Flags Flying." *Redbook* 137 (June 1971): 88-89+. [Reprinted in *Prize Stories 1972: The O. Henry Awards*. Ed. William Abrahams. Garden City: Doubleday, 1972: 116-26; and in *Redbook's Famous Fiction*. New York: Redbook Publishing Co., 1972: 84-87].

S-21   "Outside." *Southern Review* NS 7 (Autumn 1971): 1130-44.

1972

S-22   "The Bride in the Boatyard." *McCall's* June 1972: 92-93+.

S-23   "Respect." *Mademoiselle* June 1972: 146-47+.

S-24   "A Misstep of the Mind." *Seventeen* Oct. 1972: 118-19+.

1973

S-25   "Spending." *Shenandoah* 24 (Winter 1973): 58-68.

S-26   "The Base-Metal Egg." *Southern Review* NS 9 (Summer 1973): 682-86.

1974

S-27   "Neutral Ground." *Family Circle* Nov. 1974: 36+.

S-28   "Half-Truths and Semi-Miracles." *Cosmopolitan* Dec. 1974: 264-65+.

1975

S-29   "A Knack for Languages." *New Yorker* 13 Jan. 1975: 32-37.

S-30   "The Artificial Family." *Southern Review* NS 11 (Summer 1975): 615-21. [Reprinted in *The Pushcart Prize: Best of the Small Presses*. Ed. Bill

Henderson. New York: Pushcart Book Press, 1976: 11-18; in *Love Stories for the Time Being*. Eds. Genie D. Chipps and Bill Henderson. Wainscott: Pushcart Press, 1987: 137-46; and in *Selected Stories from the* Southern Review, *1965-85*. Ed. Lewis P. Simpson, et al. Baton Rouge: Louisiana State UP, 1988: 355-61].

S-31   "The Geologist's Maid." *New Yorker* 28 July 1975: 29-33. [Reprinted in *Stories of the Modern South*. Eds. Benjamin Forkner and Patrick Samway, S.J. New York: Bantam, 1978: 343-54].

S-32   "Some Sign That I Ever Made You Happy." *McCall's* Oct. 1975: 90+.

1976

S-33   "Your Place is Empty." *New Yorker* 22 Nov. 1976: 45-54. [Reprinted in *The Best American Short Stories 1977: And the Yearbook of the American Short Story*. Ed. Martha Foley. Boston: Houghton Mifflin, 1977: 317-37; and in *Elements of Literature: Fifth Course, the Literature of the United States*. Austin: Holt, Rinehart, and Winston, 1989: 960-71].

1977

S-34   "Holding Things Together." *New Yorker* 24 Jan. 1977: 30-35. [Reprinted in *We Are the Stories We Tell: The Best Short Stories by North American Women Since 1945*. Ed. Wendy Martin. New York: Pantheon Books, 1990: 150-63].

S-35   "Average Waves in Unprotected Waters." *New Yorker* 28 Feb. 1977: 32-36. [Reprinted in *Literature: An Introduction to Fiction, Poetry, and Drama*. Ed. X. J. Kennedy. 5th ed. New York: HarperCollins, 1991: 136-42; in *The American Experience*. Englewood Cliffs: Prentice-Hall, 1989: 1064-70; and in *The American Experience*. Ed. George Perkins and Barbara Perkins. New York: McGraw-Hill, 1994: 2030-37].

S-36   "Under the Bosom Tree." *Archive* Spring 1977: 72-77.

S-37   "Foot-Footing On." *Mademoiselle* Nov. 1977: 82+.

S-38   "Uncle Ahmad." *Quest/77* Nov.-Dec. 1977: 76-82.

1978

S-39   "Linguistics." *Washington Post Magazine* 12 Nov. 1978: 38-40+.

1981

S-40   "Laps." *Parents* Aug. 1981: 66-67+.

1982

S-41   "The Country Cook." *Harper's* Mar. 1982: 54-62.

1983

S-42   "Teenage Wasteland." *Seventeen* Nov. 1983: 144-45+. [Reprinted in *The Editors' Choice: New American Short Stories*. Vol. 1. Ed. George E. Murphy, Jr. New York: Bantam, 1985: 256-66; and in *New Women and New Fiction*. Ed. Susan Cahill. New York: New American Library, 1986: 133-45].

1988

S-43   "Rerun." *New Yorker* 4 July 1988: 20-32.

1989

S-44   "A Woman Like a Fieldstone House." *Ladies Home Journal* Aug. 1989: 86+. [Reprinted in *Louder Than Words: 22 Authors Donate New Stories to Benefit Share Our Strength's Fight Against Hunger, Homelessness and Illiteracy*. Ed. William Shore. New York: Vintage, 1989: 1-15].

1991

S-45   "People Who Don't Know the Answers." *New Yorker* 26 Aug. 1991: 26-36.

III. Nonfiction

NF-1   "Because I Want More than One Life." *Washington Post* 15 Aug. 1976: G1+. [Reprinted as "Confessions of a Novelist" in *Duke Alumni Register* Feb. 1977: 20]. Extremely revealing essay in which Tyler describes the stark room in which she writes, her use of fictive characters not based on actual people, and how her characters take control of a work once they are created. She admits her dread of publicity, explains how she has gradually acknowledged her limitations as a writer, and expresses her feelings about her literary reputation.

NF-2   "Books Past, Present and to Come." *Washington Post Book World* 6 Dec. 1992: 4. Tyler reveals the books that have most influenced her in the past (*The Little House*), the present (*The Macmillan Visual Dictionary*, which has names and diagrams for "even the most obscure thingamadoodle" [4]), and the future (the book she is yet to write).

NF-3   Introduction. *The Available Press/PEN Short Story Collection*. New York: Ballantine, 1985: ix-x. Summation of Tyler's task in selecting the stories for the PEN Syndicated Fiction Project in this collection. She particularly liked the variety of characters.

NF-4   Introduction. *The Best American Short Stories 1983*. Edited by Anne Tyler with Shannon Ravenel. Boston: Houghton Mifflin, 1983: xi-xx. [Reprinted as *The Year's Best American Short Stories*. London: Severn House, 1984]. Tyler's defense of the short story as an art form and explanation of the difficult time she had in selecting the twenty "best" short stories for this collection. She settled on those stories whose authors were "spendthrift" with details and created a "magnificent vitality" in their work.

NF-5 "My Summer." *New York Times Book Review* 4 June 1978: 9+. Several contemporary writers reveal their summer plans. Tyler's revolve around home and family. She hopes that the characters in her new novel (*Morgan's Passing*) will not have "crumbled away to nothing" (35-36) when she returns to them in the fall.

NF-6 "Olives Out of a Bottle." *Archive* 87 (Spring 1975): 70-90. [Reprinted in *Critical Essays on Anne Tyler*. Ed. Alice Hall Petry. New York: G.K. Hall, 1992: 28-39]. Partial transcript of a panel discussion at Duke University in 1974 in which Tyler, Reynolds Price, and others examine her work in particular and writing in general. Tyler discusses her reading, the evolving voice in her novels, the planning of her novels, and her use of dialogue. On a more personal level, she reveals how she started writing, influences on her writing, and her concern for privacy.

NF-7 "Please Don't Call It Persia." *New York Times Book Review* 18 Feb. 1979: 3+. Tyler's review of three Iranian novels (*Identity Card*, by F.M. Esfandiary; *The Caspian Circle*, by Donné Raffat; and *The Foreigner*, by Nahid Rachlin), as well as an anthology of modern Persian poetry, prefaced by her recollections of her 1964 visit to Iran and a contemplation of the subsequent changes in that country, as evidenced in the fiction.

NF-8 "Reynolds Price: Duke of Writers." *Vanity Fair* July 1986: 82-85. Affectionate reminiscence of Tyler's mentor, overviewing his life from early childhood to his early teaching days when she was his student to his battle with spinal cancer and subsequent return to teaching.

NF-9 "Still Just Writing." In *The Writer on Her Work: Contemporary Women Writers Reflect on Their Art and Situation*. Ed. Janet Sternburg. New York: Norton, 1980: 3-16. Tyler's longest and most revealing personal essay, in which she discusses balancing the role of wife and mother with her writing career. She writes in great detail of the interruptions she faced the year she was working on *Morgan's Passing* and of her attempts to create partitions between her life as a writer and her "real life."

NF-10 "Trouble in the Boys' Club: The Trials of Marvin Mandel." *New Republic* 30 July 1977: 16-19. Satiric analysis of the rise and fall of Maryland governor Marvin Mandel.

NF-11 "A Visit with Eudora Welty." *New York Times Book Review* 2 Nov. 1980: 33-34. Tyler's admiring account of her interview with her most important literary influence. Tyler captures Welty's enthusiasm for words and writing as she describes, with obvious affection, Welty's home, working habits, and personality.

NF-12 "Why I Still Treasure 'The Little House.'" *New York Times Book Review* 9 Nov. 1986: 56. Nostalgic appraisal of the influence of Virginia Lee Burton's children book "The Little House" on Tyler. Over the years, the book has comforted her and given her a partial understanding of the passage of time.

NF-13 "Writers' Writer: Gabriel Garcia Marquez." *New York Times Book Review* 4 Dec. 1977: 70. Brief explanation of why Tyler's favorite author is Marquez: his control of time and belief in the world's infinite possibilities.

NF-14 "Youth Talks about Youth: 'Will This Seem Ridiculous?'" *Vogue* 1 Feb. 1965: 85+. Reminiscence by a 23-year-old Tyler, who ponders youth, aging, time, and Model A's. Most of all she wonders if she'll ever reach a point in her life where she feels "sure of things" (206).

IV. Poetry

P-1 "The Ice-Pond Alien." In "Have Yourself a Gorey Little Christmas." *New York Times Book Review* 2 Dec. 1980: 16-18.

V. Children's Books

C-1 *Tumble Tower*.   New York: Orchard Press, 1993.   (Illustrations by Mitra Modarressi).

VI. Book Reviews

1972

R-1 "For Barthelme, 'Words Are What Matters.'" [*Sadness*, by Donald Barthelme]. *National Observer* 4 Nov. 1972: 21.

1974

R-2 "Stories of Escape and Love in 'Beasts of the Southern Wild.'" [*Beasts of the Southern Wild and Other Stories*, by Doris Betts]. *National Observer* 5 Jan. 1974: 15.

R-3 "In Unerring Detail, the Story of a Good Woman." [*The Mystic Adventures of Roxie Stoner*, by Berry Morgan]. *National Observer* 9 Nov. 1974: 25.

1975

R-4 "Of Bitches, Sad Ladies, and Female 'Politics.'" [*Bitches and Sad Ladies: An Anthology of Fiction by and About Women*, edited by Pat Rotter]. *National Observer* 22 Feb. 1975: 31.

R-5 "The Nabokov Act Returns, Dazzling Us with Mirrors." [*Tyrants Destroyed and Other Stories*, by Vladimir Nabokov]. *National Observer* 22 Mar. 1975: 25.

R-6   "Thought? Action? Or a Bit of Both?" [*Emily Stone*, by Anne Redmon; *Hers*, by
        A. Alvarez; and *Are We There Yet?*, by Diane Vreuls]. *National Observer* 19
        Apr. 1975: 25.

R-7   "Stead Pulls a Surprise: A Hotelful of Madmen." [*The Little Hotel*, by Christina
        Stead]. *National Observer* 17 May 1975: 23.

R-8   "When the Novel Turns Participant, the Reader Switches Off." [*Looking for Mr.
        Goodbar*, by Judith Rossner]. *National Observer* 14 June 1975: 19.

R-9   "The Topic Is Language--with Love and Skill." [*The Message in the Bottle*, by
        Walker Percy]. *National Observer* 19 July 1975: 21.

R-10   "'The Lonely Hunter': The Ballad of a Sad Lady." [*The Lonely Hunter*, by
        Virginia Spencer Carr]. *National Observer* 16 Aug. 1975: 17.

R-11   "Georges: Two Women Who Chose to Write as Men." [*George Sand: A
        Biography*, by Curtis Cate; and *George Eliot: The Emergent Self*, by Ruby V.
        Redinger]. *National Observer* 20 Sept. 1975: 23.

R-12   "A Photo Album of Snips and Surprises." [*Beyond the Bedroom Wall: A Family
        Album*, by Larry Woiwode]. *National Observer* 18 Oct. 1975: 21.

R-13   "Tales of an Apocalypse Served Up in a Tureen." [*The Collected Stories of
        Hortense Calisher*]. *National Observer* 22 Nov. 1975: 21.

R-14   "Barthelme's Joyless Victory." [*The Dead Father*, by Donald Barthelme].
        National Observer 27 Dec. 1975: 17.

1976

R-15   "'The Voice Hangs on, Gay, Tremulous.'" [*Letters Home*, by Sylvia Plath].
        National Observer 10 Jan. 1976: 19.

R-16   "When the Camera Looks, It Looks for All of Us." [*Jacob A. Riis:
        Photographer and Citizen*, by Alexander Alland, Sr.; *The Light of Other Days:
        Irish Life at the Turn of the Century in the Photographs of Robert French*, text by
        Kieran Hickey; *Through Camera Eyes*, by Nelson B. Wadsworth; *The
        Photographic Eye of Ben Shahn*, edited by Davis Pratt; *Native Americans: 500
        Years After*, by Joseph Farber and Michael Dorris; and *Gypsies*, by Joseph
        Koudelka]. *National Observer* 14 Feb. 1976: 19.

R-17   "Stretching the Short Story." [*Mr. Wrong*, by Elizabeth Jane Howard; and
        Dream Children, by Gail Godwin]. *National Observer* 13 Mar. 1976: 21.

R-18   "Women Writers: Equal but Separate." [*Literary Women: The Great Writers*,
        by Ellen Moers]. *National Observer* 10 Apr. 1976: 21.

R-19   "Fairy Tales: More than Meets the Ear." [*The Uses of Enchantment: The
        Meaning and Importance of Fairy Tales*, by Bruno Bettelheim]. *National
        Observer* 8 May 1976: 21.

R-20 "Gregory Hemingway Remembers Papa." [*Papa: A Personal Memoir*, by Gregory Hemingway]. *National Observer* 5 June 1976: 21.

R-21 "On the Uses of Genius, Daydreams, and Idle Hours." [*Creativity: The Magic Synthesis*, by Silvano Arieti]. *National Observer* 10 July 1976: 17.

R-22 [Review of *The Master and Other Stories*, by Sue Kaufman; and *Angels at the Ritz and Other Stories*, by William Trevor]. *New York Times Book Review* 11 July 1976: 7.

R-23 [Review of *Crossing the Border, Fifteen Tales*, by Joyce Carol Oates]. *New York Times Book Review* 18 July 1976: 8+.

R-24 "The New Improved Short Story." [*Mademoiselle Prize Stories, 1951-1975*; *Prize Stories 1976: The O. Henry Awards*; *The Talisman and Other Stories*, by Carlos Baker; *Children and Lovers: Fifteen Stories*, by Helga Sandburg; and *The Lists of the Past*, by Julie Hayden]. *National Observer* 7 Aug. 1976: 17.

R-25 "A Breathless Dash through a Whirlwind Life." [*Miss Herbert (the Suburban Wife)*, by Christina Stead]. *National Observer* 14 Aug. 1976: 17.

R-26 "Writers Talk about Writing." [*Writers at Work: The Paris Review Interviews*, edited by George Plimpton]. *National Observer* 11 Sept. 1976: 19.

R-27 [Review of *A Sea-Change*, by Lois Gould]. *New York Times Book Review* 19 Sept. 1976: 4-5.

R-28 "The Woman Who Fled From Her Self." [*Lady Oracle*, by Margaret Atwood]. *National Observer* 9 Oct. 1976: 25.

R-29 "'The Autumn of the Patriarch': Marquez's Latest Examines a Dictator's Empty Power." [*The Autumn of the Patriarch*, by Gabriel Garcia Marquez]. *National Observer* 13 Nov. 1976: 23.

R-30 [Review of *Polonaise*, by Piers Paul Read]. *New York Times Book Review* 28 Nov. 1976: 8+.

R-31 "Boundaries and Bonds: Concerning Strangers in Strange Lands." [*Sleep It Off, Lady*, by Jean Rhys; and *How I Became a Holy Mother and Other Stories*, by Ruth Prawer Jhabvala]. *National Observer* 11 Dec. 1976: 18.

R-32 "Books for Those Awkward, In-Between Years." [*What About Me?*, by Colby F. Rodowsky; *Girl Missing*, by Christine Nostlinger; *The Amazing Miss Laura*, by Hila Colman; *Father's Arcane Daughter*, by E.L. Konigsburg; *Very Far Away From Anywhere Else*, by Ursula K. Le Guin; and *Allegra Maud Goldman*, by Edith Konecky]. *National Observer* 25 Dec. 1976: 15.

1977

R-33 The What-Ifs Enliven an X-Shaped Novel." [*Henry and Cato*, by Iris Murdoch]. *National Observer* 5 Feb. 1977: 19.

R-34   "Life in Prison with a Sunny Innocent." [*Falconer*, by John Cheever]. *National Observer* 12 Mar. 1977: 19.

R-35   "Even in Crisis, That Inner Voice Goes On." [*A Quiet Life*, by Beryl Bainbridge]. *National Observer* 9 Apr. 1977: 21.

R-36   "Farewell to the Story as Imperiled Species." [*Prize Stories 1977: the O. Henry Awards*, edited by William Abrahams; *Winter's Tales 22*, edited by James Wright; *The Sea Birds Are Still Alive*, by Toni Cade Bambara; *Yellow Roses*, by Elizabeth Cullinan; *Slow Days, Fast Company: The World, the Flesh, and L.A.*, by Eve Babitz; and *In the Miro District and Other Stories*, by Peter Taylor]. *National Observer* 9 May 1977: 23.

R-37   "Herbert Gold, Two Bags, $20, and California. What?" [*Waiting for Cordelia*, by Herbert Gold]. *National Observer* 6 June 1977: 19.

R-38   "Repeat Performance." [*The Pushcart Prize, II*, edited by Bill Henderson]. *New York Times Book Review* 19 June 1977: 15+.

R-39   "The 'Ad! Da!' of Mr. Nabokov." [*Nabokov: His Life in Part*, by Andrew Field]. *National Observer* 4 July 1977: 17.

R-40   "Meg and Hannah and Elaine." [*Flight of the Seabird*, by William Lavender; *The Goat, the Wolf, and the Crab*, by Gillian Martin; and *Landfill*, by Julius Horowitz]. *New York Times Book Review* 31 July 1977: 14.

R-41   "Three Novels." [*Gilliam Unbuttoned*, by Alfred Gillespie; *Not Quite a Hero*, by Milton Bass; and *Water Under the Bridge*, by Sumner Locke Elliott]. *New York Times Book Review* 28 Aug. 1977: 7.

R-42   "Apocalypse in a Teacup." [*The Collected Stories of Hortense Calisher*]. *Washington Post Book World* 18 Sept. 1977: E3.

R-43   "Starting Out Submissive." [*The Women's Room*, by Marilyn French]. *New York Times Book Review* 16 Oct. 1977: 7+.

R-44   "Rank Smell of Success." [*The Ice Age*, by Margaret Drabble]. *Washington Post Book World* 23 Oct. 1977: E1-2.

R-45   "Chocolates in the Afternoon and Other Temptations of a Novelist." *Washington Post Book World* 4 Dec. 1977: E3.

1978

R-46   "Mother and Daughter and the Pain of Growing Up." [*Listening to Billie*, by Alice Adams; and *The Grab*, by Maria Katzenbach]. *Detroit News* 5 Feb. 1978: G2.

R-47   "Her World of Everyday Chaos." [*Injury Time*, by Beryl Bainbridge]. *Detroit News* 19 Mar. 1978: G3.

R-48 "After the Prom." [*Burning Questions*, by Alix Kates Shulman]. *Washington Post Book World* 26 Mar. 1978: G3.

R-49 "Looking Backward." [*Victim of the Aurora*, by Thomas Keneally; and *The Caspian Circle*, by Donné Raffat]. *New York Times Book Review* 26 Mar. 1978: 12-13.

R-50 "Two Women." [*Listening to Billie*, by Alice Adams; and *I Hardly Knew You*, by Edna O'Brien]. *Quest/78* 2 (Mar.-Apr. 1978): 84-85.

R-51 "Lady of the Lone Star State." [*A Prince of a Fellow*, by Shelby Hearon]. *Washington Post Book World* 2 Apr. 1978: E4.

R-52 "Letters from Bess about Bess." [*A Woman of Independent Means*, by Elizabeth Forsythe Hailey]. *New York Times Book Review* 28 May 1978: 4+.

R-53 "The Artist as an Old Photographer." [*Picture Palace*, by Paul Theroux]. *New York Times Book Review* 18 June 1978: 10+.

R-54 "The Poe Perplex." [*The Tell-Tale Heart: The Life and Works of Edgar Allan Poe*, by Julian Symons]. *Washington Post Book World* 9 July 1978: E3.

R-55 "Pretty Boy." [*Splendora*, by Edward Swift]. *New York Times Book Review* 6 Aug. 1978: 14+.

R-56 "Till Death Do Us Part." [*A Death of One's Own*, by Gerda Lerner]. *Washington Post Book World* 13 Aug. 1978: E1+.

R-57 "An Affair to Remember." [*Adjacent Lives*, by Ellen Schwamm]. *Washington Post Book World* 3 Sept. 1978: E1+.

R-58 "The Resilient Institution." [*Families*, by Jane Howard]. *Quest/78* 2 (Sept.-Oct. 1978): 61-62.

R-59 "Betty the Likeable Lady." [*The Times of My Life*, by Betty Ford]. *Washington Post Book World* 29 Oct. 1978: E1+.

R-60 [Review of *The Stories of John Cheever*]. *New Republic* 4 Nov. 1978: 45-47.

R-61 [Review of *I, etcetera*, by Susan Sontag]. *New Republic* 25 Nov. 1978: 29-30.

R-62 "Mirage of Love Past." [*The Sea, the Sea*, by Iris Murdoch]. *Washington Post Book World* 26 Nov. 1978: E5.

R-63 "Damaged People." [*The Cement Garden*, by Ian McEwan]. *New York Times Book Review* 26 Nov. 1978: 11+.

R-64 "The Books of Christmas One." [Tyler's seven favorite books of 1978]. *Washington Post Book World* 3 Dec. 1978: E1+.

R-65 "Generations on a Farm." [*A Woman's Place*, by Anne Eliot Crompton]. *New York Times Book Review* 10 Dec. 1978: 69.

1979

R-66 "Brother A and Brother B." [*The Cutting Edge*, by Penelope Gilliatt]. *New York Times Book Review* 21 Jan. 1979: 14.

R-67 "Of Different Feathers." [*Happy Endings*, by Margaret Logan]. *Washington Post* 16 Feb. 1979: D8.

R-68 "Chile: The Novel as History." [*Sweet Country*, by Caroline Richards]. *Washington Post Book World* 18 Feb. 1979: E1+.

R-69 [Review of *Stealing Home*, by Philip O'Connor]. *Washington Post Book World* 18 Mar. 1979: E1+.

R-70 "Unlikely Heroines." [*Sanjo*, by Evelyn Wilde Mayerson; and *Favours* by Bernice Rubens]. *New York Times Book Review* 6 May 1979: 13+.

R-71 [Review of *Territorial Rights*, by Muriel Spark]. *New Republic* 26 May 1979: 35-36.

R-72 "A Family Fugue." [*The Blood of Paradise*, by Stephen Goodwin]. *Washington Post Book World* 27 May 1979: G3.

R-73 "California Nightmares." [*The White Album*, by Joan Didion]. *Washington Post Book World* 17 June 1979: C1+.

R-74 "Two Novels: Growing Up." [*Wild Oats*, by Jacob Epstein; and *The Ballad of T. Rantula*, by Kit Reed]. *New York Times Book Review* 17 June 1979: 14+.

R-75 [Review of *The Basement*, by Kate Millet]. *New Republic* 7 and 14 July 1979: 35-36.

R-76 "Two Sets of Bleak Lives." [*Where the Cherries End Up*, by Gail Henley; and *Days*, by Mary Robison]. *New York Times Book Review* 29 July 1979: 13.

R-77 "Her Younger Self." [*About Time*, by Penelope Mortimer]. *New York Times Book Review* 19 Aug. 1979: 14+.

R-78 [Review of *Endless Love*, by Scott Spencer]. *New Republic* 15 Sept. 1979: 35-36.

R-79 "European Plots and People." [*From the Fifteenth District*, by Mavis Gallant]. *New York Times Book Review* 16 Sept. 1979: 13.

R-80 "Dreams of Inertia." [*Burger's Daughter*, by Nadine Gordimer]. *Saturday Review* 29 Sept. 1979: 44+.

R-81   "Mary McCarthy." [*Cannibals and Missionaries*, by Mary McCarthy]. *Washington Post Book World* 14 Oct. 1979: 4-5.

R-82   "Novel with Notes." [*Love, Etc.*, by Bel Kaufman]. *New York Times Book Review* 21 Oct. 1979: 14.

R-83   "Moments Sealed in Glass." [*Vanishing Animals and Other Stories*, by Mary Morris]. *Washington Post Book World* 23 Dec. 1979: 11.

1980

R-84   "Artistic Ambivalence." [*I Passed This Way*, by Sylvia Ashton-Warner]. *Quest/80* Jan. 1980: 77.

R-85   [Review of *The Transit of Venus*, by Shirley Hazzard]. *New Republic* 26 Jan. 1980: 29-30.

R-86   "Woman Coping." [*A Woman's Age*, by Rachel Billington]. *New York Times Book Review* 10 Feb. 1980: 15+.

R-87   "Pale People, but Rich Cosmic Dreams." [*Life Before Man*, by Margaret Atwood]. *Detroit News* 17 Feb. 1980: C2.

R-88   "Everyday Events." [*A Matter of Feeling*, by Janine Boissard]. *New York Times Book Review* 9 Mar. 1980: 10+.

R-89   "Gardner Wrestles Anew with the Devil." [*Freddy's Book*, by John Gardner]. *Chicago Sun-Times Book Week* 9 Mar. 1980: 11.

R-90   "At the Still Center of a Dream." [*The Salt Eaters*, by Toni Cade Bambara]. *Washington Post Book World* 30 Mar. 1980: 1-2.

R-91   "A Master's Voice: When Robert Penn Warren Speaks, the Words Are Golden." [*Robert Penn Warren Talking*, edited by Floyd C. Watkins and John T. Hiers]. *Chicago Sun-Times Book Week* 13 Apr. 1980: 12.

R-92   [Review of *Three by Irving*, by John Irving]. *New Republic* 26 Apr. 1980: 32-33.

R-93   "Adventures in a Charmed Universe." [*Stone Fox*, by John Reynolds Gardiner]. *New York Times Book Review* 27 Apr. 1980: 45+.

R-94   "In the 'Wood,' Mere Flashes of a Wicked Mind." [*Another Part of the Wood*, by Beryl Bainbridge]. *Detroit News* 27 Apr. 1980: F4.

R-95   [Review of *The Girl in a Swing*, by Richard Adams]. *New York* 19 May 1980: 72-73.

R-96   "Bridging Gaps of Dazzling Width." [*Maybe*, by Lillian Hellman]. *Detroit News* 1 June 1980: E2.

R-97   [Review of *Off Center*, by Barbara Grizzuti Harrison]. *New Republic* 7 June
        1980: 31-32.

R-98   "Feminism and Power: A New Social Contract?" [*Powers of the Weak*, by
        Elizabeth Janeway]. *Chicago Sun-Times Book Week* 8 June 1980: 12.

R-99   "Clothes Make the Man." [*Sunday Best*, by Bernice Rubens]. *Washington Post
        Book World* 15 June 1980: 5.

R-100   [Review of *China Men*, by Maxine Hong Kingston]. *New Republic* 21 June 1980:
        32-34.

R-101   "Finding the Right Voices: No Writer's Skill Can Beat Real People's Stories."
        [*Women in Crisis II*, by Robert Coles and Jane Hallowell Coles; and *Flannery
        O'Connor's South*, by Robert Coles]. *Detroit News* 22 June 1980: E2.

R-102   "Capote Cleans Out His Attic." [*Music for Chameleons*, by Truman Capote].
        Chicago Sun-Times Book Week 3 Aug. 1980: 13.

R-103   "The Return of Sarah Stern." [*The School Book*, by Anne Bernays]. *New York
        Times Book Review* 3 Aug. 1980: 14.

R-104   "An Honorable Heroine." [*Rich Rewards*, by Alice Adams]. *New York Times
        Book Review* 14 Sept. 1980: 13+.

R-105   "A Chance to Spill Out the Soul." [*American Dreams: Lost and Found*, by Studs
        Terkel]. *Detroit News* 21 Sept. 1980: E2.

R-106   "Mary Lee Settle: Mining a Rich Vein." [*The Scapegoat*, by Mary Lee Settle].
        Washington Post Book World 28 Sept. 1980: 1+.

R-107   "A Good Family." [*Hard Laughter*, by Anne Lamott]. *New York Times Book
        Review* 12 Oct. 1980: 11+.

R-108   "The Fine, Full World of Welty." [*The Collected Stories of Eudora Welty*].
        Washington Star 26 Oct. 1980: D1+.

R-109   "A Czech in Mourning for His Country." [*The Book of Laughter and Forgetting*,
        by Milan Kundera]. *Chicago Sun-Times Book Week* 2 Nov. 1980: 12.

R-110   "The Tenants of Tothill House." [*Setting the World on Fire*, by Angus Wilson].
        New Republic 8 Nov. 1980: 33-34.

R-111   "Coming of Age on Rass Island." [*Jacob Have I Loved*, by Katherine Paterson].
        Washington Post Book World 9 Nov. 1980: 11+.

R-112   "Staking Out Her Territory." [*A Place Apart*, by Paula Fox]. *New York Times
        Book Review* 9 Nov. 1980: 55.

R-113   "Novels of Other Times and Other Places." [*Clear Light of Day*, by Anita
        Desai]. *New York Times Book Review* 23 Nov. 1980: 1+.

R-114 "Portrait of a Bag Lady." [*If Birds Are Free*, by Evelyn Wilde Mayerson]. *Washington Post Book World* 23 Nov. 1980: 10.

R-115 "A Clamor of Voices." [*First-Person America*, edited by Ann Banks]. *Detroit News* 28 Dec. 1980: F2.

1981

R-116 [Review of *When No One Was Looking*, by Rosemary Wells]. *New York Times Book Review* 1 Feb. 1981: 28.

R-117 "An Art of Distance." [*The Collected Stories of Elizabeth Bowen*]. *New Republic* 7 Feb. 1981: 36-38.

R-118 "The Stoics and Trudgers." [*American Rose*, by Julia Markus]. *New York Times Book Review* 8 Mar. 1981: 9+.

R-119 "An Elegant First Novel." [*Dale Loves Sophie to Death*, by Robb Forman Dew]. *New Republic* 4 Apr. 1981: 35-36.

R-120 "The South Without the Scent of Lavender." [*The Collected Stories of Caroline Gordon*]. *New York Times Book Review* 19 Apr. 1981: 6+.

R-121 "Looking for Mom." [*Rainbow Jordan*, by Alice Childress; *Anna to the Infinite Power,* by Mildred Ames; and *I'm Still Me*, by Betty Jean Lifton]. *New York Times Book Review* 26 Apr. 1981: 52-53+.

R-122 "Men Will Be Boys." [*The Men's Club*, by Leonard Michaels]. *New Republic* 2 May 1981: 31-32.

R-123 "South Africa after Revolution." [*July's People*, by Nadine Gordimer]. *New York Times Book Review* 7 June 1981: 1+.

R-124 "Varieties of Ambitious Experience." [*The Fast Track: Texans and Other Strivers*, by Nicholas Lemann]. *New Republic* 13 June 1981: 31-32.

R-125 "The View from the Village." [*Dandil: Stories from Iranian Life*, by Gholam-Hossein Sa'edi]. *New Republic* 25 July 1981: 36-37.

R-126 "Girl Mothers." [*Baby Love*, by Joyce Maynard]. *New York Times Book Review* 16 Aug. 1981: 8-9.

R-127 [Review of *The Indian in the Cupboard*, by Lynne Reid Banks]. *New York Times Book Review* 11 Oct. 1981: 38.

R-128 "A Community Portrait." [*Neighborhood: A State of Mind*, by Linda G. Rich, et al]. *New Republic* 25 Nov. 1981: 26+.

R-129 "The Fall of a Star." [*Poppa John*, by Larry Woiwode]. *New Republic* 9 Dec. 1981: 36-38.

R-130 "The Glass of Fashion." [*The Language of Clothes*, by Alison Lurie]. *New Republic* 23 Dec. 1981: 32+.

1982

R-131 "Life in an Ingrown Household." [*Against the Stream*, by James Hanley]. *New York Times Book Review* 17 Jan. 1982: 7+.

R-132 "All in the Family." [*A Mother and Two Daughters*, by Gail Godwin]. *New Republic* 17 Feb. 1982: 39-40.

R-133 "Novels by Three Emerging Writers." [*A Bigamist's Daughter*, by Alice McDermott]. *New York Times Book Review* 21 Feb. 1982: 1+.

R-134 "Ordinary Family, With a Difference." [*White Horses*, by Alice Hoffman]. *New York Times Book Review* 28 Mar. 1982: 11+.

R-135 "The Imagination of Disgust." [*Flaws in the Glass*, by Patrick White]. *New Republic* 31 Mar. 1982: 40-42.

R-136 "The Wit and Wisdom of Rebecca West." [*The Young Rebecca: Writings of Rebecca West, 1911-17*, edited by Jane Marcus; and *1900*, by Rebecca West]. *Saturday Review* Apr. 1982: 55-56.

R-137 "The Civil War and Elegant Parties." [*Watchfires*, by Louis Auchincloss]. *New York Times Book Review* 2 May 1982: 12+.

R-138 "South Bronx Story." [*Forsaking All Others*, by Jimmy Breslin]. *New Republic* 19 and 26 July 1982: 42-43.

R-139 "The Complexities of Ordinary Life." [*Dancing Girls and Other Stories*, by Margaret Atwood]. *New York Times Book Review* 19 Sept. 1982: 3+.

R-140 "The Mosaic of Life." [*Grace Abounding*, by Maureen Howard]. *New Republic* 4 Oct. 1982: 35-36.

R-141 "The Growing Up of Lily Shields." [*My Old Sweetheart*, by Susanna Moore]. *New York Times Book Review* 17 Oct. 1982: 14.

R-142 "Kentucky Cameos." [*Shiloh and Other Stories*, by Bobbie Ann Mason]. *New Republic* 1 Nov. 1982: 36+.

R-143 "Good Things Come in Twos." [*Herbert Rowbarge*, by Natalie Babbitt]. *New York Times Book Review* 14 Nov. 1982: 44.

R-144 "Avignon at War." [*Constance; or Solitary Practices*, by Lawrence Durrell]. *New Republic* 6 Dec. 1982: 36-37.

1983

R-145 "Death to the Dictator." [*A Coin in Nine Hands*, by Marguerite Yourcenar]. *New Republic* 10 and 17 Jan. 1983: 42-43.

R-146 "From England to Brooklyn to West Virginia." [*No Fond Return of Love*, by Barbara Pym]. *New York Times Book Review* 13 Feb. 1983: 1+.

R-147 "A Widow's Tale." [*Praisesong for the Widow*, by Paule Marshall]. *New York Times Book Review* 20 Feb. 1983: 7+.

R-148 "The Ladies and the Tiger." [*Right-Wing Women*, by Andrea Dworkin]. *New Republic* 21 Feb. 1983: 34-35.

R-149 "Stories within Stories." [*Ararat*, by D.M. Thomas]. *New Republic* 4 Apr. 1983: 30-32.

R-150 "Phaedra in the Rural South." [*Pretty Redwing*, by Helen Henslee]. *Washington Post Book World* 10 Apr. 1983: 8.

R-151 "Mother Lived Well." [*Natural Victims*, by Isabel Eberstadt]. *New York Times Book Review* 24 Apr. 1983: 13.

R-152 "Home Folks at One Another's Throats." [*The Feud*, by Thomas Berger]. *New York Times Book Review* 8 May 1983: 1+.

R-153 "Writers in Place and Writers in Motion." [*Mississippi Writers Talking*, by John Griffin Jones; and *Black Women Writers at Work*, by Claudia Tate]. *New York Times Book Review* 29 May 1983: 6+.

R-154 "A Civilized Sensibility." [*Bartleby in Manhattan and Other Essays*, by Elizabeth Hardwick]. *New Republic* 20 June 1983: 32-33.

R-155 "Male and Lonely." [*Modern Baptists*, by James Wilcox]. *New York Times Book Review* 31 July 1983: 1+.

R-156 "The Other Elizabeth Taylor." [*The Sleeping Beauty, In a Summer Season, The Soul of Kindness,* and *Mrs. Palfrey at the Claremont*, all by Elizabeth Taylor]. *Washington Post Book World* 21 Aug. 1983: 1-2.

R-157 "Varieties of Inspiration." [*In Praise of What Persists*, edited by Stephen Berg]. *New Republic* 12 Sept. 1983: 32-33.

R-158 "The Ledfords and All of Us." [*Generations: An American Family*, by John Egerton]. *New York Times Book Review* 6 Nov. 1983: 3+.

R-159 "Danger, Defiance and Survival." [*I Will Call It Georgie's Blues*, by Suzanne Newton]. *New York Times Book Review* 13 Nov. 1983: 40.

R-160 "End of a Love Affair." [*Pitch Dark*, by Renata Adler]. *New Republic* 5 Dec. 1983: 27-28.

R-161 "Mothers and Mysteries." [*At the Bottom of the River*, by Jamaica Kincaid].
New Republic 31 Dec. 1983: 32-33.

1984

R-162 "The War Between the Swifts." [*Time After Time*, by Molly Keane]. *Washington
Post Book World* 22 Jan. 1984: 6.

R-163 "You Can't Put It Down--But Is It Good?" [*Fly Away Home*, by Marge Piercy].
Baltimore Sun 11 Mar. 1984: D8.

R-164 "1944 and All That." [*I Wish This War Were Over*, by Diana O'Hehir]. *New
Republic* 19 Mar. 1984: 36-37.

R-165 "Dreaminess and True Grit in South Dakota." [*Leaving the Land*, by Douglas
Unger]. *Washington Post Book World* 25 Mar. 1984: 3+.

R-166 "Affairs of State." [*Democracy*, by Joan Didion]. *New Republic* 9 Apr. 1984:
35-36.

R-167 "Bellow's Gifts on Display in Five Stories." [*Him with His Foot in His Mouth
and Other Stories*, by Saul Bellow]. *Chicago Tribune Bookworld* 13 May 1984:
39.

R-168 "Uncommon Characters." [*Dear Mr. Capote* and *What I Know So Far*, by
Gordon Lish]. *New Republic* 28 May 1984: 33-34.

R-169 "The Wounds of War." [*Machine Dreams*, by Jayne Anne Phillips]. *New York
Times Book Review* 1 July 1984: 3.

R-170 "The Holes in Sara's Life." [*In Another Country*, by Susan Kenney]. *New York
Times Book Review* 5 Aug. 1984: 8.

R-171 "Caught in the Web of Words." [*Modus Vivendi*, by Deirdre Levinson].
Washington Post Book World 26 Aug. 1984: 3-4.

R-172 "Poor Me." [*The Letters of Jean Rhys*, edited by Francis Wyndham and Diana
Melly]. *New Republic* 10 Sept. 1984: 29-30.

R-173 "Albany Warm-Up." [*The Ink Trunk*, by William Kennedy]. *New Republic* 15
Oct. 1984: 39-40.

R-174 "Trying to Be Perfect." [*One-Eyed Cat*, by Paula Fox]. *New York Times Book
Review* 11 Nov. 1984: 48.

R-175 "Coming Up for Eire." [*Secrets and Other Stories*, by Bernard MacLaverty].
New Republic 26 Nov. 1984: 39-40.

R-176 "Ebenezer LePage." [*The Book of Ebenezer LePage*, by G.B. Edwards]. In
"Revealed! The Secret Fantasies of Fiction Reviewers," by Jonathan Yardley.
Washington Post Book World 2 Dec. 1984: 4-6.

1985

R-177 "Go East, Young Man." [*Equal Distance*, by Brad Leithauser]. *New Republic* 21 Jan. 1985: 37-38.

R-178 "A Solitary Life Is Still Worth Living." [*Hotel du Lac*, by Anita Brookner]. *New York Times Book Review* 3 Feb. 1985: 1+.

R-179 "Mothers in the City." [*Later the Same Day*, by Grace Paley]. *New Republic* 29 Apr. 1985: 38-39.

R-180 "Growing Up Is Hard to Do." [*It's an Aardvark-Eat-Turtle World*, by Paula Danziger; *Healer*, by Peter Dickinson; *I Stay Near You*, by M.E. Kerr; and *Spanish Hoof*, by Robert Newton Peck]. *Washington Post Book World* 12 May 1985: 16.

R-181 "Come to Canada." [*Home Truths: Sixteen Stories*, by Mavis Gallant]. *New Republic* 13 May 1985: 40-42.

R-182 "Down in New Orleans." [*Lives of the Saints*, by Nancy Lemann; and *The Sioux*, by Irene Handl]. *New Republic* 24 June 1985: 36-38.

R-183 "Roar of the Greasepaint: Elegant but Airy Caricature of an Acting School." [*At Freddie's*, by Penelope Fitzgerald]. *Washington Post Book World* 13 Sept. 1985: B3.

R-184 "'Galapagos' Gives Darwin a New Twist." [*Galapagos*, by Kurt Vonnegut]. *Chicago Tribune Bookworld* 22 Sept. 1985: 37.

R-185 "Spark Flies." [*The Stories of Muriel Spark*]. *New Republic* 14 Oct. 1985: 40-41.

R-186 "Disorder at 4 A.M." [*The Relatives Came*, by Cynthia Rylant]. *New York Times Book Review* 10 Nov. 1985: 37.

R-187 "Spots of Time." [*Midair*, by Frank Conroy]. *New Republic* 18 Nov. 1985: 48-50.

1986

R-188 "The Private Life of Count Tolstoy." [*Tolstoy's Diaries*, edited and translated by R.F. Christian]. *Washington Post Book World* 19 Jan. 1986: 1-2.

R-189 "'Southern Light': Magnificent Disaster." [*Southern Light*, by J.R. Salamanca]. *Raleigh News and Observer* 23 Mar. 1986: D4.

R-190 "Daughter's-Eye View." [*Collaborators*, by Janet Kauffman]. *New Republic* 21 Apr. 1986: 34-35.

R-191 "The Undertones of Modern Marriage." [*Another Marvelous Thing*, by Laurie Colwin]. *Raleigh News and Observer* 11 May 1986: D4.

R-192 "2 Books in 1 Puts Strain on Reader." [*Jack Rivers and Me*, by Paul John Radley]. *Chicago Tribune Books* 11 May 1986: 44.

R-193 "Maryland, My Maryland: America in Miniature." [*Maryland Lost and Found: People and Places from Chesapeake to Appalachia*, by Eugene L. Meyer]. *Washington Post Book World* 1 June 1986: 6.

R-194 "He Did It All for Jane Elizabeth Firesheets." [*Off for the Sweet Hereafter*, by T.R. Pearson]. *New York Times Book Review* 15 June 1986: 9.

R-195 "The Art of Omission." [*Monkeys*, by Susan Minot]. *New Republic* 23 June 1986: 34+.

R-196 "A Talented Writer and a Novel of Sorts." [*Ghost Dance*, by Carole Maso]. *Raleigh News and Observer* 10 Aug. 1986: D4.

R-197 "After 'Love Medicine,' a Still Better Novel from Erdrich." [*The Beet Queen*, by Louise Erdrich]. *Raleigh News and Observer* 31 Aug. 1986: D4.

R-198 "The Heart Hangs On in 'Tuxedo Park.'" [*Tuxedo Park*, by Laura Furman]. *USA Today* 12 Sept. 1986: D4.

R-199 "The Czar's Poet: A Romance of Pushkin." [*The Fourth King*, by Glen Petrie]. *Washington Post Book World* 14 Sept. 1986: 9.

R-200 "Canadian Club." [*The Progress of Love*, by Alice Munro]. *New Republic* 15 and 22 Sept. 1986: 54-55.

R-201 "The Cream of Southern Short Stories." [*New Stories from the South*, edited by Shannon Ravenel]. *Raleigh News and Observer* 9 Nov. 1986: D4.

1987

R-202 [Review of *Anywhere But Here*, by Mona Simpson]. *USA Today* 16 Jan. 1987: D2.

R-203 "Marriage and the Ties That Bind." [*Intimate Partners: Patterns in Love and Marriage*, by Maggie Scarf]. *Washington Post Book World* 15 Feb. 1987: 3+.

R-204 "Inside History's Kaleidoscope." [*The Red, White and Blue*, by John Gregory Dunne]. *New York Times Book Review* 1 Mar. 1987: 3.

R-205 "A Celebration of Coping in a Family Way." [*A Wrestling Season*, by Sharon Sheehe Stark]. *Raleigh News and Observer* 22 Mar. 1987: D4.

R-206 "Bright Scraps of Fiction from Mary Gordon." [*Temporary Shelter*, by Mary Gordon]. *Chicago Tribune Books* 29 Mar. 1987: 6-7.

R-207 "The Sentimental Education of Mary McCarthy." [*How I Grew*, by Mary McCarthy]. *Washington Post Book World* 5 Apr. 1987: 9.

R-208 "The Mission." [*The Messiah of Stockholm*, by Cynthia Ozick]. *New Republic* 6 Apr. 1987: 39-41.

R-209 "Jean Rhys' Lean Prose." [*Jean Rhys: The Collected Short Stories*]. *Boston Globe* 12 Apr. 1987: B42-43.

R-210 "Elspeth Huxley: To Kenya Again, Disappointingly." [*Out in the Midday Sun*, by Elspeth Huxley]. *Raleigh News and Observer* 26 Apr. 1987: D4.

R-211 "Donald Hall: The Storyteller Fails the Poet." [*The Ideal Bakery*, by Donald Hall]. *Raleigh News and Observer* 31 May 1987: D4.

R-212 "Read, Drink and Be Merry." [*Food for Thought: An Anthology of Writings Inspired by Food*, edited by Joan and John Digby]. *Washington Post Book World* 28 June 1987: 9.

R-213 "A Time to Party and a Time to Protest." [*Campus Life*, by Helen Lefkowitz Horowitz]. *Raleigh News and Observer* 9 Aug. 1987: D5.

R-214 "Swimming Dangerous Waters." [*Three Continents*, by Ruth Prawer Jhabvala]. *Boston Globe* 16 Aug. 1987: A12-13.

R-215 "Morrison's Magical Words Evoke Agony." [*Beloved*, by Toni Morrison]. *Baltimore Sun* 6 Sept. 1987: N14.

R-216 "If It's Not Russian, He Hates It." [*The Frigate Pallada*, by Ivan Aleksandrovich Goncharov]. *New York Times Book Review* 20 Sept. 1987: 9.

1988

R-217 "The Poetic Stories of Francine Prose." [*Women and Children First and Other Stories*, by Francine Prose]. *Washington Post Book World* 20 Mar. 1988: 3.

R-218 "How to Hang Loose, Grow Up Resilient in the Ersatz Family." [*The Beginner's Book of Dreams*, by Elizabeth Benedict]. *Chicago Tribune Books* 3 Apr. 1988: 4.

R-219 "Life Moves Too Fast for the Picture." [*Moon Tiger*, by Penelope Lively]. *New York Times Book Review* 17 Apr. 1988: 9.

R-220 "The Right Guy From the Wrong Side of the Tracks." [*The Bride Who Ran Away*, by Diana O'Hehir]. *Washington Post Book World* 24 Apr. 1988: 1+.

R-221 "Vivid, Quirky Characters from the Spark Gallery." [*A Far Cry from Kensington*, by Muriel Spark]. *Boston Globe* 10 July 1988: 98-99.

R-222 "Up from Misery." [*Letourneau's Used Auto Parts*, by Carolyn Chute]. *New Republic* 11 July 1988: 40-41.

R-223 "Dallas, Echoing Down the Decades." [*Libra*, by Don DeLillo]. *New York Times Book Review* 24 July 1988: 1+.

R-224 "The Enduring Enigma of Lev Tolstoy." [*Tolstoy*, by A.N. Wilson]. *Washington Post Book World* 28 Aug. 1988: 3.

R-225 "In the Midst of Life." [*Saying Good-bye to Grandma*, by Jane Resh Thomas]. *New York Times Book Review* 13 Nov. 1988: 48.

R-226 "Robertson Davies' Pictures From an Institution." [*The Lyre of Orpheus*, by Robertson Davies]. *Washington Post Book World* 18 Dec. 1988: 3.

1989

R-227 "Master of Moments." [*Selected Stories*, by Andre Dubus]. *New Republic* 6 Feb. 1989: 41-42.

R-228 "An American Boy in Gangland." [*Billy Bathgate*, by E.L. Doctorow]. *New York Times Book Review* 26 Feb. 1989: 1+.

R-229 "Burmese Days." [*John Dollar*, by Marianne Wiggins]. *New Republic* 27 Mar. 1989: 35-36.

R-230 "Painting with Words." [*In the Night Cafe*, by Joyce Johnson]. *Chicago Tribune* 16 Apr. 1989, sec. 14: 6-7.

R-231 "Manic Monologue." [*Tripmaster Monkey: His Fake Book*, by Maxine Hong Kingston]. *New Republic* 17 Apr. 1989: 44-46.

R-232 "Troyat's Biography of Gorky Doesn't Plumb Depths." [*Gorky*, by Henri Troyat]. *Baltimore Sun* 14 May 1989: M13.

R-233 "John Casey's Yankee Waterman." [*Spartina*, by John Casey]. *Washington Post Book World* 4 June 1989: 3-4.

R-234 "Pursued by They." [*Life with a Star*, by Jiri Weil; translated by Ruzena Kovarikova with Rosyln Schloss]. *New York Times Book Review* 18 June 1989: 3.

R-235 "The Best Thing About This Book Is Its Heroine." [*The Way to Cook*, by Julia Child]. *Houston Post* 17 Sept. 1989: C6.

R-236 "Just a Little Something She Cooked Up." [*The Way to Cook*, by Julia Child]. *Washington Post Book World* 17 Sept. 1989: 1+.

R-237 "The Plodding Life: Dispatches from a Writer's Desk." [*The Writing Life*, by Annie Dillard]. *Baltimore Sun* 17 Sept. 1989: M9.

R-238 "Lamott Tracks an Eccentric California Clan." [*All New People*, by Anne Lamott]. *San Francisco Chronicle* 15 Oct. 1989: REV 1+.

R-239 "Class Wars." [*Among School Children*, by Tracy Kidder]. *New Republic* 13 Nov. 1989: 40-41.

R-240 "In the Russian Grain." [*The Wooden Architecture of Russia: Houses, Fortifications, Churches*, by Alexander Opolovnikov and Yelena Opolovnikova]. *Washington Post Book World* 3 Dec. 1989: 7.

1990

R-241 "Portrait of a Modern Barbarian." [*The Knight, Death and the Devil: A Novel of Life Corrupted by Evil*, by Ella Leffland]. *San Francisco Chronicle* 4 Feb. 1990: REV 1+.

R-242 "Tea and Milquetoast." [*Lewis Percy*, by Anita Brookner]. *Washington Post Book World* 18 Feb. 1990: 3+.

R-243 The Outsider May Be You." [*The Collected Stories of Wallace Stegner*]. *New York Times Book Review* 18 Mar. 1990: 2.

R-244 "A Loving Carelessness." [*Family Pictures*, by Sue Miller]. *Chicago Tribune* 22 Apr. 1990, sec. 14: 1+.

R-245 "Comic Mourning for a Funky Youth." [*Goodbye Without Leaving*, by Laurie Colwin]. *San Francisco Chronicle* 13 May 1990: REV 3+.

R-246 "How to Read a Chinese Menu." [*Swallowing Clouds*, by A. Zee]. *Washington Post Book World* 23 Sept. 1990: 4.

R-247 "'Karamazov': Finding What Was Lost in the Translation." [*The Brothers Karamazov*, by Fyodor Dostoevsky; translated by Richard Pevear]. *Baltimore Sun* 30 Sept. 1990: 9C.

R-248 "'Minor' Writings by E.B. White Provide Major Pleasure." [*Writings from the New Yorker*, by E.B. White; edited by Rebecca M. Dale]. *Baltimore Sun* 18 Nov. 1990: G8.

R-249 "Raising a Glass to the American Dream." [*The Last Fine Time*, by Verlyn Klinkenborg]. *Boston Globe* 30 Dec. 1990: A15-16.

1991

R-250 [Review of *Magic Hour*, by Susan Isaacs]. *Vogue* Feb. 1991: 224+.

R-251 "Barbara Pym's Secret Life." [*A Lot to Ask: A Life of Barbara Pym*, by Hazel Holt]. *Washington Post Book World* 17 Mar. 1991: 1+.

R-252 "Fiercely Precise: Kaye Gibbons' World of Southern Womanhood." [*A Cure for Dreams*, by Kaye Gibbons]. *Chicago Tribune* 24 Mar. 1991, sec. 14: 3.

R-253 "'Tibet': The Flight of a Wounded Heart." [*The House Tibet*, by Georgia Savage]. *USA Today* 5 Apr. 1991: D5.

R-254 "Tribal Rites in Westchester." [*Object Lessons*, by Anna Quindlen]. *New York Times Book Review* 14 Apr. 1991: 7+.

R-255 "Kentucky Housewife's Prose Cooks Up Picture of Mid-19th Century Daily Life." [*The Kentucky Housewife*, by Lettice Bryan]. *Baltimore Sun* 21 Apr. 1991: E6.

R-256 "Recipe for Living." [*Long Ago in France: The Years in Dijon* and *The Boss Dog*, by M.F.K. Fisher; and *Among Friends: M.F.K. Fisher and Me*, by Jeannette Ferrary]. *Washington Post Book World* 28 Apr. 1991: 4-5.

R-257 "Tan's 'Wife' Tells More Tales." [*The Kitchen God's Wife*, by Amy Tan]. *USA Today* 13 June 1991: D2.

R-258 "Moscow on the Seine." [*The Tattered Cloak and Other Novels*, by Nina Berberova]. *New Republic* 17 June 1991: 48-49.

R-259 "In the Land of Lolita." [*Vladimir Nabokov: The American Years*, by Brian Boyd]. *Atlantic* Oct. 1991: 128-30.

The Anne Tyler Papers

Special Collections Library
Duke University
Durham, NC 27708-0185

Researchers working on scholarly or academic projects may be granted access to these materials and may make selected photocopies for research purposes only. Nothing may be published without prior written permission from Anne Tyler. The collection contains manuscripts, typescripts, and holographs of Tyler's novels and short stories. In addition, the collection contains several boxes of uncatalogued correspondence, reviews, and newspaper clippings.

Novels

The Accidental Tourist (handwritten draft)
Breathing Lessons (handwritten draft)
Celestial Navigation (holograph)
The Clock Winder (holograph)
Dinner at the Homesick Restaurant (two holographs, typed draft, and final typescript)
Earthly Possessions (holograph)
"I Know You, Rider" (typescript)
If Morning Ever Comes (holograph)
Morgan's Passing (holograph and typescript; three related clippings)
"Pantaleo" (holograph and typescript; correction sheets)
Searching for Caleb (typescript; one related clipping)
A Slipping-Down Life (holograph)
The Tin Can Tree (holograph)
"Winter Birds, Winter Apples" (holograph)

Short Stories

Group One

"Alaska"
"Average Waves in Unprotected Waters"
"The Base-Metal Egg"
"Believable Lies"
"The Bride in the Boatyard"
"Children"
"The Common Courtesies"
"The Death Nurse"
"Dreams in Another Language"
"Earthman"
"An Exxon Love Story"
"Final Reductions"
"Foot-Footing On"
"The Geologist's Maid"
"Getting Rid of Otis"
"Ground Search"
"Half-Truths and Semi-Miracles"
"I Was Not Always as You See Me Now"
"Joey Getting Older"

"A Knack for Languages"
"Laps"
"Letters from Home"
"Linguistics"
"The Magic Eight Ball"
"Mr. Bucket"
"The Needlewoman's Husband"
"Notes for the Next Life"
"The Registration of Aliens"
"Sequestered"
"Spending"
"Take-Alongs"
"Things That Matter"
"Uncle Ahmad"
"Under the Bosom Tree"
"You Choose How You Lose"
"Your Place Is Empty"

Group Two
According to Tyler's written instructions, these stories "are not to be re-published, anthologized, or put in any collections due to inferiority."

"The Artificial Family" (holograph and typescript)
"As the Earth Gets Old" (holograph, typescript, and printed copy)
"The Baltimore Birth Certificate" (typescript)
"Dry Water" (typescript)
"Eloping Again" (holograph and typescript)
"Empty Houses" (holograph and typescript)
"The Feather Behind the Rock" (holograph, typescript, and printed copy)
"A Flaw in the Crust of the Earth" (holograph)
"Foreign Prayers" (holograph)
"Glass Wind" (holograph)
"The Genuine Fur Eyelashes" (holograph and typescript)
"The Half-Decent Symphony" (typescript)
"Here We Sit With Smiles" (typescript)
"Horses in the Night" (typescript)
"I Play Kings" (typescript)
"I Was Born Mean" (typescript)
"I'm Not Going to Ask You Again" (typescript)
"Joey" (typescript)
"A Misstep of the Mind" (holograph and typescript)
"Neutral Ground" (holograph)
"Nobody Answers the Door" (typescript)
"Outside" (holograph and typescript)
"The Piggly Wiggly Bandit" (holograph and typescript)
"Respect" (holograph and typescript)
"The Sandals" (typescript)
"The Saints in Caesar's Household" (typescript)
"Something to Take With You" (typescript)
"A Street of Bugles" (typescript)
"The Tea Machine" (holograph and typescript)

"Tennessee Saturday Night" (typescript)
"They Don't Beat You Up in Montana" (typescript)
"Two Brothers" (typescript)
"Two People and a Clock on the Wall" (holograph, typescript, and printed copy)
"The Witch-Woman" (holograph and typescript)
"Youth Is the Only Age" (typescript)

Other Materials

Letters to Tyler (from her editor at Knopf, Judith B. Jones, her agent, and others)
Clippings of articles associated with her novels (such as the article on a phony doctor
   that prompted the character Morgan Gower or the catalogue page with a picture
   of one of Morgan's hats)
Book reviews of Tyler's novels from newspapers and magazines
Newspaper and journal articles about Tyler

Secondary Sources

I. Books

B-1   Evans, Elizabeth. *Anne Tyler*. New York: Twayne, 1993. Comprehensive appraisal of Tyler's work, with commentary on both her novels and short stories, as well as her book reviews. Evans finds intriguing connections between Tyler's characters and characters in the works of various other (usually Southern or feminist) writers. Other chapters explore Tyler's humor, the role of women, and the functioning of families in her works.

B-2   Linton, Karin. *The Temporal Horizon: A Study of the Theme of Time in Anne Tyler's Major Novels*. Uppsala, Sweden: Acta Universitatis Upsaliensis, 1989. Exploration of the theme of time in Tyler's first eleven novels through the use of Paul Fraisse's concept of a "temporal horizon." By focussing on various characters' views of time, Linton considers their reactions to changes in their lives as indicative of their ability to achieve a balanced temporal perspective. She finds that all Tyler's characters (except Jeremy Pauling in *Celestial Navigation*) achieve, at least partly, a fairly balanced view of time. Each, therefore, becomes capable of positive change.

B-3   Petry, Alice Hall, ed. *Critical Essays on Anne Tyler*. New York: G.K. Hall, 1992. Comprehensive reference guide to Tyler with an excellent introduction that highlights the major events of Tyler's life and assesses the current state of scholarship on her work. In addition, the volume includes reprints of hard-to-find interviews, Tyler's essay "Because I Want More Than One Life," selected reviews of her first eleven published novels (including four by John Updike), reprints of five early scholarly articles about Tyler's fiction, and three new essays on her work.

B-4   Petry, Alice Hall. *Understanding Anne Tyler*. Columbia: U of South Carolina P, 1990. Comprehensive and cogent study of Tyler's first eleven novels' themes and motifs, illustrating (in chapter-length discussions of each novel) the development of Tyler's four main concerns: "the dynamics of the individual and the family; man's inability or unwillingness to communicate; his response, constructive or otherwise, to the exigencies of change and of passing time; and his quest for the patterns, and ultimately the meanings, underlying a world of seeming chaos" (23). Additionally, insightful excerpts from Petry's August 1989 interview-by-mail reveal Tyler's thoughts on her work, influences, and philosophy of writing.

B-5   Stephens, C. Ralph, ed. *The Fiction of Anne Tyler*. Jackson: UP of Mississippi, 1990. Thirteen essays about Tyler's fiction, most of them presented as papers at the first Anne Tyler Symposium at Essex Community College in Baltimore on April 21-22, 1989. The papers' subjects range from psychological readings and influence studies to explorations of theme and characterization. The volume includes a brief introduction by Stephens as well as an index.

B-6   Voelker, Joseph C. *Art and the Accidental in Anne Tyler*. Columbia: U of Missouri P, 1989. Varied interpretations of Tyler's first eleven novels (excluding *Morgan's Passing*). Voelker's introduction examines Tyler's Quaker consciousness and her characters' "extreme individualism" (11). Later chapters explore such topics as narrative perspective and artistic method in *Celestial Navigation*, the lyrical mode of *Breathing Lessons*, genetic patterning in *Searching for Caleb*, "idealization" in *Earthly Possessions*, psychological growth in *The Accidental Tourist*, and the development of Tyler's subjects and style in her earliest novels.

II. Articles

A-1   Almond, Barbara R.   "The Accidental Therapist: Intrapsychic Change in a Novel."   *Literature and Psychology* 38 (Spring-Summer 1992): 84-104. Exploration of the relationship between Macon Leary and Muriel Pritchett in *The Accidental Tourist*. Muriel functions as an "accidental therapist" to promote psychological change in Macon as he works through his grief over his son's death.

A-2   "Anne Tyler." (The 25 Most Intriguing People of the Year). *People Weekly* 26 Dec. 1988: 76-77. Short article focussing on Tyler's growing popular and critical recognition. A full-page recent photograph of Tyler appears on page 76.

A-3   Baum, Rosalie Murphy. "Boredom and the Land of Impossibilities in Dickey and Tyler." *James Dickey Newsletter* 6 (Fall 1989): 12-20. Comparison of Macon Leary in *The Accidental Tourist* to Ed Gentry, hero of James Dickey's *Deliverance*. Leary paradigmatically represents the female search for meaning through social relationships while Gentry represents the male paradigm of the adventurous quest for meaning outside the home and society.   Yet both protagonists experience adventure and ultimately accept feminine resolutions of domestic happiness and interpersonal relationships.

A-4   Betts, Doris. "The Fiction of Anne Tyler." *Southern Quarterly* 21 (Summer 1983): 23-37. [Reprinted in *Women Writers of the Contemporary South*. Ed.

Peggy Whitman Prenshaw. Jackson: U of Mississippi P, 1984: 23-37]. A comprehensive study of Tyler's adaptation of short story methods in her first nine books, especially in expanding the dimensions of her work in the areas of chronology, characterization, and multiple perspectives.

A-5 Betts, Doris. "Tyler's Marriage of Opposites." In *The Fiction of Anne Tyler*. Ed. C. Ralph Stephens. Jackson: UP of Mississippi, 1990: 1-15. Tyler's technique of juxtaposing opposites in her fiction produces her enduring vision of life. Focussing mainly on *Breathing Lessons*, but with abundant references to Tyler's other novels as well, Betts explains how Tyler's characters reach reconciliation and resolution, achieving synthesis after periods of crisis and conflict.

A-6 Binding, Paul. "Anne Tyler." In *Separate Country: A Literary Journey through the American South*. New York: Paddington Press, 1979: 198-209. [Reprinted by UP of Mississippi, 1988: 171-81]. An exploration of the "Southern" qualities inherent in Tyler's works (sense of place and family), as well as her positive view of men and tender view of sex. Binding utilizes examples from Tyler's first six novels to make his points. The 1988 edition mentions the later novels only in passing.

A-7 Birns, Margaret Boe. "Ibsen's Lady, Tyler's Housewife: Animus Possession in the Modern Heroine." *Anima: An Experiential Journal* 10 (Spring 1984): 86-92. Psychoanalytic feminist reading of *Earthly Possessions* (and Ibsen's *Lady from the Sea*) considering the influence of Jung's concept of the male "animus" figure on the main female characters. Charlotte Emory's psychological wholeness improves as she interacts with Jake Simms, who represents the masculine side of her psyche.

A-8 Blais, Madeleine. "Still Just Writing." *Washington Post Magazine* 25 Aug. 1991: 8-12+. Appreciative response to Tyler's fiction, which begins with a review of the biographical information available in Tyler's published interviews and essays, then adds personal anecdotes and, most interestingly, descriptions of the Baltimore neighborhoods and locales used in Tyler's fiction, as well as an examination of how Baltimoreans respect Tyler's privacy.

A-9 Bloom, Alice. "George Dennison, *Luisa Domic*, Bobbie Ann Mason, *In Country*, Anne Tyler, *The Accidental Tourist*." *New England Review and Bread Loaf Quarterly* 8 (Summer 1986): 513-25. An analysis of the new image of the hero in three contemporary American novels. Bloom asserts that these novels treat the family as a group rather than as individuals, explore the conservative rather than adventurous aspects of life, and emphasize maternal rather than paternal social structures. In *The Accidental Tourist*, Macon Leary's personality exemplifies this trend toward the passive.

A-10 Bond, Adrienne. "From Addie Bundren to Pearl Tull: The Secularization of the South." *Southern Quarterly* 24 (Spring 1986): 64-73. A comparison of Pearl Tull in *Dinner at the Homesick Restaurant* and Addie Bundren in William Faulkner's *As I Lay Dying*. Despite some parallels between the two women's lives, Bond thinks that the differences between the two illustrate changes in Southern society over the past century.

A-11   Bowers, Bradley R.   "Anne Tyler's Insiders." *Mississippi Quarterly* 42 (Winter 1988-89): 47-56.   Exploration of Tyler's use of various narrative techniques to admit her readers into her texts, often conveying to them "inside" knowledge of which her characters remain unaware.

A-12   Brooks, Mary Ellen.   "Anne Tyler."   In *The Dictionary of Literary Biography: American Novelists Since World War II*. Ed. James E. Kibler, Jr. Detroit: Gale Research, 1980, vol. 6: 336-45. Overview of Tyler's life which discusses her early interest in art, use of humor, and predominant themes. The article includes synopses of Tyler's novels (through *Morgan's Passing*) with limited analyses, a brief bibliography (with information on British publication of her novels), and a copy of the first page of the handwritten manuscript of *Celestial Navigation*.

A-13   Brown, Laurie L.   "Interviews with Seven Contemporary Writers." *Southern Quarterly* 21 (Summer 1983): 3-22. A compilation of interviews with seven women writers: Lisa Alther, Ellen Douglass, Gail Godwin, Shirley Ann Grau, Mary Lee Settle, Elizabeth Spencer, and Tyler. Tyler discusses the early days of her writing career, her methods of composition, her work as a book reviewer, and her fondness for *The Little House* (a children's book by Virginia Lee Burton) because of its theme of time and change. In addition, she reveals her superstition about not talking about works in progress, awareness of her audience, and reactions to her growing fame.

A-14   Brush, Mary Anne.   "The Two Worlds of Anne Tyler." *Baltimore Towne Magazine* Apr. 1989: 28-37. Photographic essay with text contrasting the two Baltimore neighborhoods prominent in Tyler's work: Roland Park and downtown Baltimore. Although the two areas seem quite different, Tyler's characters bridge the gap between the two worlds through a shared humanity.

A-15   Carroll, Virginia Schaefer.   "The Nature of Kinship in the Novels of Anne Tyler." In *The Fiction of Anne Tyler*. Ed. C. Ralph Stephens. Jackson: UP of Mississippi, 1990: 16-27. An insightful description of the often contradictory functions of families in Tyler's novels (especially *The Clock Winder*, *Celestial Navigation*, *The Accidental Tourist*, and *Breathing Lessons*). Carroll asserts that in these novels Tyler's families both nurture and isolate their individual members. Yet, despite the homogenizing influences of twentieth-century American culture, they somehow manage to retain their uniqueness amid familial alliances.

A-16   Carson, Barbara Harrell.   "Art's Internal Necessity: Anne Tyler's *Celestial Navigation*." In *The Fiction of Anne Tyler*. Ed. C. Ralph Stephens. Jackson: UP of Mississippi, 1990: 47-54. Psychological reading of *Celestial Navigation* that examines the interplay of life and art in the character Jeremy Pauling. Jeremy fails to achieve psychic wholeness because he can not successfully connect the inner creative world of his art with the external world of his family.

A-17   Carson, Barbara Harrell.   "Complicate, Complicate: Anne Tyler's Moral Imperative." *Southern Quarterly* 31 (Fall 1992): 24-34. Tyler's characters contradict the traditional view in American literature of the individual as isolated hero. Instead, in *Earthly Possessions*, *The Accidental Tourist*, and *Breathing Lessons*, Tyler creates characters who embrace complexity, thus enriching their lives. Tyler prefers characters who do not cut themselves off from the past, the possibility of hurt, or the chance of failure. In her fiction, "connectedness," not isolation, produces "selfhood."

A-18   Chevalier, Tracy. "Tyler, Anne." *Contemporary Novelists*. Ed. Lesley Henderson. 5th ed. Chicago: St. James Press, 1991: 891-93. Complete summary of Tyler's novels and awards to date, along with a lengthy, though not comprehensive, list of her short stories and of critical books about her work. Chevalier discusses Tyler's thematic use of family in many of her novels and praises her escaping easy categorization, especially in *The Accidental Tourist*.

A-19   Commire, Anne. "Anne Tyler 1941-." *Something About the Author*. Detroit: Gale, 1975, vol. 7: 198-199. Outdated and sometimes inaccurate short biographical sketch, which does, however, contain an interesting photo of Tyler as a young woman.

A-20   Cook, Bruce. "New Faces in Faulkner Country." *Saturday Review* 4 Sept. 1976: 39-41. [Reprinted in *Critical Essays on Anne Tyler*. Ed. Alice Hall Petry. New York: G.K. Hall, 1992: 157-58]. Article on new Southern writers that includes an interview with Tyler. The emphasis is on whether she is a Southern writer. Tyler discounts the influence of Faulkner, preferring instead Eudora Welty. She also discusses Baltimore as the setting for her latest works.

A-21   Cook, Bruce. "A Writer--During School Hours." *Detroit News* 6 Apr. 1980: E1+. [Reprinted in *Critical Essays on Anne Tyler*. Ed. Alice Hall Petry. New York: G.K. Hall, 1992: 50-52]. Personal interview with Tyler following publication of *Morgan's Passing*, in which she expresses concern that Morgan be well received by her readers. She also comments on how the Iranian hostage crisis has affected her family.

A-22   Crane, Gwen. "Anne Tyler, 1941-." In *Modern American Women Writers*. Eds. Lea Baechler and A. Walton Litz. New York: Scribner's, 1991: 499-510. Following a brief summary of Tyler's background, Crane discusses recurring themes, motifs, and character types in Tyler's first eleven novels, including the imperfect love that holds families together, her runaway characters, and their attempts at self-determination. Attempting to identify Tyler's literary influences, Crane finally concludes that while Tyler "absorb[s] influences from various literary schools, she subscribes to none, and continues to chart her own literary course" (509). The article ends with a brief selected bibliography.

A-23   Currie, Marianne D. "'Stringtail Man': Music as Motif in *Searching for Caleb*." *South Carolina Review* 24 (Fall 1991): 135-40. Appraisal of the pervasive use of music to delineate character and theme in *Searching for Caleb*. Characters' musical preferences, as well as their family's response to that music, reveal an underlying tension between conformity and individuality.

A-24   Dorner, George. "Anne Tyler: A Brief Interview with a Brilliant Author from Baltimore." *The Rambler* 2 (1979): 22. Tyler's written answers to a few questions about her response to critics and her views on being Southern and on Southern writing.

A-25   Doyle, Paul A.   "Tyler, Anne." *Contemporary Novelists*. Ed. James Vinson.
        1st ed. New York: St. Martin's Press, 1972: 1264-66. [Reprinted (with expanded
        lists of works and additional brief comments on new novels) in 2nd ed. (1976:
        1395-97), 3rd ed. (1982: 648-49), and 4th ed. (1986: 824-25)].   Brief
        biographical data and listing of works to date. The article discusses the treatment
        of families and death in *If Morning Ever Comes* and *The Tin Can Tree*. Doyle
        compares Tyler's dialogue to Hemingway's (in the 2nd edition he compares her
        to Carson McCullers instead) but wonders whether she will flesh out her
        characterizations, vary her themes, and expand her narrow range of subjects in
        future work.

A-26   Durham, Joyce R.   "City Perspectives in Anne Tyler's 'Morgan's Passing' and
        'The Accidental Tourist.'"   *Midwest Quarterly* 34 (Autumn 1992):   42-56.
        Examination of the characters Morgan Gower and Macon Leary as urban
        survivors. Though both respond differently (Morgan with a lack of order and
        Macon with an overabundance of it), they both define their urban environments
        through endurance and adaptation.

A-27   Dvorak, Angeline Godwin.   "Cooking as Mission and Ministry in Southern
        Culture: The Nurturers of Clyde Edgerton's *Walking Across Egypt*, Fannie
        Flagg's *Fried Green Tomatoes at the Whistle Stop Cafe* and Anne Tyler's *Dinner
        at the Homesick Restaurant*." *Southern Quarterly* 30 (Winter-Spring 1992): 90-
        98. In contrast to Edgerton's and Flagg's novels in which characters use cooking
        to create nurturing environments for the people around them, Tyler's *Dinner at
        the Homesick Restaurant* presents Pearl Tull's failure to provide emotional
        nourishment in the meager meals she provides for her children. Ezra's restaurant
        provides him with the opportunity to fulfill both his need for nourishment and his
        need for nurturing others.

A-28   Eckard, Paula Gallant.   "Family and Community in Anne Tyler's *Dinner at the
        Homesick Restaurant*." *Southern Literary Journal* 22 (Spring 1990): 33-44. An
        examination of the variety of familial relationships and the contrasting
        perspectives of family members in *Dinner at the Homesick Restaurant*.
        Juxtaposing the book against Faulkner's *As I Lay Dying*, Eckard compares Pearl
        to Addie Bundren, Jenny to Dewey Dell, and Cody to Darl. Ezra's Homesick
        Restaurant she compares to Carson McCuller's sad cafe in *The Ballad of the Sad
        Cafe*.

A-29   Elkins, Mary J.   *"Dinner at the Homesick Restaurant*:   The Faulkner
        Connection." *Atlantis: A Women's Studies Journal* 10 (Spring 1985): 93-105.
        [Reprinted in *The Fiction of Anne Tyler*. Ed. C. Ralph Stephens. Jackson: UP
        of Mississippi, 1990: 119-35]. Comparison of Tyler's *Dinner at the Homesick
        Restaurant* to William Faulkner's *As I Lay Dying*, downplaying the parallels
        between the novels. The real connection to Faulkner lies in Tyler's treatment of
        time, yet in the end, Tyler's novel retains her optimistic view rather than
        accepting Faulkner's deterministic one.

A-30   English, Sarah.   "An Interview with Anne Tyler." *The Dictionary of Literary
        Biography Yearbook: 1982*. Detroit: Gale Research, 1983: 193-94. Insightful
        interview by mail in which Tyler briefly discusses personal topics such as her

work schedule and her feelings about childhood, as well as more general issues related to her writing and the critical reception of her work.

A-31   Evans, Elizabeth. "'Mere Reviews': Anne Tyler as Book Reviewer." In *Critical Essays on Anne Tyler*. Ed. Alice Hall Petry. New York: G.K. Hall, 1992: 233-42. Tyler's book reviews reveal as much about her (including rare biographical insights) as they do about the wide range of books she reviews. In the reviews Tyler expresses opinions on social issues, the "narrative obligation" of writers to their readers, a predilection for style over experimentation, and, most importantly, her belief that, through skillful attention to detail, successful writers must convince their readers to care about their characters.

A-32   Evans, Elizabeth. "Anne Tyler." In *American Women Writers: A Critical Reference Guide from Colonial Times to the Present*. Ed. Lina Mainiero. New York: Frederick Ungar, 1982: 275-76. Brief biographical overview, including a discussion of Tyler's themes and characterization, followed by short comments on *Celestial Navigation*, *Searching for Caleb*, *Earthly Possessions*, and *Morgan's Passing*.

A-33   Farrell, Grace. "Killing off the Mother: Failed Matricide in *Celestial Navigation*." In *Critical Essays on Anne Tyler*. Ed. Alice Hall Petry. New York: G.K. Hall, 1992: 221-32. Excellent psychological reading of *Celestial Navigation* focussing on the failure of its characters to come to terms with the loss of a mother or mother-figure. The refusal of the characters "to acknowledge [this] primal loss" (229) prevents their moving from dependency to autonomy.

A-34   Ferry, Margaret. "Recommended: Anne Tyler." *English Journal* Feb. 1987: 93-94. Brief appraisal of nine of the first ten novels (*Morgan's Passing* is inexplicably omitted), focussing on Tyler's various presentations of family conflict and her experiments with point of view.

A-35   Foote, Audrey C. "Writing Other Lives, Making Other Chances." *World and I* Feb. 1992: 359-64. Short biographical sketch appraising Tyler's career, Quakerism, and penchant for privacy.

A-36   Freiert, William K. "Anne Tyler's Accidental Ulysses." *Classical and Modern Literature* 10 (Fall 1989): 71-79. Comparison of Macon Leary's quest in *The Accidental Tourist* to Odysseus's voyage in *The Odyssey*. Both characters search for fulfillment in similar ways.

A-37   Gardiner, Elaine, and Catherine Rainwater. "A Bibliography of Writings by Anne Tyler." In *Contemporary American Women Writers: Narrative Strategies*. Eds. Catherine Rainwater and William J. Scheik. Lexington: U of Kentucky P, 1985: 142-52. Bibliography of Tyler's novels (through *Dinner at the Homesick Restaurant*), short stories (through Nov. 1983), essays and articles (up to Nov. 1980), and a thorough listing of her book reviews (from Nov. 1972 through March 1984).

A-38   Garland, Jeanne. "Who's Who in the Baltimore Writing Establishment." *Baltimore Magazine* Dec. 1979: 55-59. Overview of Baltimore writers with statements from Tyler concerning her writing habits, her dislike of publicity, and her other life as a housewife.

A-39   Gibson, Mary Ellis. "Family as Fate: The Novels of Anne Tyler." *Southern Literary Journal* 16 (Fall 1983): 47-58. [Reprinted in *Critical Essays on Anne Tyler*. Ed. Alice Hall Petry. New York: G.K. Hall, 1992: 165-74]. Exploration of Tyler's attempt in *Dinner at the Homesick Restaurant, Searching for Caleb*, and *Celestial Navigation* to use her characters to express her ironic, almost metaphysical view of fate and its effects on families.

A-40   Gilbert, Susan. "Private Lives and Public Issues: Anne Tyler's Prize-winning Novels." In *The Fiction of Anne Tyler*. Ed. C. Ralph Stephens. Jackson: UP of Mississippi, 1990: 136-46. Re-evaluation of Tyler's treatment of contemporary political and social issues in her later works, such as abortion (*Breathing Lessons*), gun control and crime (*The Accidental Tourist*), and the state of public education (*The Accidental Tourist*). Gilbert notes that Tyler is not as ahistorical as some critics aver and that she actually depicts the social class structure of Baltimore fairly accurately. But, in choosing to view simple endurance as the principal virtue of her stories, Tyler wastes valuable opportunities to effect social change.

A-41   Gilbert, Susan. "Anne Tyler." In *Southern Women Writers: The New Generation*. Ed. Tonette Bond Inge. Tuscaloosa: U of Alabama P, 1990: 251-78. Excellent feminist analysis of the recurring themes, motifs, and character types in Tyler's first ten novels. Gilbert emphasizes Tyler's tendency to avoid social issues as if her families live oblivious to time, without "historical dimension" (251). The article ends with a brief biographical sketch and an appraisal of Tyler's anti-feminist and slightly anachronistic place in contemporary literature.

A-42   Gullette, Margaret Morganroth. "The Tears (and Joys) Are in the Things: Adulthood in Anne Tyler's Novels." *New England Review and Bread Loaf Quarterly* 7 (Spring 1985): 323-34. [Reprinted as Chapter 5 in *Safe at Last in the Middle Years: The Invention of the Midlife Progress Novel: Saul Bellow, Margaret Drabble, Anne Tyler, John Updike*. Berkeley: U of California P, 1988: 105-19; and in *The Fiction of Anne Tyler*. Ed. C. Ralph Stephens. Jackson: UP of Mississippi, 1990: 97-109]. Using examples from *Celestial Navigation, The Clock Winder, A Slipping-Down Life, The Accidental Tourist, Earthly Possessions*, and *Morgan's Passing*, Gullette discusses Tyler's treatment of responsibility, the tension between family and self, personal growth, childhood, mother figures, and gender roles and paradigms. Tyler's protagonists increasingly learn to seek their own happiness in ways that come naturally to them. The trick is not attaining these goals, but discovering what they really want and learning to accept and live with that knowledge.

A-43   Harper, Natalie. "Searching for Anne Tyler." *Simon's Rock of Bard College Bulletin* 4 (Fall 1984): 6-7. Interesting account of a 1984 interview with Tyler, in which her discussion of the creation of the characters in *Searching for Caleb* provides the main focus.

A-44   Iannone, Carol. "Novel Events." *National Review* 1 Sept. 1989: 46-49. Unfavorable assessment of Tyler's fiction as lightweight. Focussing on the cultural appeal of Tyler's fiction, her dependence on obtrusive metaphors, and her repetitive character types and plot structures, Iannone derides Tyler's lack of feminist stances and labels her writing mediocre in technique and subject matter, claiming that while her writing satisfies the minimal demands set by her loyal readers, it ultimately fails to recreate the complexity of real life.

A-45   Inman, Sue Lile. "The Effects of the Artistic Process: A Study of Three Artist Figures in Anne Tyler's Fiction." In *The Fiction of Anne Tyler*. Ed. C. Ralph Stephens. Jackson: UP of Mississippi, 1990: 55-63. Character study of Jeremy Pauling in *Celestial Navigation*, Morgan Gower in *Morgan's Passing*, and Ezra Tull in *Dinner at the Homesick Restaurant* as artist figures. Jeremy fails to achieve an identity outside his art, Morgan's identity remains constant, but Ezra succeeds in creating his own artistic vision.

A-46   Johnston, Sue Ann. "The Daughter as Escape Artist." *Atlantis: A Women's Studies Journal* 9 (Spring 1984): 10-22. Psychological reading of three novels by women (Margaret Drabble's *Jerusalem the Golden*, Margaret Atwood's *Lady Oracle*, and Anne Tyler's *Earthly Possessions*), exploring the attempts of daughters to achieve an identity separate from their restrictive mothers. What these daughters discover is that their flight from mother is actually a journey towards their true selves. In taking on the role of mother herself, Charlotte Emory (*Earthly Possessions*) finally accepts her role as a daughter.

A-47   Jones, Anne. "Home at Last and Homesick Again: The Ten Novels of Anne Tyler." *Hollins Critic* 23 (Apr. 1986): 1-13. Extended discussion of prominent themes and motifs in Tyler's first ten novels. Brief plot summaries chronicle the psychic growth of the protagonists as they seek to resolve the tension between their opposing needs for autonomy and relatedness, between separation and union.

A-48   Kanoza, Theresa. "Mentors and Maternal Role Models: The Healthy Mean between Extremes in Anne Tyler's Fiction." In *The Fiction of Anne Tyler*. Ed. C. Ralph Stephens. Jackson: UP of Mississippi, 1990: 28-39. Study of the role of the mother-in-law (usually as a foil to a more traditional mother or mother figure) in *Earthly Possessions*, *Celestial Navigation*, and *The Clock Winder*. Inspired by unconventional mothers-in-law, the female protagonists of these novels evolve into self-sufficient, autonomous individuals, combining the best of their stable and passive mothers with the energetic openness to life represented by their mothers-in-law.

A-49   Koenig, Rhoda. "Books." *New York* 12 Sept. 1988: 110-11. Essay review of *Breathing Lessons*, complete with a full-page, color photograph of Tyler. Tyler symbolically appropriates the ordinary aspects of life in her work, rendering them "momentous and magical." The article also includes a brief biographical sketch of Tyler's life.

A-50   Koppel, Gene. "Maggie Moran, Anne Tyler's Madcap Heroine: A Game Approach to *Breathing Lessons*." *Essays in Literature* 18 (Fall 1991): 276-87. Examination of Tyler's contrasting (yet complementary) approaches to life and art as a game in *Breathing Lessons*. She juxtaposes joyousness and unpredictability ("the game-spirit" embodied in Maggie) with responsibility and stability (as represented by Ira) to create a realistic vision of marriage and life.

A-51   Lamb, Wendy. "An Interview with Anne Tyler." *Iowa Journal of Literary Studies* 3 (1981): 59-64. Interview with Tyler following her reading and fiction workshop at the University of Iowa in May 1979. Tyler answers questions about the writing process, her fondness for her characters, her portrayal of ministers, her trouble in writing *Morgan's Passing*, her reclusiveness, the ending of *Celestial Navigation*, her negative feelings about *If Morning Ever Comes* and *The Tin Can Tree*, and other aspects of her writing.

A-52   Lueloff, Jorie. "Authoress Explains Why Women Dominate in South." (Baton Rouge) *Morning Advocate* 8 Feb. 1965: A11. [Reprinted in *Critical Essays on Anne Tyler*. Ed. Alice Hall Petry. New York: G.K. Hall, 1992: 21-23]. One of the earliest published interviews with Tyler, who openly discusses the role of women in Southern literature, her own interest in Southern dialect, and her feelings about the South.

A-53   "Mademoiselle's Annual Merit Awards." *Mademoiselle* Jan. 1966: 45-49. Early article in which Tyler discusses her writing habits, her feelings about women writers, and her literary tastes and influences--Woolf, McCullers, and Welty. Page 46 contains a photo of Tyler at age 24.

A-54   Manning, Carol S. "Agrarianism, Female-Style." *Southern Quarterly* 30 (Winter-Spring 1992): 69-76. Revisionist argument of how the often overlooked female side of agrarianism is expressed metaphorically through the process of food preparation in several novels by Southern women writers: Edith Summers Kelley's *Weeds*, Eudora Welty's *Delta Wedding*, Ellen Douglas's *A Family's Affairs*, and Tyler's *Dinner at the Homesick Restaurant*, which in some ways represents the death of female agrarianism. In her role as mother, Pearl fails to live up to the agrarian ideal.

A-55   Manning, Carol S. "Welty, Tyler, and Traveling Salesmen: The Wandering Hero Unhorsed." In *The Fiction of Anne Tyler*. Ed. C. Ralph Stephens. Jackson: UP of Mississippi, 1990: 110-18. Comparison of Eudora Welty's character King MacLain in *The Golden Apples* to Beck Tull in *Dinner at the Homesick Restaurant*. Both men desert their families, seemingly for freedom and adventure. But Welty and Tyler turn around the traditional image of the wandering adventurer to reveal the enormous loss both men actually suffer by staying away from home.

A-56   Marovitz, Sanford. "Anne Tyler's Emersonian Balance." In *Critical Essays on Anne Tyler*. Ed. Alice Hall Petry. New York: G.K. Hall, 1992: 207-20. Important exploration of Tyler's Emersonian foundation, which begins by discussing her view of time as a continuum. The article also discusses Tyler's use of light imagery to reveal the developing character of Elizabeth Abbott in *The Clock Winder*, the failure of Jeremy Pauling and the success of Mary Tell in *Celestial Navigation* to achieve Emerson's "organic wholeness" (213), and Jenny Tull's growth towards self-reliance in *Dinner at the Homesick Restaurant*.

A-57 Michaels, Marguerite. "Anne Tyler, Writer 8:05 to 3:30." *New York Times Book Review* 8 May 1977: 13+. [Reprinted in *Critical Essays on Anne Tyler*. Ed. Alice Hall Petry. New York: G.K. Hall, 1992: 40-44]. Revealing personal interview with Tyler that describes her home, study, writing habits, affinity with Jeremy Pauling of *Celestial Navigation*, and interest in character, as well as her thoughts on fame and literary reputation.

A-58 Nesanovich, Stella. "The Individual in the Family: Anne Tyler's *Searching for Caleb* and *Earthly Possessions*." *Southern Review* 14 (Winter 1978): 170-76. [Reprinted in *Critical Essays on Anne Tyler*. Ed. Alice Hall Petry. New York: G.K. Hall, 1992: 159-64]. Analysis of family relationships in these two novels, especially the characters' contrasting responses to life and their corresponding restlessness.

A-59 Nesanovich, Stella. "An Anne Tyler Checklist, 1959-80." *Bulletin of Bibliography* 38 (Apr.-June 1981): 53-64. Initial Tyler bibliography that lists early book reviews of Tyler's first seven novels, as well as Tyler's fiction and book reviews.

A-60 Olendorf, Donna. "Tyler, Anne." In *Contemporary Authors*. Eds. Ann Evory and Linda Metzger. Detroit: Gale Research, 1984. New Revision Series, vol. 11: 510-13. Comprehensive, short biographical sketch of Tyler's life and career through *Dinner at the Homesick Restaurant* that includes a basic overview of Tyler's life, literary influences, and achievements. Olendorf skillfully intersperses comments from interviews and book reviews into short analyses of six of Tyler's first nine novels.

A-61 Papadimas, Julie Persing. "America Tyler Style: Surrogate Families and Transiency." *Journal of American Culture* 15 (Fall 1992): 45-51. Sociological investigation of Tyler's creation of surrogate family groups to compensate for or replace weakened nuclear ones (such as the three-house family of *The Tin Can Tree*, the boarding house family of *Celestial Navigation*, and Ezra's homelike restaurant and Jenny's pediatric practice in *Dinner at the Homesick Restaurant*). Furthermore, transient characters (such as Charlotte in *Earthly Possessions* and Justine and Duncan in *Searching for Caleb*) convey the sense of impermanence felt by an increasingly mobile American culture.

A-62 Petry, Alice Hall. "Bright Books of Life: The Black Norm in Anne Tyler's Novels." *Southern Quarterly* 31 (Fall 1992): 7-13. An interesting look at Tyler's positive depiction of African-American characters, focussing on *If Morning Ever Comes*, *The Tin Can Tree*, *A Slipping-Down Life*, *The Clock Winder*, *Searching for Caleb*, and *Breathing Lessons*. Though sometimes serving a mere "choral function," Tyler's African-American characters are always rendered with humanity and dignity. Often they even exhibit human qualities with more complexity than some of Tyler's dysfunctional white families. In fact, relatively minor African-American characters in *The Tin Can Tree* and *Breathing Lessons* actually articulate the central theme of each novel.

A-63 Reed, J.D. "Postfeminism: Playing for Keeps." *Time* 10 Jan. 1983: 60-61. Brief analysis of postfeminism, which includes Tyler among several women writers whose subjects extend beyond the range of "women's novels." Tyler dislikes being labeled "a mother of two" who writes.

A-64   Ridley, Clifford. "Anne Tyler: A Sense of Reticence Balanced by 'Oh, Well, Why Not?'" *National Observer* 22 July 1972: 23. [Reprinted in *Critical Essays on Anne Tyler*. Ed. Alice Hall Petry. New York: G.K. Hall, 1992: 24-27]. Personal interview with Tyler soon after the publication of *The Clock Winder*. Tyler's passivity is apparent as she discusses her distaste for her first two novels, her curiosity about the South and Southern families, the source for *A Slipping-Down Life*, and her affection for the book because of its characters' ability to change. Additionally, she relates her thoughts on the ending of *The Clock Winder*, her respect for the privacy of others, and her lack of enthusiasm for feminist novels.

A-65   Robertson, Mary F. "Anne Tyler: Medusa Points and Contact Points." In *Contemporary American Women Writers: Narrative Strategies*. Eds. Catherine Rainwater and William J. Scheik. Lexington: U of Kentucky P, 1985: 119-42. [Reprinted in *Critical Essays on Anne Tyler*. Ed. Alice Hall Petry. New York: G.K. Hall, 1992: 184-204]. Complicated discussion of Tyler's narrative strategy of bringing family insiders into contact with outsiders. Tyler uses the family as "a sign of order or disorder in personality and society" (122) through the use of "Medusa points," which allow individuals to retain their individuality within the family structure, and "contact points," which provide characters with the necessary connection to the world outside the family. The article focuses primarily on *Dinner at the Homesick Restaurant* but also refers to *Earthly Possessions* and *Morgan's Passing*.

A-66   Ross-Bryant, Lynn. "Anne Tyler's *Searching for Caleb*: The Sacrality of the Everyday." *Soundings: An Interdisciplinary Journal* 73 (Spring 1990): 191-207. Feminist reading of Tyler's *Searching for Caleb*, which explores Tyler's use of the ordinary to subvert a traditionally dualistic (and masculine) view of life and families. Caleb Peck teaches Justine Peck that her need for family does not replace her need for individuality. She learns to accept both continuity and change. With Justine's new vision of wholeness (a feminine view of cyclical rather than linear time), Tyler reveals the extraordinary qualities of ordinary life.

A-67   Shafer, Aileen Chris. "Anne Tyler's 'The Geologist's Maid': 'till human voices wake us and we drown.'" *Studies in Short Fiction* 27 (Winter 1990): 65-71. Interesting comparison of the character of Professor Bennett Johnson in Tyler's short story "The Geologist's Maid" to Prufrock in T.S. Eliot's "The Love Song of J. Alfred Prufrock." Noting Tyler's "Prufrockian allusory framework" (65), Shafer compares Johnson's inability to communicate with his black maid Maroon, despite his desperate desire to do so, to Prufrock's isolation. Despite Johnson's almost living through his maid by listening to her deeply emotional responses to life, he can't break out of his own introspective Prufrockian isolation long enough to communicate with her. Ironically, for her own part, Maroon doesn't realize the importance of the events in her life to him or for herself.

A-68   Shelton, Frank W. "Anne Tyler's Houses." In *The Fiction of Anne Tyler*. Ed. C. Ralph Stephens. Jackson: UP of Mississippi, 1990: 40-46. Revisionist view of Tyler's domesticity explaining how Tyler strays from the feminist tradition of viewing houses as prisons for female characters. Tyler sees houses in such novels as *Earthly Possessions*, *Celestial Navigation*, *The Clock Winder*, *Searching for Caleb*, *Morgan's Passing*, and *The Accidental Tourist* as being as potentially repressive to the male characters as to the female. Yet these houses also act as "physical and spiritual correlatives" (45) for the characters. The most successful characters combine and reconcile in their homes the "opposing human needs for permanence and mobility" (46).

A-69 Shelton, Frank W. "The Necessary Balance: Distance and Sympathy in the Novels of Anne Tyler." *Southern Review* 20 (Autumn 1984): 851-60. [Reprinted in *Critical Essays on Anne Tyler*. Ed. Alice Hall Petry. New York: G.K. Hall, 1992: 175-83). A convincing exploration of Tyler's characters' attempt to balance distance and sympathy, disengagement and engagement in their lives and relationships. Tyler's first three novels are mentioned briefly as preludes to her fuller development of conflict between the individual's opposing needs for freedom and for connectedness. In *The Clock Winder* Elizabeth Abbott first seeks independence but then becomes involved in the Emerson family; in *Searching for Caleb*, Justine Peck's compromise balances "movement and rootedness" (857); in *Morgan's Passing*, Morgan Gower achieves a similar balance; and in *Dinner at the Homesick Restaurant*, each of the three Tull children attempts to counterbalance these contradictory impulses.

A-70 Taylor, Gordon O. "Morgan's Passion." In *The Fiction of Anne Tyler*. Ed. C. Ralph Stephens. Jackson: UP of Mississippi, 1990: 64-72. Uneven study of the evolution of Morgan Gower in *Morgan's Passing*. Morgan's shifting identities mirror Tyler's own exercises in storymaking.

A-71 Town, Caren J. "Rewriting the Family During *Dinner at the Homesick Restaurant*." *Southern Quarterly* 31 (Fall 1992): 14-23. Exploration of the ways in which Cody, Ezra, and Jenny Tull revise their individual concepts of family. Each character creates an idea of family to suit his or her own needs for emotional sustenance and nourishment.

A-72 Trouard, Dawn. "'Teaching the Cat to Yawn': Criticisms of St. Anne." *Southern Quarterly* 30 (Fall 1991): 83-89. Unfavorable review essay of Alice Hall Petry's *Understanding Anne Tyler* and C. Ralph Stephens's *The Fiction of Anne Tyler*. Trouard castigates the books for their conventional approaches and their dependence on Tyler interviews rather than critical perspective. Only Susan Gilbert's essay in the Stephens book suggests a new approach to Tyler.

A-73 Voelker, Joseph C. "The Semi-Miracle of Time." *World and I* Feb. 1992: 347-57. Tyler creates chronicles, not histories, of family life, recording moments that produce subtle epiphanies about her characters' lives. Focussing on *Saint Maybe*, Voelker expresses interesting views on religion (especially the similarities between Tyler's Quaker upbringing and the beliefs of the Church of the Second Chance) and on the unconventional format of her books' endings. Finally, he notes the parallels between the ages of Tyler's characters and her own age when she writes her books.

A-74 Wagner, Joseph B. "Beck Tull: "The absent presence" in *Dinner at the Homesick Restaurant*." In *The Fiction of Anne Tyler*. Ed. C. Ralph Stephens. Jackson:

UP of Mississippi, 1990: 73-83. Psychological exploration of the effects of an absent father on the three children in *Dinner at the Homesick Restaurant*. Because of their father's absence, Ezra's sexual identity remains confused (he is never able to sustain a relationship with a woman), Jenny becomes marginalized and anorexic (never able to risk complete intimacy with men), and Cody's attempts to replace his father make him bitter until, after his father's return, he can forgive him and finally accept his mother and siblings.

A-75   Weatherby, W.J. "The Family Business." *Guardian* 17 Jan. 1989: 17. Brief appraisal of Tyler's recent rise to prominence. Weatherby examines Tyler's literary influences and subjects.

A-76   Willrich, Patricia Rowe. "Watching through Windows: A Perspective on Anne Tyler." *Virginia Quarterly Review* 68 (Summer 1992): 497-516. Excellent overview of Tyler's life and career, containing some comments from Tyler herself not found elsewhere. Tyler's perspective remains objective and aloof, concentrating on character.

A-77   Woizesko, Helene, and Michael Scott Cain. "Anne Tyler." *Northeast Rising Sun* 1 (June-July 1976): 28-30. Interesting account of an interview with Tyler that focusses on her creation of the characters in *Celestial Navigation* and *Searching for Caleb*.

A-78   Yardley, Jonathan. "Women Write the Best Books." *Washington Post* 16 May 1983: B1+. Tyler is included in a list of more than twenty contemporary women writers who now dominate American fiction. Tyler, along with Gail Godwin, has been able to "shake off the strictures of feminist orthodoxy and to establish [her] individual [voice] and themes" (B11).

A-79   Zahlan, Anne R. "Anne Tyler." In *Fifty Southern Writers After 1900: A Bio-Bibliographical Sourcebook*. Eds. Joseph M. Flora and Robert Bain. Westport: Greenwood Press, 1987: 491-504. Biographical essay that includes a sketch of Tyler's life, a summary of the themes and plots of her novels (through *The Accidental Tourist*), a limited survey of criticism, and a brief bibliography.

A-80   Zahlan, Anne Ricketson. "Traveling Towards the Self: The Psychic Drama of Anne Tyler's *The Accidental Tourist*." In *The Fiction of Anne Tyler*. Ed. C. Ralph Stephens. Jackson: UP of Mississippi, 1990: 84-96. Psychological reading of *The Accidental Tourist* (with brief references to *Earthly Possessions* and *Searching for Caleb*). Referring to Freudian and Lacanian principles, she explains Macon Leary's "journey through psychic despair to rebirth" (86). To overcome the psychological effects of his son's death, Macon must, with the help of Muriel Pritchett, move through several stages until he can achieve a healthy, "integrated self" (95).

III. Dissertations and Theses

D-1 Askew, Jennifer Y. "*The Accidental Tourist*: Novel and Film." Thesis. Florida Atlantic U, 1991. Comparison of *The Accidental Tourist* with its film adaptation by director Lawrence Kasdan. In general, the adaptation is successful, especially the film's direct use of Tyler's dialogue. Thematically, however, the film's tone is more melancholy than the book's quirky, comic tone.

D-2 Brock, Dorothy Faye Sala. "Anne Tyler's Treatment of Managing Women." Diss. North Texas State U, 1985. Identifies the major female characters of Tyler's first nine novels as "managing women" whose most important characteristic is endurance. Brock divides these women into two subgroups: regenerative managing women (who adapt and grow, renewing themselves and their families) and rigid managing women (who fail to adapt, stifling their development and hurting their families). Brock also describes Tyler's typical narrative structure as a cyclical pattern of escape, crisis, return, and renewal.

D-3 Cooper, Barbara Eck. "The Difficulty of Family Life: The Creative Force in the Domestic Fictions of Six Contemporary Women Novelists." Diss. U of Missouri, 1986. Study of family conflict and creativity in six novels (*Housekeeping* by Marilynne Robinson, *Brown Girl* by Paule Marshall, *The Color Purple* by Alice Walker, *Song of Solomon* by Toni Morrison, *Dale Loves Sophie to Death* by Robb Foreman, and Tyler's *Dinner at the Homesick Restaurant*). Ezra Tull reacts to family conflict by attempting to stage a series of perfect family dinners, creating hope both for the family as a group and for his own creative life.

D-4 Crowe, Brenda Stone. "Anne Tyler: Building Her Own 'House of Fiction.'" Diss. U of Alabama, 1993. Presentation of Tyler as a book reviewer and reader followed by a discussion of her aesthetics and their application to her own writing. Finally, the study investigates Tyler's growth as a novelist and her sympathetic presentation of characters.

D-5 Dunstan, Angus Michael. "The Missing Guest: Dinner Parties in British and American Literature." Diss. U of California, Santa Barbara, 1986. Examination of the typical failure of dinner parties in British and American fiction due to forces of dissent and dissolution. Most dinner parties include a Missing Guest, who symbolizes the change necessary to create communal harmony at the party (and, in some cases, within society itself). Ezra Tull, in acting as the Metaphysical Host in *Dinner at the Homesick Restaurant*, attempts to maintain balance by creating unity and restraining discord.

D-6 Gainey, Karen Fern Wilkes. "Subverting the Symbolic: The Semiotic Fictions of Anne Tyler, Jayne Anne Phillips, Bobbie Ann Mason, and Grace Paley." Diss. U of Tulsa, 1990. Kristevan reading of novels by Tyler and three other contemporary American women writers. In these works, Gainey finds contradictory strains of Emersonian transcendentalism (desires to escape and a belief in transformation) and a self-questioning of that transcendental self. Through manipulating language, characters subvert conventional views of a unified self.

D-7   Gaitens, Judi. "The Web of Connection: A Study of Family Patterns in the Fiction of Anne Tyler." Diss. Kent State U, 1988. Using Tyler's first ten novels and several short stories, Gaitens examines Tyler's large, happy families and her smaller, weaker ones. Both groups tend to compound family identity (to the point of stagnation) through inbreeding, or to dilute it through the inclusion of outsiders. The introduction includes a review of Tyler scholarship and an overview of her life.

D-8   Hill, Darlene Reimers. "From Aunt Mashula's Coconut Cake to Big Macs: References to Food in Recent Southern Women's Fiction (Welty, Tyler, Mason, Hill, Smith, Shivers)." Diss. U of Rhode Island, 1989. Examination of the way in which changing eating habits reveal sociological transitions in individual families and in the structure of Southern society itself. Hill finds Tyler particularly interesting because her books' settings span both the transitional period of midcentury and the fragmented contemporary era.

D-9   Landis, Robyn Gay. "The Family Business: Problems of Identity and Authority in Literature, Theory, and the Academy (Patriarchal Family)." Diss. U of Pennsylvania, 1990. Analysis of traditional Christian and Freudian concepts of patriarchal family models, from a literary and critical perspective, followed by a discussion of the problems inherent in these models for both male and female family members. Using works by Tyler, other women writers, and feminist critics, Landis revises historically patriarchal paradigms. These alternative family models affect both the creation of individual identity and the use of authority within family structures.

D-10   Lovenheim, Barbara Pitlick. "Dialogues with America: Androgyny, Ethnicity, and Family in the Novels of Anne Tyler, Joanne Greenberg, and Toni Morrison." Diss. U of Rochester, 1990. Investigation of the novels of Anne Tyler, Joanne Greenberg, and Toni Morrison as a redefinition of the extended family across traditional boundaries (Tyler here is treated as Southern) to create an androgynous character type capable of nurturing both masculine and feminine traits.

D-11   Naulty, Patricia Mary. "'I Never Talk of Hunger': Self-Starvation as Women's Language of Protest in Novels by Barbara Pym, Margaret Atwood, and Anne Tyler." Diss. Ohio State U, 1988. Feminist treatment of anorexia nervosa in three novels (Barbara Pym's *Quartet in Autumn*, Margaret Atwood's *The Edible Woman*, and Tyler's *Dinner at the Homesick Restaurant*). Focussing on mother/daughter relationships and societally imposed, ideologically restrictive perceptions of women's roles, Naulty argues that the daughters in these novels reject traditional female roles and express their defiance through the language of starvation.

D-12   Nesanovich, Stella. "The Individual in the Family: A Critical Introduction to the Novels of Anne Tyler." Diss. Louisiana State U, 1979. Earliest dissertation on Tyler, focussing on family relationships in her first seven novels and the often contradictory effects of families upon individual members. Some aspects of family life nurture and support the individual, while other aspects repress or stifle individualism.

D-13   Peters, Deborah. "With Hearts Expanding: The Journey Motif in Novels by Anne Tyler." Diss. St. Louis U, 1989. Investigation of Tyler's use of the archetypal journey motif in her first eleven novels. Most of the journeys involve circular patterns of escape and return in which the characters seek identity or freedom outside the restrictions of family or marriage. Usually, by the end of her novels, most of Tyler's characters have resolved their internal conflict through a new perspective and/or a new relationship.

D-14   Pope, Deborah Lee. "Character and Characterization in the Novels of Anne Tyler." Diss. U of Mississippi, 1989. Exploration of Tyler's focus on familial relationships among the characters of her first eleven novels. Each main character seeks to maintain his or her individuality in the context of various family configurations. Pope divides Tyler's characters into two groups: retreating males and competent females.

D-15   Powell, Candace Alaide. "Missed Connections: A Horneyan Analysis of Anne Tyler's Characters." Thesis. Stephen F. Austin State U., 1991. Application of psychologist Karen Horney's psychoanalytic personality theories to Tyler's characters. Powell identifies several Horneyan personality traits in Tyler's characters and concludes that her characterizations are both realistic and psychologically accurate.

D-16   Quiello, Rose Maria. "Breakdowns and Breakthroughs: The Figure of the Hysteric in Contemporary Novels by Women." Diss. U of Connecticut, 1991. Feminist exploration of the subversion of conventional social structures by female characters in novels by Anne Tyler, Kate O'Brien, and Margaret Drabble. Tyler's female characters often accomplish this subversion through language and through their renunciation of traditional gender roles as mother and wife.

D-17   Whitesides, Mary Parr. "Marriage in the American Novel from 1882 to 1982." Diss. U of South Carolina, 1984. Analysis of the often contradictory and changing views of marriage (and divorce) in American novels from the late nineteenth century to the late twentieth. The gradual social acceptance of divorce is outlined in examples from the nineteenth-century novels, while the contemporary novels (Tyler's *Dinner at the Homesick Restaurant*) illustrate society's appropriation of the family unit to create boundaries previously established through marriage.

D-18   Wolpert, Ilana Paula. "Crossing the Gender Line: Female Novelists and Their Male Voices." Diss. Ohio State U, 1988. Study of the male protagonists in novels by female authors (George Eliot, Toni Morrison, Charlotte Bronte, Virginia Woolf, and Tyler). Such "crossover writing" illuminates changes in gender roles over the past two hundred years. In particular, *Celestial Navigation* presents in Jeremy Pauling the figure of a man attempting to redefine his role as a man at a time when gender roles are changing and becoming increasingly complex.

IV. Selected Reviews of Tyler's Novels

If Morning Ever Comes

V-1   "Age Without Wisdom." *Times Literary Supplement* 15 July 1965: 593.

V-2   *Booklist* 15 Oct. 1964: 193.

V-3   Eckberg, Carol A. *Library Journal* 15 Nov. 1964: 4563.

V-4   Gloag, Julian. "Home Was a House Full of Women." *Saturday Review* 26 Dec. 1964: 37-38.

V-5   Hill, William B. *America* 28 Nov. 1964: 722.

V-6   Jackson, Katherine Gauss. "Mad First Novel, but Without Madness." *Harper's* Nov. 1964: 152.

V-7   *Kirkus Reviews* 15 Aug. 1964: 837.

V-8   Long, John Allan. "'New' Southern Novel." *Christian Science Monitor* 21 Jan. 1965: 9.

V-9   Mara, Maura. *Best Sellers* 1 Nov. 1964: 317.

V-10   "Paperbacks: New and Noteworthy." *New York Times Book Review* 25 Sept. 1977: 49.

V-11   Prescott, Orville. "Return to the Hawkes Family." *New York Times* 11 Nov. 1964: 41. [Reprinted in *Critical Essays on Anne Tyler*. Ed. Alice Hall Petry. New York: G.K. Hall, 1992: 61-62].

V-12   Ridley, Clifford A. "From First Novels to the Loves of William Shakespeare." *National Observer* 16 Nov. 1964: 21.

V-13   Saal, Rollene W. "Loveless Household." *New York Times Book Review* 22 Nov. 1964: 52.

V-14   Sullivan, Walter. "Worlds Past and Future: A Christian and Several from the South." *Sewanee Review* 73 (Autumn 1965): 719-26.

V-15   *Time* 1 Jan. 1965: 71.

V-16   Vansittart, Peter. "Landscapes, People." *Spectator* 9 July 1965: 56.

V-17   *Virginia Quarterly Review* 41 (Winter 1965): viii-ix.

The Tin Can Tree

V-18 Bell, Millicent. "Tobacco Road Updated." *New York Times Book Review* 21 Nov. 1965: 77.

V-19 *Booklist* 15 Oct. 1965: 196.

V-20 Brooks, Gwendolyn. "Soup's On." *Book Week* 7 Nov. 1965: 24.

V-21 Bunker, Patricia. *Saturday Review* 2 Oct. 1965: 49.

V-22 Conley, John. "A Clutch of Fifteen." *Southern Review* NS 3 (July 1967): 776-87.

V-23 Fasick, Adele M. *Library Journal* 15 Oct. 1965: 4367.

V-24 Flavin, Ian. *Books and Bookmen* Feb. 1967: 30.

V-25 Fleischer, Leonore. *Publisher's Weekly* 12 Sept. 1966: 90-91.

V-26 Frankel, Haskel. "Closing a Family Wound." *Saturday Review* 20 Nov. 1965: 50. [Reprinted in *Critical Essays on Anne Tyler*. Ed. Alice Hall Petry. New York: G.K. Hall, 1992: 63-64].

V-27 Gardner, Marilyn. "Figurines in a Paperweight." *Christian Science Monitor* 10 Feb. 1966: 7.

V-28 Jackson, Katherine Gauss. *Harper's* Dec. 1965: 133.

V-29 *Kirkus Reviews* 15 Aug. 1965: 849.

V-30 *Kliatt Young Adult Paperback Book Guide* 11 (Fall 1977): 9.

V-31 Lehmann-Haupt, Christopher. "A Small Pebble with a Big Splash." *New York Times* 23 Dec. 1965: 25.

V-32 McNiff, Mary Stack. *America* 30 Oct. 1965: 507-08.

V-33 Richardson, D.E. "Grits and Mobility: Three Southern Novels." *Shenandoah* 17 (Winter 1966): 102-05.

V-34 Ridley, Clifford A. "Spark and Tyler Are Proof Anew of Knopf Knowledge of Top Fiction." *National Observer* 29 Nov. 1965: 25.

V-35 Stedmond, J.M. "Fiction." *University of Toronto Quarterly* 36 (July 1967): 379-89.

A Slipping-Down Life

V-36   Bannon, Barbara A. *Publisher's Weekly* 12 Jan. 1970: 59.

V-37   "Best Books for Young Adults 1970." *Top of the News* Apr. 1971: 307-09.

V-38   *Booklist* 15 June 1970: 1261.

V-39   Earl, Pauline J. *Best Sellers* 1 May 1970: 57-58.

V-40   Edelstein, Arthur. "Art and Artificiality in Some Recent Fiction." *Southern Review* NS 9 (July 1973): 736-44. [Reprinted in *Critical Essays on Anne Tyler*. Ed. Alice Hall Petry. New York: G.K. Hall, 1992: 65-66].

V-41   *Kirkus Reviews* 1 Jan. 1970: 24-25; also 1 Feb. 1970: 119.

V-42   Lee, Hermione. "Frantic Obsessions." (London) *Observer* 29 May 1983: 30.

V-43   Levin, Martin. "Reader's Report." *New York Times Book Review* 15 Mar. 1970: 44.

V-44   "New and Noteworthy." *New York Times Book Review* 3 Apr. 1977: 53-54.

V-45   Wadsworth, Carol Eckberg. *Library Journal* 15 Mar. 1970: 1050.

The Clock Winder

V-46   Bannon, Barbara A. *Publisher's Weekly* 14 Feb. 1972: 67-68.

V-47   Blackburn, Sara. "Novels." *Washington Post Book World* 14 May 1972: 13. [Reprinted in *Critical Essays on Anne Tyler*. Ed. Alice Hall Petry. New York: G.K. Hall, 1992: 68].

V-48   *Booklist* 1 July 1972: 930.

V-49   *Choice* Nov. 1972: 1134.

V-50   Davies, Russell. "Californian Wilderness." (London) *Observer* 11 Feb. 1973: 37.

V-51   Doyle, Paul A. *Best Sellers* 15 June 1972: 148-49.

V-52   Easton, Elizabeth. *Saturday Review* 17 June 1972: 77.

V-53   Gell, Marilyn. *Library Journal* 15 Mar. 1972: 1035.

V-54   Greacen, Robert. *Books and Bookmen* Aug. 1973: 87-88.

V-55   Hill, George. (London) *Times* 25 Jan. 1973: 12.

V-56   Hunter, Jim. "Fine Revolution." *Listener* 1 Feb. 1973: 156.

V-57   Kammermeyer, Janet. *Library Journal* 15 Sept. 1972: 2971.

V-58   *Kirkus Reviews* 1 Feb. 1972: 158-59.

V-59   Levin, Martin. "New & Novel." *New York Times Book Review* 21 May 1972:
       31. [Reprinted in *Critical Essays on Anne Tyler*. Ed. Alice Hall Petry. New
       York: G.K. Hall, 1992: 67].

V-60   *New Republic* 13 May 1972: 29.

V-61   *New Yorker* 29 Apr. 1972: 140.

V-62   Smith, Catharine Mack. "Indian File." *New Statesman* 16 Feb. 1973: 240-41.

V-63   *Virginia Quarterly Review* 48 (Autumn 1972): cxx.

Celestial Navigation

V-64   Allen, Bruce. *Library Journal* 1 Mar. 1974: 679.

V-65   Bannon, Barbara A. *Publisher's Weekly* 10 Dec. 1973: 30.

V-66   Barnes, Julian. "Kidding." *New Statesman* 4 Apr. 1975: 457.

V-67   Bell, Pearl K. "The Artist as Hero." *New Leader* 4 Mar. 1974: 17-18.

V-68   *Booklist* 1 July 1974: 1182.

V-69   Clapp, Susannah. "In the Abstract." *Times Literary Supplement* 23 May 1975:
       577. [Reprinted in *Critical Essays on Anne Tyler*. Ed. Alice Hall Petry. New
       York: G.K. Hall, 1992: 69-70].

V-70   Godwin, Gail. "Two Novels." *New York Times Book Review* 28 Apr. 1974: 34-
       35. [Reprinted in *Critical Essays on Anne Tyler*. Ed. Alice Hall Petry. New
       York: G.K. Hall, 1992: 71-72].

V-71   Grumbach, Doris. "Women's Work." *New Republic* 25 May 1974: 32-33.

V-72   Halio, Jay L. "Love and the Grotesque." *Southern Review* NS 11 (Autumn
       1975): 942-48.

V-73   Kennedy, Eileen. *Best Sellers* 1 May 1974: 63.

V-74   *Kirkus Reviews* 15 Dec. 1973: 1380.

V-75   Pryce-Jones, Alan. "Five Easy Pieces: One Work of Art." *Washington Post
       Book World* 24 Mar. 1974: 2. [Reprinted in *Critical Essays on Anne Tyler*.
       Ed. Alice Hall Petry. New York: G.K. Hall, 1992: 73-74].

V-76   Ridley, Clifford A.   "Novels: A Hit Man, a Clown, a Genius." *National Observer* 4 May 1974: 23.

                              Searching for Caleb

V-77   Bannon, Barbara A. *Publisher's Weekly* 3 Nov. 1975: 63.

V-78   *Booklist* 15 Apr. 1976: 1166.

V-79   *Choice* July 1976: 668.

V-80   Chura, Walt. *America* 10 Apr. 1976: 319-20.

V-81   de Usabel, Frances E. *Library Journal* 15 Dec. 1975: 2345.

V-82   Grumbach, Doris. "Psychic Trip in Search of Caleb." *Los Angeles Times Book Review* 8 Feb. 1976: 6.

V-83   Howard, Philip. (London) *Times* 13 May 1976: 16.

V-84   Howes, Victor. "Freedom: Theme of Pecks' Battle Hymns." *Christian Science Monitor* 14 Jan. 1976: 23.

V-85   Janeway, Michael. *Atlantic Monthly* Mar. 1976: 107.

V-86   Just, Ward. "A 'Wonderful' Writer and Her 'Magical' Novel." *Washington Post* 10 Mar. 1976: B9.

V-87   *Kirkus Reviews* 1 Nov. 1975: 1253-54.

V-88   *Kliatt Young Adult Paperback Book Guide* 11 (Spring 1977): 8.

V-89   Mellors, John. "Japanese Cross." *Listener* 20 May 1976: 654.

V-90   Neville, Jill. "Fiction: Mayhem in the Antipodes." (London) *Sunday Times* 16 May 1976: 41.

V-91   Ostermann, Robert. "Breathing New Life Into Old Conventions." *National Observer* 24 Jan. 1976: 19.

V-92   Peters, Catherine. "Opting Out." *Times Literary Supplement* 27 Aug. 1976: 1060. [Reprinted in *Critical Essays on Anne Tyler*. Ed. Alice Hall Petry. New York: G.K. Hall, 1992: 80-81].

V-93   Pollitt, Katha. "Two Novels." *New York Times Book Review* 18 Jan. 1976: 22. [Reprinted in *Critical Essays on Anne Tyler*. Ed. Alice Hall Petry. New York: G.K. Hall, 1992: 82-83].

V-94   Sage, Lorna. "Turning Out the Attic." (London) *Observer* 9 May 1976: 27.

V-95   Schwartz, Lynn Sharon. *Saturday Review* 6 Mar. 1976: 28.

V-96   Sullivan, Walter. "Gifts, Prophecies, and Prestidigitations: Fictional Frameworks, Fictional Modes." *Sewanee Review* 85 (Winter 1977): 116-25.

V-97   Tack, Martha B. "Pecking Order." *Village Voice* 1 Nov. 1976: 95.

V-98   Updike, John. "Family Ways." *New Yorker* 29 Mar. 1976: 110-12. [Reprinted in *Critical Essays on Anne Tyler*. Ed. Alice Hall Petry. New York: G.K. Hall, 1992: 75-79; and in his *Hugging the Shore: Essays and Criticism*. New York: Knopf, 1983: 273-78].

Earthly Possessions

V-99   Ackroyd, Peter. "Giving Up in America." *Spectator* 22 Oct. 1977: 24.

V-100   Bannon, Barbara A. *Publisher's Weekly* 14 Mar. 1977: 91.

V-101   *Booklist* 1 May 1977: 1327.

V-102   Bouton, Katherine. *Ms.* Aug. 1977: 35-36.

V-103   Broyard, Anatole. "Tyler, Tracy and Wakefield." *New York Times Book Review* 8 May 1977: 12.

V-104   *Choice* Sept. 1977: 867.

V-105   Clapperton, Jane. *Cosmopolitan* July 1977: 18.

V-106   Cosgrave, Mary Silva. *Horn Book Magazine* Oct. 1977: 562.

V-107   Delbanco, Nicholas. *New Republic* 28 May 1977: 35-36. [Reprinted in *Critical Essays on Anne Tyler*. Ed. Alice Hall Petry. New York: G.K. Hall, 1992: 85-87].

V-108   de Usabel, Frances E. *Library Journal* 15 May 1977: 1213.

V-109   Freiert, William K. *Classical and Modern Literature* 10 (Fall 1989): 59-60.

V-110   Fuller, Edmund. "Two Women Casting Off Encumbrances." *Wall Street Journal* 30 June 1977: 8.

V-111   Glendinning, Victoria. "Running on the Spot." *Times Literary Supplement* 9 Dec. 1977: 1456.

V-112   Jefferson, Margo. "Two for the Road." *Newsweek* 2 May 1977: 75-76.

V-113   Johnson, Diane. "Your Money or Your Life." *Washington Post Book World* 29 May 1977: F1+.

V-114 *Kirkus Reviews* 1 Mar. 1977: 244.

V-115 Larson, Charles R. "Anne Tyler, Storyteller." *National Observer* 30 May 1977:
21.

V-116 Leonard, John. "A Loosening of Roots." *New York Times* 3 May 1977: 39.

V-117 Neville, Jill. "Journey to Treason." (London) *Sunday Times* 23 Oct. 1977: 41.

V-118 Perez, Gilberto. "Narrative Voices." *Hudson Review* 30 (Winter 1977-78): 607-
20.

V-119 *Progressive* July 1977: 44.

V-120 Reed, Nancy Gail. "Novel Follows Unpredictable Escape Routes." *Christian
Science Monitor* 22 June 1977: 23.

V-121 Sale, Roger. "Hostages." *New York Review of Books* 26 May 1977: 39-42.

V-122 Sullivan, Walter. "The Insane and the Indifferent Walker Percy and Others."
Sewanee Review 86 (Winter 1978): 153-59. [Reprinted in *Critical Essays on
Anne Tyler*. Ed. Alice Hall Petry. New York: G.K. Hall, 1992: 92-93].

V-123 Updike, John. "Loosened Roots." *New Yorker* 6 June 1977: 130+. [Reprinted
in *Critical Essays on Anne Tyler*. Ed. Alice Hall Petry. New York: G.K. Hall,
1992: 88-91; and in his *Hugging the Shore: Essays and Criticism*. New York:
Knopf, 1983: 278-83].

V-124 Wigan, Angela. "Wilderness Course." *Time* 9 May 1977: 86-87.

V-125 Wolf, Jamie. "Anne Tyler Civilizes the Bizarre." *Los Angeles Times Book
Review* 22 May 1977: 22.

Morgan's Passing

V-126 *Atlantic Monthly* May 1980: 102.

V-127 Bannon, Barbara A. *Publisher's Weekly* 25 Jan. 1980: 325.

V-128 Binding, Paul. "North of South." *New Statesman* 5 Dec. 1980: 25-26.

V-129 *Booklist* 1 Mar. 1980: 930.

V-130 *British Book News* Feb. 1981: 120.

V-131 Cohen, George. *Chicago Tribune BookWorld* 23 Mar. 1980: 3.

V-132 de Usabel, Frances E. *Library Journal* 15 Mar. 1980: 746.

V-133 Disch, Thomas M. "The Great Imposter." *Washington Post Book World* 16 Mar. 1980: 5.

V-134 Evanier, David. "Song of Baltimore." *National Review* 8 Aug. 1980: 972-73.

V-135 Fuller, Edmund. "Micawber as a Hardware Store Manager." *Wall Street Journal* 21 Apr. 1980: 26.

V-136 Gray, Francine du Plessix. *Commonweal* 5 Dec. 1980: 696.

V-137 Gray, Paul. "The Rich Are Different." *Time* 17 Mar. 1980: 91.

V-138 Grier, Peter. "Bright Novel That Overstretches Credibility." *Christian Science Monitor* 14 Apr. 1980: B9. [Reprinted in *Critical Essays on Anne Tyler*. Ed. Alice Hall Petry. New York: G.K. Hall, 1992: 101-02].

V-139 Hoffman, Eva. "When the Fog Never Lifts." *Saturday Review* 15 Mar. 1980: 38-39. [Reprinted in *Critical Essays on Anne Tyler*. Ed. Alice Hall Petry. New York: G.K. Hall, 1992: 95-97].

V-140 Hudacs, Martin J. *Best Sellers* Aug. 1980: 171.

V-141 *Kirkus Reviews* 1 Jan. 1980: 35.

V-142 *Kliatt Young Adult Paperback Book Guide* 16 (Winter 1982): 17-18.

V-143 Kubal, David. "Fiction Chronicle." *Hudson Review* 33 (Autumn 1980): 437-48.

V-144 Mojtabai, A.G. "A State of Continual Crisis." *New York Times Book Review* 23 Mar. 1980: 14+. [Reprinted in *Critical Essays on Anne Tyler*. Ed. Alice Hall Petry. New York: G.K. Hall, 1992: 98-100].

V-145 Murray, James G. "Fiction in the (very) Low 80s: An Early Retrospective with (mostly) Regrets for the Future." *Critic* Dec. 1980: 1-7.

V-146 Naughton, John. "Fascinating Faust." *Listener* 16 Oct. 1980: 513.

V-147 Nesanovich, Stella. "Anne Tyler's *Morgan's Passing*." *Southern Review* 17 (Summer 1981): 619-21.

V-148 Olson, Clarence E. "Many Acts to a Life." *St. Louis Post-Dispatch* 18 May 1980: D4.

V-149 Prescott, Peter S. "Mr. Chameleon." *Newsweek* 24 Mar. 1980: 82-83+.

V-150 Spoliar, Nicholas. "Taking of Parts." *Times Literary Supplement* 31 Oct. 1980: 1221.

V-151 Towers, Robert. *New Republic* 22 Mar. 1980: 28+. [Reprinted in *Critical Essays on Anne Tyler*. Ed. Alice Hall Petry. New York: G.K. Hall, 1992: 103-06].

V-152 Updike, John. "Imagining Things." *New Yorker* 23 June 1980: 94+.
[Reprinted in his *Hugging the Shore: Essays and Criticism*. New York: Knopf, 1983: 283-92].

V-153 *Virginia Quarterly Review* 56 (Autumn 1980): 138-39.

V-154 Willison, Marilyn Murray. "The Warp and Woof of Contrasting Life Styles."
Los Angeles Times Book Review 30 Mar. 1980: 8.

V-155 Wolcott, James. "Some Fun." *New York Review of Books* 3 Apr. 1980: 34.

Dinner at the Homesick Restaurant

V-156 Bailey, Katherine. *English Journal* Oct. 1990: 84.

V-157 Bannon, Barbara A. *Publisher's Weekly* 19 Feb. 1982: 60.

V-158 Barnet, Andrea. *Saturday Review* Mar. 1982: 62.

V-159 Baumgaertner, Jill. "Poetry in Bed and Board." *Cresset* Sept. 1982: 29-31.

V-160 de Mott, Benjamin. "Funny, Wise and True." *New York Times Book Review* 14
Mar. 1982: 1+. [Reprinted in *Critical Essays on Anne Tyler*. Ed. Alice Hall
Petry. New York: G.K. Hall, 1992: 111-14].

V-161 de Usabel, Frances E. *Library Journal* 15 Feb. 1982: 476.

V-162 Dillin, Gay Andrews. "Meaty Fiction with a Draft of Sadness." *Christian
Science Monitor* 9 July 1982: 14.

V-163 Ehresmann, Julia M. *Booklist* 15 Dec. 1981: 522.

V-164 Felts, Virginia C. *Book Report* 2 (May/June 1983): 40.

V-165 Fuller, Edmund. "Feuding Mountain Clans and a Poignant Family Comedy."
Wall Street Journal 20 Apr. 1982: 30.

V-166 Garner, Marilyn. *Antigonish Review* 50 (Summer 1982): 49-51.

V-167 Gornick, Vivian. "Anne Tyler's Arrested Development." *Village Voice* 30 Mar.
1982: 40-41.

V-168 Greenwell, Bill. "Real Life." *New Statesman* 1 Oct. 1982: 27-28.

V-169 Johnson, Priscilla. *School Library Journal* Aug. 1982: 132.

V-170 Kearns, George. "Fiction Chronicle." *Hudson Review* 35 (Autumn 1982): 499-
512.

V-171 *Kirkus Reviews* 15 Jan. 1982: 94-95; also 15 Feb. 1982: 211-12.

V-172 Lee, Hermione. "Heart of Urban Darkness." (London) *Observer* 3 Oct. 1982: 33.

V-173 Linehan, Eugene J. *Best Sellers* June 1982: 94-95.

V-174 Lorenz, Sarah. *English Journal* Jan. 1988: 76.

V-175 Mars-Jones, Adam. "Family Mealtimes." *Times Literary Supplement* 29 Oct. 1982: 1188.

V-176 McMurtry, Larry. "Tyler Artfully Mixes Domestic Fare, Tragedy." *Chicago Tribune BookWorld* 21 Mar. 1982: 3.

V-177 Meades, Jonathan. *Books and Bookmen* Nov. 1982: 38.

V-178 Mellors, John. "Food for Love." *Listener* 21 Oct. 1982: 23-24.

V-179 Olson, Clarence E. "Legacy of Dreams Turned Sour." *St. Louis Post-Dispatch* 28 Mar. 1982: B4.

V-180 Ramsey, Nancy. *San Francisco Review of Books* 7 (Summer 1982): 21.

V-181 Schiff, Robbin. *Ms.* June 1982: 75.

V-182 See, Carolyn. "The Family's Hold--A Caress or Grip?" *Los Angeles Times* 30 Mar. 1982, sec. VI: 6.

V-183 Seton, Cynthia Propper. "Generations at Table." *Washington Post Book World* 4 Apr. 1982: 7.

V-184 Sheppard, R.Z. "Eat and Run." *Time* 5 Apr. 1982: 77-78.

V-185 Strouse, Jean. "Family Arsenal." *Newsweek* 5 Apr. 1982: 72-73.

V-186 Taubman, Robert. "Beckett's Buttonholes." *London Review of Books* 21 Oct.-3 Nov. 1982: 16-17.

V-187 Updike, John. "On Such a Beautiful Green Little Planet." *New Yorker* 5 Apr. 1982: 189+. [Reprinted in *Critical Essays on Anne Tyler*. Ed. Alice Hall Petry. New York: G.K. Hall, 1992: 107-10; and in his *Hugging the Shore: Essays and Criticism*. New York: Knopf, 1983: 292-99].

V-188 *West Coast Review of Books* 8 (May 1982): 23.

V-189 Wolcott, James. "Strange New World." *Esquire* Apr. 1982: 123-24. [Reprinted in *Critical Essays on Anne Tyler*. Ed. Alice Hall Petry. New York: G.K. Hall, 1992: 115-16].

The Accidental Tourist

V-190 *Antioch Review* 44 (Spring 1986): 249-50.

V-191 Blades, John. "For NutraSweet Fiction, Tyler Takes the Cake." *Chicago Tribune BookWorld* 20 July 1986: 37.

V-192 Bloom, Alice. *New England Review and Bread Loaf Quarterly* 8 (Summer 1986): 513-25.

V-193 Craig, Patricia. "Angela and the Beast." *London Review of Books* 5 Dec. 1985: 24.

V-194 Eder, Richard. *Los Angeles Times Book Review* 15 Sept. 1985: 3+.

V-195 Flanagan, Mary. "Return Flights." *Books and Bookmen* Oct. 1985: 40-41.

V-196 Fletcher, Janet, et al. "The Best Books of 1985." *Library Journal* Jan. 1986: 45-50.

V-197 Freiert, William K. *Classical and Modern Literature* 10 (Fall 1989): 60.

V-198 Hooper, Brad. *Booklist* Aug. 1985: 1597.

V-199 Hulbert, Ann. *Commonweal* 29 Nov. 1985: 679-80.

V-200 Johnson, Diane. "Southern Comfort." *New York Review of Books* 7 Nov. 1985: 15-17.

V-201 Kakutani, Michiko. "Books of the Times." *New York Times* 28 Aug. 1985: C21.

V-202 Koenig, Rhoda. "Back in Your Own Backyard." *New York* 2 Sept. 1985: 59-60.

V-203 Larson, Charles. "Quirky Types Are Heart of Tyler Tale." *Chicago Tribune BookWorld* 25 Aug. 1985: 31.

V-204 Mars-Jones, Adam. "Despairs of a Time-and-Motion Man." *Times Literary Supplement* 4 Oct. 1985: 1096.

V-205 Mathewson, Joseph. "Taking the Anne Tyler Tour." *Horizon* Sept. 1985: 14. [Reprinted in *Critical Essays on Anne Tyler*. Ed. Alice Hall Petry. New York: G.K. Hall, 1992: 123-25].

V-206 McMurtry, Larry. "Life Is a Foreign Country." *New York Times Book Review* 8 Sept. 1985: 1+. [Reprinted in *Critical Essays on Anne Tyler*. Ed. Alice Hall Petry. New York: G.K. Hall, 1992: 132-36].

V-207 Mellors, John. "All for Love." *Listener* 7 Nov. 1985: 28-29.

V-208 Mutter, John. *Publisher's Weekly* 11 July 1986: 67.

V-209 Olson, Clarence E. "The Wonderfully Wacky World of Anne Tyler." *St. Louis Post-Dispatch* 8 Sept. 1985: B4.

V-210 Prescott, Peter S. "Watching Life Go By." *Newsweek* 9 Sept. 1985: 92. [Reprinted in *Critical Essays on Anne Tyler*. Ed. Alice Hall Petry. New York: G.K. Hall, 1992: 117-18].

V-211 Rich, Barbara. "Class of 1985." *Women's Review of Books* Apr. 1986: 11-12.

V-212 Scholar, Nancy. *Wilson Library Bulletin* Dec. 1985: 72.

V-213 Sitton, Jessica. *San Francisco Review of Books* 11 (Spring 1986): 12.

V-214 Updike, John. "Leaving Home." *New Yorker* 28 Oct. 1985: 106-08+. [Reprinted in *Critical Essays on Anne Tyler*. Ed. Alice Hall Petry. New York: G.K. Hall, 1992: 126-31].

V-215 *Virginia Quarterly Review* 62 (Summer 1986): 90-91.

V-216 *West Coast Review of Books* 11 (Summer 1985): 24.

V-217 Yardley, Jonathan. "Anne Tyler's Family Circles." *Washington Post Book World* 25 Aug. 1985: 3. [Reprinted in *Critical Essays on Anne Tyler*. Ed. Alice Hall Petry. New York: G.K. Hall, 1992: 119-22].

Breathing Lessons

V-218 Andrew, Nigel. "Que Sera Sera." *Listener* 19 Jan. 1989: 50.

V-219 Angier, Carole. "Small City America." *New Statesman & Society*. 20 Jan. 1989: 34.

V-220 Anthony, Carolyn A. *Library Journal* 1 May 1989: 44.

V-221 Beverly, Elizabeth. "The Tidy Plans That Crumbled." *Commonweal* 24 Feb. 1989: 120-21.

V-222 Bolotin, Susan. "Anne Tyler's Eccentric Circles." *Vogue* Sept. 1988: 446.

V-223 Brace, Marianne. "Keeping Off the Straight and Narrow." *Books* Feb. 1989: 17.

V-224 Brett, Simon. "Mustn't Try Harder." *Punch* 20 Jan. 1989: 48.

V-225 Brookner, Anita. "Things Fall Apart and Cannot Be Glued." *Spectator* 21 Jan. 1989: 36.

V-226 Curran, Ronald. *World Literature Today* 64 (Winter 1990): 112-13.

V-227 Davis, Hope Hale. "Watching the Ordinary People." *New Leader* 28 Nov. 1988: 19-21.

V-228 Eder, Richard. "Crazy for Sighing and Crazy for Loving You." *Los Angeles Times Book Review* 11 Sept. 1988: 3.

V-229 Flower, Dean. "Barbaric Yawps and Breathing Lessons." *Hudson Review* 42 (Spring 1989): 133-40.

V-230 Friedman, Melvin J. "A Day, a Life." *Progressive* Dec. 1988: 44-45.

V-231 Gernes, Sonia. *America* 12 Nov. 1988: 382.

V-232 Golden, Marita. "New Wives' Tales." *Ms.* Sept. 1988: 86+.

V-233 Hoagland, Edward. "About Maggie, Who Tried Too Hard." *New York Times Book Review* 11 Sept. 1988: 1+. [Reprinted in *Critical Essays on Anne Tyler*. Ed. Alice Hall Petry. New York: G.K. Hall, 1992: 140-44].

V-234 Hooper, Brad. *Booklist* July 1988: 1756.

V-235 James, Darlene. "A Trio of Conjurers: New Novels Portray Enduring Characters." *Maclean's* 10 Oct. 1988: 48c-e.

V-236 Kaganoff, Penny. *Publisher's Weekly* 11 Aug. 1989: 454.

V-237 Kakutani, Michiko. "Anne Tyler's Couple on a Journey." *New York Times* 3 Sept. 1988: 14.

V-238 *Kirkus Reviews* 1 July 1988: 931.

V-239 *Kliatt Young Adult Paperback Book Guide* Jan. 1990: 15.

V-240 Klinghoffer, David. "Ordinary People." *National Review* 30 Dec. 1988: 48-49. [Reprinted in *Critical Essays on Anne Tyler*. Ed. Alice Hall Petry. New York: G.K. Hall, 1992: 137-39].

V-241 Lee, Hermione. "Made in Baltimore." (London) *Observer* 15 Jan. 1989: 48.

V-242 Lescaze, Lee. "Mid-life Ups and Downs." *Wall Street Journal* 6 Sept. 1988: 28.

V-243 Manuel, Diane. "Meaningful Moments at the Foot of the Cellar Steps." *Christian Science Monitor* 7 Sept. 1988: 17-18.

V-244 McPhillips, Robert. "The Baltimore Chop." *Nation* 7 Nov. 1988: 464-66. [Reprinted in *Critical Essays on Anne Tyler*. Ed. Alice Hall Petry. New York: G.K. Hall, 1992: 150-54].

V-245 *New Yorker* 28 Nov. 1988: 121.

V-246 Olson, Clarence E. "Odd Ties That Bind." *St. Louis Post-Dispatch* 11 Sept. 1988: F5.

V-247 Prescott, Peter S. *Newsweek* 26 Sept. 1988: 73.

V-248 Rich, Barbara. "Exquisite Eccentrics." *Women's Review of Books* Nov. 1988: 20-21.

V-249 Sheppard, R.Z. "In Praise of Lives Without Life-Styles." *Time* 5 Sept. 1988: 75.

V-250 Skenazy, Paul. "Sublime Slices of Daily Life." *San Francisco Chronicle Review* 11 Sept. 1988: 1+.

V-251 Spalding, Frances. *Times Educational Supplement* 3 Feb. 1989: B2.

V-252 Stegner, Wallace. "The Meddler's Progress." *Washington Post Book World* 4 Sept. 1988: 1+. [Reprinted in *Critical Essays on Anne Tyler*. Ed. Alice Hall Petry. New York: G.K. Hall, 1992: 148-49].

V-253 Steinberg, Sybil. *Publisher's Weekly* 1 July 1988: 67.

V-254 Taylor, Maurice. *Library Journal* 1 Sept. 1988: 184.

V-255 Thwaite, Anthony. "Family Romances." *London Review of Books* 2 Feb. 1989: 14-15.

V-256 Towers, Robert. "Roughing It." *New York Review of Books* 10 Nov. 1988: 40-41. [Reprinted in *Critical Essays on Anne Tyler*. Ed. Alice Hall Petry. New York: G.K. Hall, 1992: 145-47].

V-257 *Virginia Quarterly Review* 65 (Spring 1989): 56.

V-258 *West Coast Review of Books* 14.1 (1988): 39.

V-259 *West Coast Review of Books* 14.2 (1988): 22-23.

V-260 Wolitzer, Hilma. "'Breathing Lessons': Anne Tyler's Tender Ode to Married Life." *Chicago Tribune Books* 28 Aug. 1988: 1+.

V-261 Wood, Michael. "Laughably Resilient Creatures." *Times Literary Supplement* 20 Jan. 1989: 57.

Saint Maybe

V-262 Andraski, Katie. *Christianity Today* 22 June 1992: 42-43.

V-263 Bawer, Bruce. "Anne Tyler: Gravity and Grace." *Washington Post Book World* 18 Aug. 1991: 1-2.

V-264 Bawer, Bruce. "Anne Tyler's Leap of Faith." *Houston Post* 1 Sept. 1991: C10.

V-265 Binding, Paul. "Conscious Goodness." *New Statesman & Society* 4 Oct. 1991: 32.

V-266 Brookner, Anita. "The Good, the Drab, and the Tacky." *Spectator* 26 Oct. 1991: 36.

V-267 Brosnahan, John. *Booklist* 1 June 1991: 1843.

V-268 Burton, Douglas. "A Quiet Hero." *World & I* Feb. 1992: 365-69.

V-269 Caldwell, Gail. "Characters with the Tyler Gift for Bearing the Unbearable." *Boston Globe* 25 Aug. 1991: 63:3.

V-270 Cherry, Kelly. "The Meaning of Guilt." *Southern Review* 28 (Winter 1992): 168-73.

V-271 Eder, Richard. "Quiescence as Art Form." *Los Angeles Times Book Review* 8 Sept. 1991: 3+.

V-272 Fialkoff, Francine. *Library Journal* 1 June 1991: 198.

V-273 Fitch, Katherine. *School Library Journal* Dec. 1991: 149-50.

V-274 Gardner, Marilyn. "Ordinariness as Art." *Christian Science Monitor* 25 Sept. 1991: 13.

V-275 Gray, Paul. "Looking for a Second Chance." *Time* 9 Sept. 1991: 67-68.

V-276 Gromer, Crystal. "Never Far from Home." *Commonweal* 8 Nov. 1991: 656-58.

V-277 Hankla, Cathryn. "A Last-Chance Life." *World & I* Feb. 1992: 339-45.

V-278 Hawley, John C. *America* 4-11 Jan. 1992: 18-19.

V-279 Johnson, Greg. "The Misfit Men of Anne Tyler." *Atlanta Journal Constitution* 25 Aug. 1991: N7.

V-280 Johnston, Darcie Conner. "A Gentle Eking Out of Lives." *Belles Lettres* 7 (Fall 1991): 27.

V-281 Jones, Daniel. *Quill & Quire* Aug. 1991: 18.

V-282 Kakutani, Michiko. "Love, Guilt and Change in a Family." *New York Times* 30 Aug. 1991: C21.

V-283 *Kirkus Reviews* 1 June 1991: 693.

V-284 Kosman, Joshua. "Anne Tyler's Balancing Act." *San Francisco Chronicle Review* 1 Sept. 1991: 1.

V-285 Lannon, Linnea. "Days of Atonement." *Detroit News* 25 Aug. 1991: L7.

V-286 Larson, Susan. "Soul Food." (New Orleans) *Times-Picayune* 1 Sept. 1991: E6.

V-287 Leithauser, Brad. "Just Folks." *New York Review of Books* 16 Jan. 1992: 53-55.

V-288 Longshore, Lydia. *Vogue* Sept. 1991: 388.

V-289 Morey, Ann-Janine. "The Making of Saint Maybe." *Christian Century* 20-27 Nov. 1991: 1090-92.

V-290 Olson, Clarence E. "The Hazard of Being a Brother's Keeper." *St. Louis Post-Dispatch* 25 Aug. 1991: H5.

V-291 Parini, Jay. "The Accidental Convert." *New York Times Book Review* 25 Aug. 1991: 1+.

V-292 Sage, Lorna. "Compassion in Clans." *Times Literary Supplement* 27 Sept. 1991: 24.

V-293 Slater, Joyce. "Road to Redemption." *Chicago Tribune Books* 25 Aug. 1991: 3.

V-294 Steinberg, Sybil. *Publisher's Weekly* 14 June 1991: 46.

V-295 Sutherland, John. "Lucky Brrm." *London Review of Books* 12 Mar. 1992: 23-24.

V-296 Timson, Judith. "Lives of a Saint." *Maclean's* 23 Sept. 1991: 70.

V-297 Walters, Colin. "A Story of Love and Forgiveness." *Washington Times* 8 Sept. 1991: B7.

V-298 Wilson, Robert. "'Saint Maybe,' a Sure Thing." *USA Today* 23 Aug. 1991: D1.

Index

NOTE: Page numbers preceded by an asterisk (*) refer to sections in the text devoted exclusively to that subject or work.

About the Author

ROBERT W. CROFT is Assistant Professor of English at Gainesville College in Gainesville, GA. He lives with his wife and two children in Athens, Georgia, and is currently working on a reference guide to Anne Tyler's works, *An Anne Tyler Companion*.